Mikael Johnsson

How to create high-performing innovation teams

Mikael Johnsson

How to create high-performing innovation teams

—

DE GRUYTER

ISBN 978-3-11-073711-0
e-ISBN (PDF) 978-3-11-073193-4
e-ISBN (EPUB) 978-3-11-073201-6

Library of Congress Control Number: 2022934379

Bibliographic information published by the Deutsche Nationalbibliothek
The Deutsche Nationalbibliothek lists this publication in the Deutsche Nationalbibliografie;
detailed bibliographic data are available from the Internet at http://dnb.dnb.de.

© 2022 Walter de Gruyter GmbH, Berlin/Boston
Coverimage: fongfong2/iStock/Getty Images Plus
Illustrations: © 2022 Linnéa Johnsson, WarmTeacup, Web: http://www.warmteacup.se
Instagram: @warm.comics
Typesetting: Integra Software Services Pvt. Ltd.
Printing and binding: CPI books GmbH, Leck

www.degruyter.com

Prologue

For as long as I can remember, I have tried to find better ways of doing things, and my passion has always been in making new creations. "Does it have to be this way?" – this is a mantra for which I was mocked several times during my various employments, before I found myself on the track with my innovation projects, innovation consulting, and applied research. I have never accepted a bad solution just because "this is what we have always done" and have, therefore, always strived to do things smarter. My motto is to try to see where the problem originates and then solve it at the root, where it begins. As I have worked, created new products, and studied innovation management, my knowledge of how to develop ideas for the market has deepened and broadened.

My previous book, *Sell the skin before the bear is shot*, is about how to contemplate and develop an idea towards the market by using different concrete tools, depending on the project's current position in the development process. Some of that content is included in this book as well, but the focus here is mainly on the innovation team that will carry out the enormously fun innovation work. Teams can be key to successful innovation work, but it is relatively complicated to begin the work. A natural thought is that you manage yourself and that teamwork does not affect you. Of course, you can do much yourself, but even if you work on your own, you almost always depend on input from the market, users, customers, suppliers, and distributors, where all these can be seen as team members with unique skills. The myth of the strong lone inventor is quite well established. It is a bit tragic, however, as most people who choose to work alone remain lonely inventors without any significant successes. If you want to be an innovator who has reached the market with your new product, you must become involved in different contexts, collaborate, form teams, and work together. It does not matter whether the work is internal to an organization, aimed at a commercial market, or provided as a public service. You are always active in a context, and therefore you must understand it and learn to collaborate within that context.

I write this book to illuminate the essential considerations for those in the process of forming or creating an innovation team, and I write it because books that detail the methods of hands-on innovation work are rare – in this case, the work of creating an innovation team. The industry or focus of the business does not matter – the approach is the same and over the years, I have worked with the same process in various businesses and public institutions. The book, as such, is especially suitable for you who are in management positions and responsible for innovation work, for innovation leaders or innovation managers, for those in innovation management implementation roles, for consultants in the field of innovation management, for those who do practical work in innovation projects, for students of innovation management at college or university, and for you who simply want to immerse yourselves in a working method aiming to create high-performance innovation teams.

https://doi.org/10.1515/9783110731934-202

Innovation is not associated with any particular field or business: it is everywhere. Therefore, I want you to think about your business during your reading, and as you read and think, try to identify a small area in need of development where you can put together an innovation team. When your thoughts have come this far, it's simple: read on, use the book's models and tips, and sketch a small and limited project to begin – the smaller and more straightforward, the better. But the project must make enough space for challenges and independent work. The first project can be limited to something estimated to take 6–12 months to complete. This horizon is long enough to provide perspective on the work and room for reflection and unexpected solutions as it progresses. At the same time, a project with this scope is clear enough to complete in a reasonable timeframe, so it is plannable.

Remember, that you will benefit most from the book before the innovation teams have been formed, as there then remains time to do something different and plan for a successful innovation project.

I would like to thank everyone who made this book possible to write, especially the financiers and participants in the research project Model Driven Decision and Development Support (MD3S) – namely KK Foundation, Blekinge Institute of Technology, Aura Light, Avalon Innovation, Dynapac Compaction Equipment AB, GKN Aerospace Engine Systems, Holje International Group, Tetra Pak Packaging Solutions AB, and Volvo Construction Equipment – and the financiers and participants in the research project Wings of Innovation – namely Sparbankstiftelsen Rekarne, Mälardalen University, Munktell Science Park, Calix AB, and Eskilstuna Elektronik-Partner AB. Finally, to my family and friends who have read the "manuscript in progress" and given feedback on the writing process, thanks!

I hope that you, the reader, will benefit from the book. Good luck in creating your high-performing innovation team, and remember, have fun!

Mikael Johnsson, PhD

Contents

1 Introduction and background

The purpose of this book – A guideline and hands-on methodology

Before we begin, I want to point out that this book is written to be used as a handbook, whereby you who have a particular interest in innovation and innovation work will, hopefully, have an extensive exchange of content. The content rests on research and practical experience – my own and others'. The end of the book contains a comprehensive reference list for in-depth studies. Feel free to underline and take notes in it. Make it your workbook, your companion on your journey. – "Okay, let's go!"

In this chapter, you will learn more about the following topics:
- how to read the book to get the most out of the content,
- recurrently used innovation-related concepts in the book,
- why innovation work is so important to prioritize for long-term success,
- how to plan for an innovation portfolio, and
- the group development process and its problems.

Before you start reading, please have a look here first

The structure of the book reflects how to read the book to fully understand the entire work of creating high-performing innovation teams. This first chapter offers insight into what innovation work is, alongside numerous innovation-related terms, as well as why innovation is essential and what role innovation teams play in the development process. It also motivates this book's focus on the group development process in the pursuit of high-performing innovation teams.

Chapter two focuses on conditions important to consider when planning for creating high-performing innovation teams. For this purpose, the creating high-performing innovation team model is used. The model enfolds three parts, as illustrated in Fig. 1.1; innovation enablers, the innovation facilitator, and the process of creating high-performing innovation teams, also referred to as the HIT process (High-performing Innovation Teams). The HIT process begins with top management commitment and ends with a kick-off as the official start of the innovation project.

For clearance, chapter two focuses on in-depth descriptions of innovation enablers (i.e., factors affecting high-performing innovation teams' work), an introduction to the innovation process and how to apply an agile approach on that, and the innovation facilitator and their role as a support system to the innovation team

https://doi.org/10.1515/9783110731934-001

throughout the entire process and innovation project. Also, we get to know about organizational structures and how they affect innovation teams.

Chapter three centers on the HIT process, step by step. You may be tempted to turn immediately to that chapter (at least I would have, for sure). Feel free to do so, but remember to come back to study the previous chapters as well, as they ground the practical work done later on. Without that overview, it is easy to overlook essential aspects as the innovation team is initiated set off.

Chapters four and five examine the future. The former discusses challenges for newly formed innovation teams, while the latter considers further innovation enablers and challenges, this time where the members of the innovation teams are distributed around the globe.

Finally, in chapter six, it's time to wrap up. There, I say some concluding words, a few key takeaways from my perspective, and a link to my LinkedIn profile if you want to reach out to me or connect.

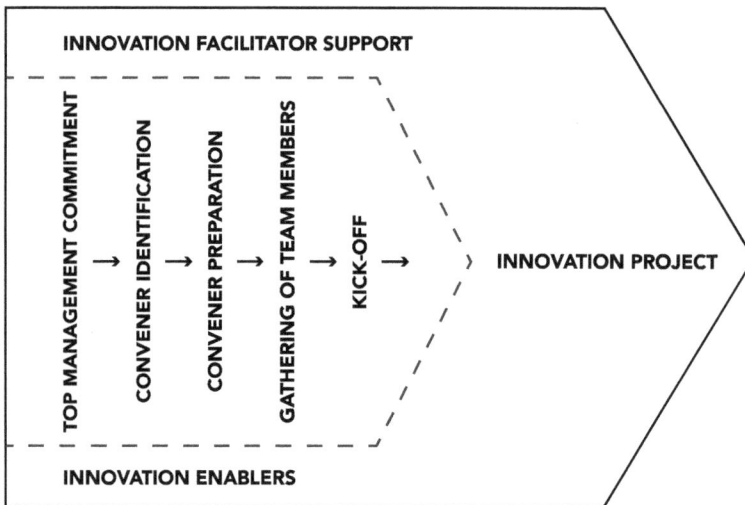

Fig. 1.1: The creating high-performing innovation team model.

Each chapter begins with a short introduction to its content and concludes with a summary and work material, phrased as questions, for reflection and practical work. The questions work just as well for personal reflection as for group discussion. One suggestion is to find a place you like and set aside an hour or two to reflect in-depth on what the questions mean to you and your organization. I do not claim the questions are easy to answer, but working with them concretely and purposefully can make a substantial difference. Depending on what your organization looks like and what assignment you have, it can be difficult to work alone on this task. Indeed, collaboration is a success factor mentioned variously throughout the book. Therefore, another suggestion is that you gather a group who can meet in a comfortable place where you can be at peace and progressively discuss the book's questions. Initially, the questions are relatively general, but as they accumulate and as the book's content becomes more and more concrete, the questions become more complex. All aim to prepare you to create, manage, and participate in high-performing innovation teams. Your first encounter with this material may pose certain challenges, so give it some time. Feel free to divide the work, taking time to reflect between the discussions and to consider your organization with new eyes. As you will notice, each question can be broken into countless follow-up questions, all of which can be starting point for change. All questions are open-ended. They intend you to think and to describe the present situation and what you can change if necessary.

Definitions of key concepts

This book features recurring key concepts related to innovation. When asked what they think innovation means, people commonly answer by referring to such concepts as invention, creativity, and new ideas. Each of these answers is partly right, but innovation is so much more. Very few see the whole picture; therefore, I have collected the concepts I refer to here to ease further reading. Those readers unfamiliar with the concepts below may find them somewhat cumbersome to use in everyday work. It might feel more natural to use words such as "product development," "development," "invention," "creative work," and similar, which are well recognized and believed to define innovation. In that case, feel free to start with that language, but my advice is to aim to apply terms accurately to facilitate communication and gradually build up knowledge of the area. Other, equally specific concepts exist in, for example, business development, plumbing, construction, and business administration. In the industries mentioned (and others, of course), it is not surprising with concepts such as business plans, flow rates, newton-meters, and profitability. Please spend some time considering what the words below really mean, using them as often as possible in daily conversations and communication with employees and external people.

Innovation: In the definition of innovation used throughout this book, three criteria must be met: It must be new, it must create value, and it must be successfully established in its market. Whether it is patented is immaterial. However, many people miss that it must be successful and must create value. Success means that it is insufficient merely to introduce something new in a market, either internal or external to the organization. If the newly introduced product does not last long, it is not an innovation. If the newly introduced product does not create value for the intended target group, the same applies. Value could include, for example, monetary values, time savings, work satisfaction, increased comfort, well-being, improved health, and other things that somehow create value. Finally, if it is neither implemented nor adding value, it can still be new; in that case, an invention has been developed. Perhaps it is patented, too. A patent can be superficially attractive but unprofitable and otherwise not valuable. Of course, there is a business in selling patents without having a fully developed product or market or in filing patents to hinder competitors from entering the market. Although these functions have value, they are not further explored in this book, and the conclusion remains that an invention is not automatically an innovation.

Innovation process: This concept is slightly simpler. In short, it is a process to guide the development of ideas for the market. Several innovation processes can be selected from, and many organizations develop their own based on one that already exists. A quick search on the Internet for "innovation process" will generate countless hits. This book takes the position that agile innovation processes support fast innovation work and that the innovation team formation is part of the innovation process, as will be explained in chapter two.

Innovation work: Since, from an operational perspective, to become an innovation an idea must be generated, developed, and launched, then create value, innovation work includes all the work necessary to successfully reach the market. Many mistakenly claim that innovation work should focus mainly on technological development. If there is no focus on market establishment, however, no innovation will be generated. Or, if there is no focus on the development of value-creating models, neither will there be innovation. From the perspective of management, innovation work involves, for example, identifying a direction, planning for resources, and making space for the operational work. Therefore, innovation work is among the most complex things to conduct, as it requires skills corresponding to all phases, from preparatory work to the market.

Innovation capability: This means the ability to perform innovation work. Some employees in an organization are somehow born to innovate. They find it easy to "see" new opportunities, such as new business opportunities, where others see only problems and approaching competitors. In this book, innovation capability means having the theoretical knowledge of what innovation work is and the drive to complete the work required to reach the market. Notably, an individual does not have to do all the work on their own, which is one reason to form innovation teams. As just mentioned, some people have a natural ability to innovate, while others find it challenging to comprehend. Yet everyone can improve their ability to innovate in the same way as they might learn to ride a bike. Once learned, it is unforgettable, and it only becomes more enjoyable the more knowledge is gained. With training in various aspects of innovation work, one's capability to innovate can surely increase.

Innovation team: The reason the teams are created in the first place is that collaboration is more efficient than is individual work. Unfortunately, far too many working groups perform work for which they do not have the skills, which affects their result.

An innovation team is not merely any work group that might get lucky in innovating. An innovation team is a team purposely created to conduct innovation work; it must therefore be created with the purpose to innovate. For example, if one wants a new house and for it to be built correctly, different professions are hired for different assignments, all experts in their area (e.g., an architect, engineers, plumbers, and electricians). Innovation work by an innovation team is the same. It is multifunctional and requires a mix of competencies. Additionally, the innovation team must be able to work under relatively abstract conditions in the early stages of the project. The message is that excellence in an innovation team requires it to be consciously created with appropriate competences and conditions. This requirement is at the core of this book.

Group-development process: This process has four phases: forming, storming, norming, and performing, from which it is said that groups emerge. Groups are converted to teams in the transitions from norming to performing phase. In the performing phase, some teams become high-performing. Additionally, after the project is completed, there is a fifth phase where the team is dissolved.

High-performing innovation team: This is an innovation team that has emerged to the status that they are high-performing.

Sponsor: A sponsor, in this case of innovation teams work, is a person who works between the management and the innovation team and acts as a communication channel between them. The sponsor supports the innovation team's work and can also open doors in the organization, if needed.

Innovation facilitator, or facilitator: The facilitator, if needed due to lack of organizational knowledge of creating innovation teams, supports the innovation team by assisting with ongoing training and advice throughout the innovation team's formation and the upcoming innovation project. The facilitator mainly communicates with the convener and sponsor, as well as with management, when needed.

Convener: All team members on an innovation team share leadership. Therefore, the innovation team does not have a dedicated project manager. However, a convening person is assigned to communicate with the facilitator and sponsor for updates and feedback. The convener's task is to form the innovation team in consultation with the management, potentially with the facilitator's support, and hold it together until the structures have appropriately settled. At first, the convener has a slightly more holistic understanding of the innovation process because of the relation to the facilitator, but as the innovation project takes off, the rest of the team members catch up.

General terms used for the sake of simplicity:

- Innovation team. At its core, this book is about how to create high-performing innovation teams. For simplicity, the terms innovation team and team are used to refer to these teams.
- Organization. In this book, the word organization captures all types of companies, businesses, public institutions, associations, and so forth.
- Product. As applied in this book, the term product indicates services, processes, systems, organizations, and so on – everything that can be developed.

Innovation – Do or die

Here in the introduction, there are two reasons to innovate that must be highlighted. The first is about long-term survival in the market and how to plan to work with incremental and radical innovation work as parallel activities. The second is that innovation projects need to be carried out at an ever-increasing pace, so there is reason to understand how it can be done as efficiently as possible.

Planning your innovation project portfolio

Innovation has become an over-exploited buzzword that appears in all possible contexts. Nevertheless, if not working actively with innovation, the business will eventually disappear from the market. Research has long shown that the organizations that actively work with innovation are both more successful and more profitable than those that do not. Those who avoid appreciable investment in innovation do so under the excuse that such investments are too costly and too risky. It absolutely requires resources, and far from all innovation investments reach the market. Still, it is not necessary to risk the whole business. A distribution of 70, 20, and 10 percent is usually considered appropriate, as illustrated in Fig. 1.2. Here, 70 percent of the work is to continually improve everyday life and slowly developing the business as the environment develops; 20 percent, to advance the business and products (or product generation) connected to the business already underway; and the remaining 10 percent, to make more radical efforts, with investments in projects whose outcomes are uncertain or whose value is not fully understood. These 10 percent have a high-risk factor, and the vast majority of these investments never achieve commercial success. However, excitingly, the organizations that function according to the 70-20-10 approach to their innovation portfolio have a strong ability to survive and profit. Over time, revenues are reversed – that is, the high-risk projects account for 70 percent of revenues – and the part of the business that felt long-term secure provides 10 percent of revenues.

The financial crisis of 2008–2009 brought disaster to many subcontractors in most business areas. Of course, there are many reasons for that. One factor that stands out in my eyes, though, was that they relied on their customers always buying from them without developing their own products to meet future technology shifts. The process was that customers in, for example the automotive industry, send drawings by email, mail, or by fax(!), and the subcontractor then produced what was ordered, with almost no questions asked. Big customers could also make annual demands for ever-cheaper prices, resulting in a very distinct focus on cost savings. There is nothing wrong with keeping costs down and developing daily operations towards perfection, but leave some room for what is to come as well.

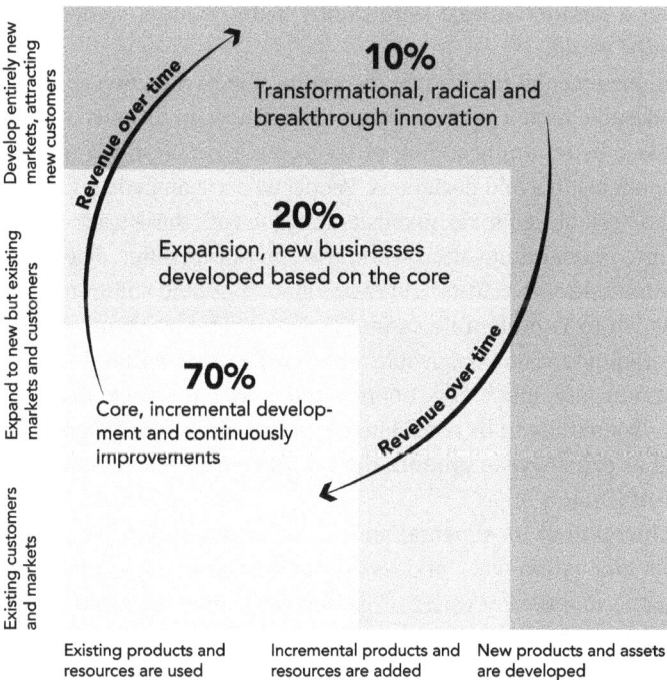

Fig. 1.2: The innovation project portfolio. The figure is inspired by Nagji, B. & Tuff, G., (2012). Managing Your Innovation Portfolio, *Harvard Business Review,* May 2012.

Notably, the different areas of the 70-20-10 innovation portfolio approach require entirely different skills, depending on which of these areas is in focus. There is no reason to expect great deeds if employees are suddenly asked to conduct radical innovation work without having knowledge of it or having received training in it. The same applies if highly visionary employees are to focus on improving some detail in an isolated context. As such, the organization must carefully plan for these totally different activities and staff with people who are suitable to the task. Doing only one or a few of these specializations often leads to business problems: Focusing on only incremental innovations or constant improvements leads to lack of preparation for inevitable technological shifts. On the other extreme, too much experimentation with radical innovations can destabilize a business.

Incremental and radical innovation

Incremental and radical innovation are two extremes of innovation work and its outcome, the product. While incremental innovation has a low degree of novelty, being at the level of *new to me* or *new to the organization*, radical innovation is highly novel, aiming for a product at least significantly better than its predecessor and at its peak, new to the world.

At the first extreme, incremental innovation, the improvements are often so small that they are barely noticeable from a product perspective. The main focus is usually on making work processes better and smother, or for example, on assuring quality and standardizing components to avoid deviations. People who are analytical and accurate in small details are well placed to do an outstanding job with these tasks.

At the other extreme, radical innovation work, the conditions differ. The work is more abstract and exploratory in nature. There are many possible solutions to a given problem, and which to is preferable cannot be known before some experimentation. Such work requires visionary people who have a great ability to think abstractly. To innovate radically, much of entrepreneurship and analytical peoples' help is also needed. For something to be considered a radical innovation, it must be five times better or half as expensive to produce than previous solutions, indicating what is required in the new solution.

All in all, the combination of incremental and radical innovation has come to be called ambidextrous innovation work and has become common. It is often described as two-handed or two-way innovation. This balance is fine, however, and it can be challenging because organizations do not always have the resources or employees to focus on both daily operation and exploratory innovation.

At the risk of complicating things a bit, I must point out that it is possible to be radical in incremental innovation work as well. For example, if the task is to improve a work process that may not be noticeable in the end product, the work process itself can be developed with substantial elements of change and a high level of innovation. Thus, this task may make the same demands for abstract thinking as radical innovation work does. We have seen it many times in the manufacturing industry with automation, robotics, digitization, and much more. As another example, internet users can chat with organization representatives around the clock. Some time ago, such services were solved with personnel working in shifts. The design is to have personnel in countries with different time zones. Today, though, smart chatbots based on Artificial intelligence (AI) handle the most common issues. When it becomes too complicated, experienced customer service personnel become involved in handling the specific issue. The connection to radical innovation is that the user notices no significant difference; he or she gets (hopefully) his or her answers. Still, the technology that delivers the solution has undergone several radical development steps.

The danger of organizations that are too slim

Nowadays, the challenge for many organizations is that they have slimmed their operations too hard through various optimization methods; these are sometimes called "anorexic" organizations. Such organizations leave absolutely no room for new development, given the available staffing. They lack the strength to do anything other than just survive. Daily activities occur in a (mild) panic or are slightly too demanding. Workers' days are mostly spent putting out fires and covering up for people who are at home with sick children or sick themselves. Sure, this picture is somewhat exaggerated, but the trend is common. The bottom line is that neither energy nor resources are available to develop the organization further.

For a manager recognizing this situation, it is essential to create space for employees to develop enough new products that a diving market does not come as a shock. There is usually no good reason to go at full speed constantly. Think of, for example, machines or vehicles used in manufacturing processes or for transport. They have both built-in fuses and overdrive protection, preventing damage to the machines or the engine. We also have fuses at home in our households or the factories to protect against overload, save money, and avoid personal injury. A common practice in the business world is to study how long different work tasks take to complete, thereby calculating the cost of an activity. What many people miss, unfortunately, is that if a job takes ten minutes to perform once, that is no indication employees will be able to do this job six times in one hour. Everything does not always flow perfectly; there are needs to visit the restroom, "stretch your legs," get some water, or just take a short break – obvious. Shifting the focus back to the too-slim organization, the individual employee will, over time, underperform, become forgetful and make strange decisions with unforeseen consequences. From an innovation perspective, the organizational approach described is suboptimal because new ideas usually arise in times of reflection, perhaps in an off-topic conversation with a colleague at the water cooler or coffee machine.

The shorter the product life cycle, the faster the innovation work

It's not just a feeling that new products are introduced on the market at an ever-increased pace – it's a fact. Accordingly, to keep pace with the market, organizations have good reason to learn new methods to develop products. One might think the methods to develop new products are already refined, from stage-gate through waterfalls-, semi-parallel and parallel development methods for agile and flexible innovation work. The latter variants of innovation processes are significantly faster to market than are the previous ones. However, they also place greater demands on the individuals who execute the work. Leadership and employees' competence in innovation work and how it is done is becoming increasingly important. Another parameter must also be considered – teams perform better than individuals do. That realization can be applied in innovation work, which is the main purpose of this book: the art of creating high-performing innovation teams.

Innovate for the future

The most significant business revolution to date is currently unfolding. Many jobs that exist today will not exist in the future. On the other hand, many others will be born. Obvious examples include self-driving vehicles that will change the entire logistics industry, as well as AI that, for example, makes design calculations faster and safer or can train the next generation of school children better than humans, or the automation and robotization of everything from inventory management to complicated surgical operations. It has long been predicted that computer-rendered animations will replace the modeling profession, and discussions about drones delivering goods have been going on for some time. For example, aircraft already today land better on their own than when physical pilots make the landing.

In the shadow of these well-known changes, another radical change is occurring in the service sector, through blockchain technology. Roughly about moving information from a sender to a recipient through a number of nodes that guarantee that the data is not distorted along the way, blockchain technology is usually associated with Bitcoin. However, it was the first practical product created in the form of an encrypted currency as a result of the financial crisis of 2008–2009. As stated, the purpose was to limit monetary inflation and to increase privacy in peer-to-peer financial transactions but also to cut out middlemen in the operation. Since then, blockchain technology has been developed full steam ahead. New solutions will soon be available for basically all existing service professions that require an intermediary for any reason. The critique of blockchain technology often regards potential bugs in smart contracts that can lead to unwanted consequences due to actions being automatically executed if triggers are activated. Further, people's employment may suffer with reduced need for human interaction in the provided service. However, this discussion has a long history, featuring examples like the Spinning Jenny, the steam engine, the tractor, the nail gun, the cement, the forklift, wireless communications, and so on. For example, as new production methods and technologies have developed over the centuries, an enormous number of jobs have disappeared. So will it be in the future as well. In this context, the interesting thing is that beyond the profession itself, the functionality or value for the end-customer usually improves.

Indeed, the effects are most often positive, for example, fewer errors, fewer unwanted variations, fewer accidents, and faster deliveries. In the future, the major difference will be how solutions are produced and who or what delivers them. Even if today's work may not remain in the future in the form it does today, there will undoubtedly be completely new jobs that are unknown today, much as app developers or influencers on social media are now established professionals, even though these professions did not exist before 2005. Further, one of the biggest opponents to blockchain-based decentralized finance (DeFi) (i.e., borrowing and lending cryptocurrencies peer-to-peer) for many years, JP Morgan (one of the major players in traditional banking), opened a lounge in the metaverse (i.e., the digital and virtual universe), offering its services in February 2022. The idea of doing so was ridiculous in 2021. For some reason they reconsidered their standpoint regarding DeFi and decided to be an early adopter aiming for first-mover advantage. JP Morgan got its first competitor in the metaverse, HSBC, about a month later.

To anticipate the rapid pace of change, we all need space to train our abilities to be observant and prepared in the workplace and the outside world. We need this space partly to be able to meet competitors but also to be able to take advantage of opportunities and develop these into value-creating products.

In conclusion – for an organization to avoid slowly vanishing, it must focus on redistributing resources and freeing up time for future survival and success. Take advantage of the opportunities out there – do or die!

The group development process and its problems – Wasted time

The group development process has been explored for many decades and may seem unnecessary to address in a book like this one. However, little attention has been paid to the prevention of problems that easily occur as a group emerges towards a team. So far, it has been a high priority to learn to identify issues that arise and to solve them by various techniques, but this approach is a bit like taking painkillers for headaches. The problem is that the damage has already occurred; the performance of the team has already decreased. Instead, I believe it better to avoid the circumstances that lead to headaches. The process of forming innovation teams is further described in chapter three.

Team building the right way

The group development process is well known in many contexts. Today, there is hardly a business that has not arranged exercises for team building. It has grown into an entire industry that offers no conferences and kick-offs without "fun" team-building games or exercises. However, team building too often focuses not on a challenge for the team that is relevant when the team returns to the workplace. Certainly, I have not often seen myself or anyone else climb very high up in a tree, throw a boot as far as possible, light a fire like ancient cavemen or throw a lasso on an artificial reindeer as part of the work. On the other hand, I have several times seen people forced into trees even though they fear heights, laughed at because they can neither throw a boot very far, hit the artificial reindeer horn with a lasso, nor get the ridiculous pile of boards to fire up – as if it mattered. These exercises can sometimes be reminiscent of the humiliation that many would recognize in a school gym class, where certain athletic people can become heroes while the rest become a burden to bear.

There is nothing wrong with having fun with the games just mentioned, yet they are not as fun for everyone. Furthermore, tasks that are part of the work of creating a high-performing innovation team are absent, such as conducting a market research, mapping a supplier chain, or perhaps pricing a product that does not exist. Instead of potentially creating an internal hierarchy, focus can be placed on creating a team based on the task it is to perform – to develop new products as quickly and efficiently as possible. As you might note, there is a kick-off later in the book, but note too that it focuses on kicking off the project and building the team for its mission, nothing else.

Group or team – It's not the same! How to know the difference?

Conversationally, the terms "group" and "team" are sometimes used interchangeably, which is understandable considering that they are used in the same way but for different purposes. However, the two differ significantly, and I would like to stress that in the context of innovation work, a person ought not shrug their shoulders and say, "Who cares?".

Groups and teams are far from the same thing. A group is generally defined as a complex social system comprising at least two people. However, these two people do not necessarily share the same goal. For example, consider two people waiting at a bus stop. They simply happen to be in the same place at the same time. Still, they are a group. In a work-related context, it may be that the group members do not even want to be part of the group and even less so want to work on the predetermined task. The members can have terrible work experiences with the very people in the group. If problems arise, they may present as people avoiding getting involved, not trying to help resolve issues, doing no more than is required, and being unhappy helping other group members with their potential problems. As long as group members lack the same goal or a desire to perform the stated task, the group will not progress towards becoming a team. Thus, their work will not be particularly efficient.

A team, on the other hand, has reached a stage of maturity at which members share goals and ambitions. They feel like members of the team and work of their own free will to solve challenges that have arisen. They want something and strive to achieve it. The team gives them a sense of belonging, and they have developed effective ways of working together. In a team, members support each other and help each other solve problems without demanding or expecting reciprocal services. Thus, a group does not have to be a team, but a team is always a group. Of course, some groups do not actively oppose each other and do progress the work, but a team functions more smoothly and with less friction between members.

The group development process: Forming, storming, norming, performing, and dissolving

As soon as a group is put together, a group development process begins to resolve how the individuals in the group develop consciously and unconsciously in relation to the new context. The group development process has been discussed in plenty of good literature. Here, it is briefly summarized to as a foundation of knowledge to support the creation of our high-performing innovation team. Usually, the group development process is described in four or five steps: forming, storming, norming, and performing, possibly followed by dissolving, after the project is completed, as illustrated in Fig. 1.3.

The group forms in the first phase, which is characterized by members seeking membership in the group. At this stage, the work is driven by dependence and acceptance rather than the group's task to solve. This phase is sometimes also called "the honeymoon" because in it, the job and group atmosphere feel nice and good. They face no problems other than being accepted by the group, and issues or problems that may arise are forgiven.

During the second phase, the group has tightened. As a result, the group's leadership develops, and relatively often, appointed leaders or leadership are questioned and criticized. The behaviors accepted by the group in the first phase are not as readily accepted in this phase, and open conflict is common. Unfortunately, group members tend to defend themselves, form subgroups, and adopt positions of hostility instead of developing a work environment in which members can feel safe expressing their opinions without being negatively criticized. A significant problem with this phase is that group members tend to focus more on group affiliation than on the work to be performed.

If the group enters the third phase, the work climate is stabilized by the development of norms, structures, and attitudes through self-organization. The effect is that group members increasingly trust each other, leading to a greater understanding of each other's work. Finally, suppose the group reaches the fourth phase, which normally takes about four to six months. In that case, the group transforms into a team, which characterized by teamwork; here, the members have found each other and take joint responsibility for their work and that of other members. The ideal outcome is for the team to become high-performing, which may be reached after some six to eight months. Sometimes, this outcome is considered to be signaled when the team has "flow." Work does not feel like work. Everything is fun, and time flies. New problems to solve are experienced only as everyday tasks resolved without hassle. Everything is possible, and life is wonderful.

The fifth phase is not really a development phase, but rather the opposite. Here, the group or team is dissolved, and the members return to their regular work or start work in a new working group with a new group development process. Hopefully, the group has developed into a team that has completed its job, but this outcome is far from certain. Countless groups and teams have been prematurely dissolved because they fail to agree about what to do or how to solve group-related problems.

Several considerations regarding the group development process are worth emphasizing. A group is not guaranteed to develop into a team, much less a high-performing team, nor is a phase sure to last a predictable duration or have a predictable sequence. The group or team can move between the different phases, both forward and backward, depending on the situation and circumstances. For example, a group that has passed the second phase and becomes a team in the third phase can easily fall back a

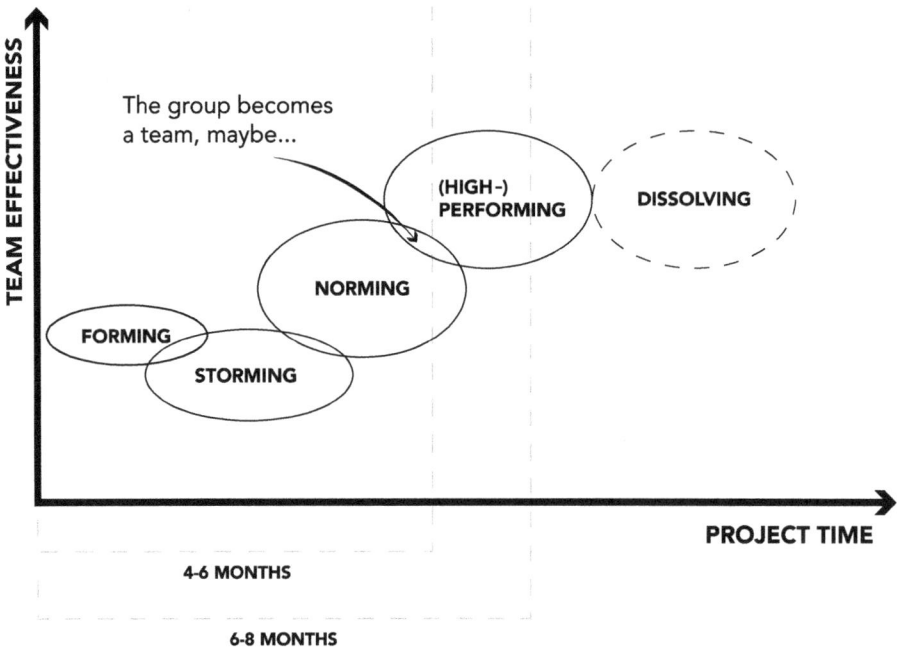

Fig. 1.3: The group development process. The figure is inspired by Wheelan, S. *et al.*, (2021). *Creating Effective Teams.*

step or two and then develop into a team again after another work period. This process can recur even during a single project.

Creating high-performing innovation teams – A methodology

As mentioned, a group starts with a given number of members and thus begins emerging towards a team through the various phases of group development. Notably, however, the group is reformed into a new group if a new member joins or drops out. The new group does not automatically retain its current status but needs time and space to stabilize. If a new person is added, he or she must feel a sense of belonging and that he or she contributes to the group's work. If a person leaves the group and is not replaced by another, all work tasks must be distributed to the remaining members, which may be problematic, given the potential loss of skills.

Another noticeable thing when a member is introduced or lost is how the new constellation communicates and interacts with each other and how tasks are delegated. Although the change may not be obvious, these are entirely new conditions. Someone may become more talkative or quieter than usual. Someone may step forward and assume more responsibility, while someone else steps back.

The emerging process takes months

To reach the desired stage when the group is transformed into a team and begins to perform, the members have first spent months of work and energy finding a structure to follow in their work. According to the most prominent researchers of the group development process, it commonly takes around four to six months to reach the stage when the group becomes a team and begins to perform. However, less than half of all groups never reach the level at which they contribute to the organization's goal, meaning that a much energy and many resources are spent on work that does not create value – energy and resources that could be spent more wisely and more effectively.

Create high-performing innovation teams following a systematic method

Clearly, it is a waste of both time and resources to appoint an innovation group that, after at least four months, becomes an innovation team, maybe. Unlike the expected group development process, which happens more or less by itself when a group of people is put together, the group development process I have focused on developing, as a researcher and practitioner, is deliberate. It comprises three steps: forming, norming, and (high-) performing, as illustrated in Fig. 1.4. Through structured work, it aims to reduce the problematic storming phase and quickly enter the phase in which the group has become a team, with the goal of becoming a high-performing one. This process, creating high-performing innovation teams, rests on group development problems, organizational theories, and the complexity of innovation work. The process has developed into a step-by-step process to give an innovation project a running start. By avoiding the storming phase, enormous time and resources can be saved, creating value for the project instead. Innovation work can be performed faster, contributing to innovations and supporting the organization's future survival.

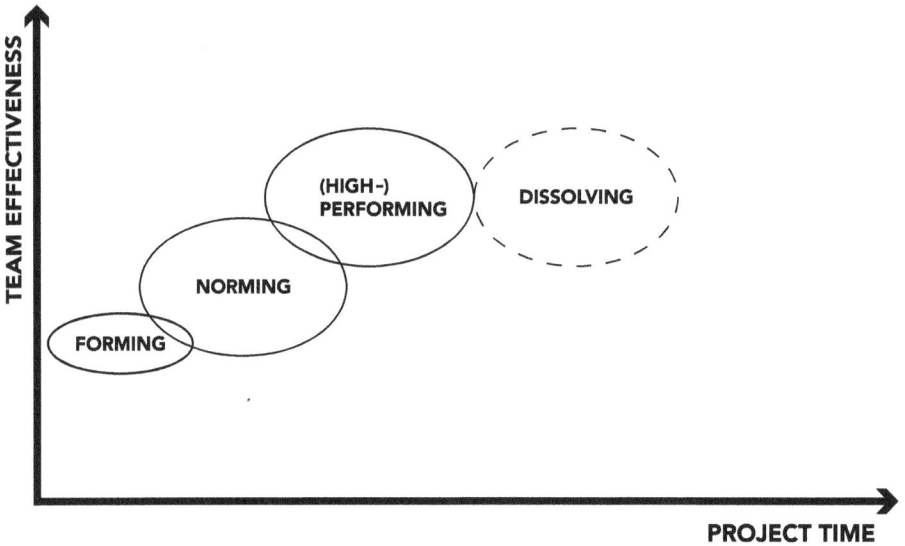

Fig. 1.4: The high-performing innovation team development process.

Regarding groups and teams – now we know they are not the same. However, to ease the further reading, however, the term "team" is used regardless of its status in the group development process unless it is specifically important to separate them in future sections.

Summary

When you flip through a book for the first time, it may be tempting to consider chapter three the point of greatest interest because that is where the detailed presentation for creating high-performing teams appears. Starting there is an excellent choice, skimming through the chapter, but do not forget to investigate the other chapters as well, especially chapter two, which describes various factors that promote the innovation team's work. These factors are divided into three perspectives: the organizational perspective, the innovation team perspective, and the team member perspective. Also, in chapter two, there is exciting knowledge about the agile innovation process and the innovation facilitator. All of these factors are important for the success and development of the innovation team, and some of them seriously impact the outcome. Also, if you're about to create a global innovation team, chapter five is probably especially interesting.

To ease the reading and create a consensus on what the various concepts in this book mean, the most central and most recurrent words related to innovation are picked out and briefly defined and explained.

- Innovation – something new, value-creating, and successfully implemented in the market
- Innovation process – a structured working method for developing innovations
- Innovation work – all work required to develop innovations
- Innovation ability – theoretical and practical skills to perform innovation work
- Innovation team – a team, purposely created to carry out innovation work
- Product – goods, services, processes, systems, business models, etc
- Team – a group emerged to team status. Henceforward, regardless of group or team status, the term "team" is used to ease reading

Innovation work is essential for all types of organizations that want to remain, and for that, a well-planned and strategic innovation portfolio is necessary. The work distribution of 70, 20, and 10 percent, respectively, is considered appropriate, where seventy percent of the work is about continuous improvement; 20 percent, extending its ongoing business; and the remaining 10 percent, radical high-risk projects where outcome and value may be unknown. Over time, nearly all the revenue will come from high-risk projects, and what was the core business's income has decreased to a fraction of what it was.

Innovation spans two extremes – incremental and radical, from "small improvements" to "new to the world." A radical innovation must be five times better or half as expensive to produce to be classified as a radical. On the other hand, the working method does not differ much between the two extremes because it is about developing new solutions to an identified problem. Although it might sound strange, it is possible to develop radical innovations even in the area of incremental improvements (the 70 percent area). The focus is then often on significantly improved processes or production methods, which may not be noticeable in the final product. However, and this is important. Innovation teams must be carefully staffed depending on the range of novelty aimed for. For radical innovation, visionary people are suitable. The same people are not as good for small improvements. However, the problem is that slim organizations tend to be constantly congested, often leading to them lacking the time to concern themselves with future income according to the 70–20–10 distribution. It is unnecessarily hard on staff to be persistently overloaded or to lack time for reflection. Reflections are one of the success factors for new ideas.

At the same time, as new products are being launched at an ever-faster pace, methods for innovating products have also been developed to become both agile and flexible. As a result, they have also become more complex and knowledge-intensive, and here the innovation team is a suggested solution because teams perform better than individuals. As proof of the constant change, there is a growing concern that many of today's jobs will not exist in the future. This is not necessarily a bad thing, at least in the long run. Take a moment and consider what professions you would not like to have from those who have disappeared in the last 40, 60, or 100 years. There are some positives to change. Right? However, from an organizational context or employee perspective, it may be challenging to constantly deal with the unknown in forms as controllable as possible.

According to the classic group development process, it may take four to six months for a group to develop into a team in four phases and dissolves in the fifth: forming, storming, norming, performing, and dissolving. If they reach the team status at all, that is. Far from all groups become teams, and even fewer perform at high levels, meaning that many resources are invested in groups that could do so much more. For groups to become a high-performing team, it's about six to eight months of work, if they reach that phase. For this reason, my research regards how to create innovation teams in three phases: forming, norming, and performing, with the goal of high performance, without the storming phase, and thereby saving valuable time and resources.

Questions for reflections and discussions

This section is intended for reflection and discussion of what has been addressed in chapter one. Take a moment to think about the questions asked below, based on your organization. As mentioned in the introduction, the questions are just as suitable for personal reflection as for group discussion. Set aside at least an hour and work your way through a few questions. Then create a recurring structure by booking a number of occasions to work your way through the questions that conclude each chapter. At the first time, you will get an idea of which people should join in for reflection and discussion. Invite them to participate.

The first chapter introduces the holistic picture of innovation and innovation teams. Therefore, the questions for reflection and discussion are more general in nature and suit readers working in a management position with an overview of the organization. They also suit readers who operate in the organization to reflect from the perspective of a sponsor, convener, and team member. As the content of the book becomes more concrete and detailed, the questions to reflect upon and discuss also become more concrete and precise.

Before you start reading

- In our organization, what is our understanding of the book's central concept of innovation?
- How can we, in our organization, communicate the central concepts of innovation to create shared understanding and increase knowledge of innovation?
- How can we, in our organization, use the questions for reflection in this book as a working material?

Innovation – Do or die

- In a comparison of our approach to the 70-20-10 innovation project portfolio approach, what does our portfolio look like?
  - If there is an imbalance – how should we reallocate projects?
  - If needed, what will be the first five actions to balance our innovation project portfolio?
- How do we create space in our organization to work radically in all areas of development, even in the area of continuous improvement?
- How should we, in our organization, face a future we do not know much about?
- How do we make sure our organization is not so slim that it hinders innovation?
- In our business, are new products launched at an ever-increased pace?
  - If so, how do we match that pace?
- In general, what, if any, new professions in our business have emerged in the past decade?
- In our organization, what, if any, new professions have emerged in the past decade?
- What new professions are about to emerge?
- How can we, in our organization, apply innovation leaders?

The group development process and its problems – Waste of time

- How do we, in our organization, make time and space for new innovation teams to develop?

2 Organizational conditions for innovation work

This chapter introduces four conditions that affect the innovation team from different perspectives: factors that enable the innovation team's work; how innovative and non-innovative organizations are structured; agile innovation work in practice and, finally, the innovation facilitator (facilitator), a support function to the innovation team. In a way, this chapter forms the basis for the innovation team and precedes the explanation of how the innovation teams themselves are created. It provides an understanding that complex but structured work awaits. This chapter presents an understanding of what awaits the innovation team when it is formed and continuously through their continued work. Feel free to return to refresh your memory after you get to the practical work.

In this chapter, you will learn more about the following:
- factors enabling innovation teams' work,
- how organizational structures affect innovation teams,
- agile innovation work, and
- how to support innovation teams through facilitation.

Innovation enablers – Factors that enable innovation

This section will acquaint you with twenty different factors that affect the innovation team's work in different ways. In this context, they are called *innovation enablers* (as highlighted in Fig. 2.1), given that they all promote or enable innovation work, especially some of them. First, I introduce all twenty innovation enablers, with explanations

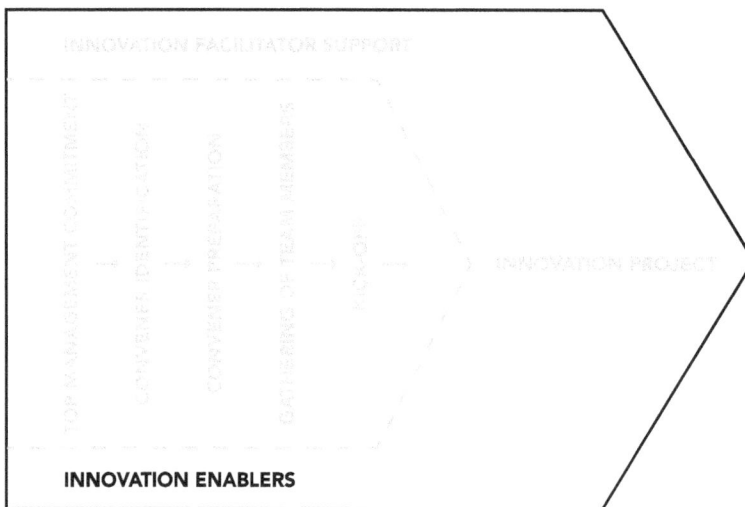

INNOVATION ENABLERS

Fig. 2.1: Innovation enablers, as part of the creating high-performing innovation team model.

https://doi.org/10.1515/9783110731934-002

for each. You will then get a more in-depth insight into which of these most impact the innovation team's work. These key enablers are therefore important to track because they invigorate an innovation project if they are fulfilled – if not, their absence diminishes a team's work.

Innovation enablers in three perspectives – The organization, the team, and the team members

The perspectives of the innovation enablers, the organizational, team, and team members are separated, as illustrated in Fig. 2.2. The innovation team is in the center, illustrated as six members, two of them as dashed circles. It demonstrates that the innovation team is preferably built on 4–6 members, further explained in chapter three, where the team size is further discussed (i.e., chapter three, the power of small teams). However, since the innovation team is built on individuals and surrounded by its organization, each constitutes another perspective to consider.

THE INNOVATION TEAM MODEL

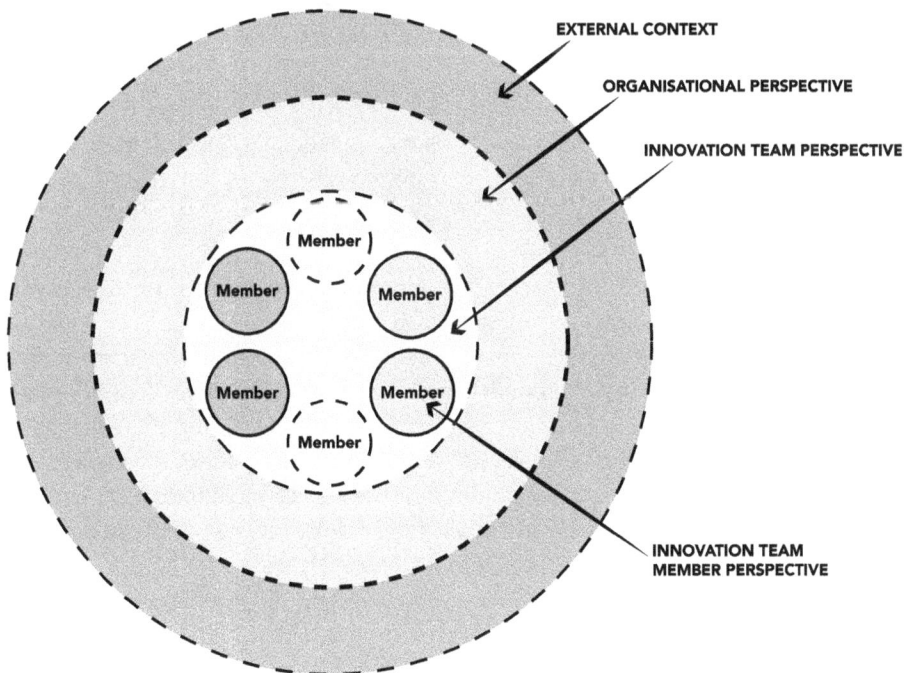

Fig. 2.2: The innovation team, its context, and related viewpoints. The figure is inspired by Johnsson, M. (2016), *Innovation Enablers and Their Importance for Innovation Teams*. Blekinge Institute of Technology.

Prior research has identified manifold factors (innovation enablers) that affect innovation teams from the perspectives of the organization, team, and team members. Here, the enablers are clustered into twenty factors (as illustrated in Fig. 2.3) to ease overview and communicate differences between them. Several of them span several perspectives, and they are therefore essential to discuss on that basis. All the factors mentioned below are more or less important for innovation teams in practical work, depending on the situation and project.

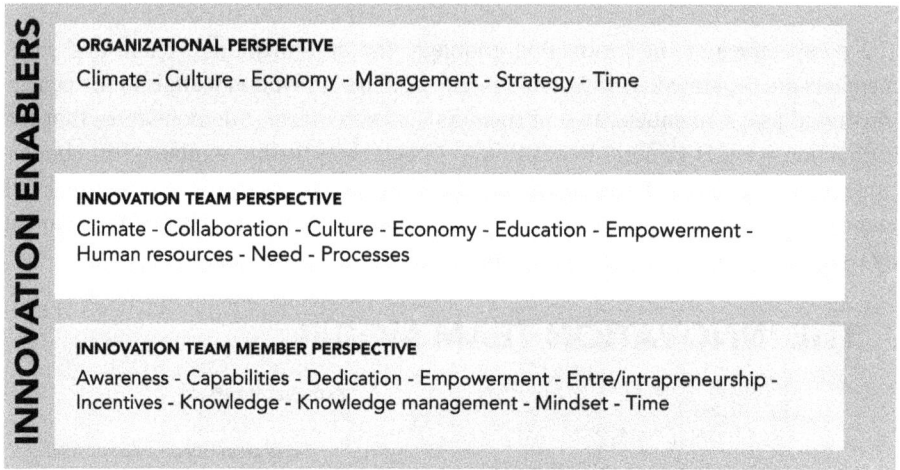

INNOVATION ENABLERS

ORGANIZATIONAL PERSPECTIVE

Climate - Culture - Economy - Management - Strategy - Time

INNOVATION TEAM PERSPECTIVE

Climate - Collaboration - Culture - Economy - Education - Empowerment - Human resources - Need - Processes

INNOVATION TEAM MEMBER PERSPECTIVE

Awareness - Capabilities - Dedication - Empowerment - Entre/intrapreneurship - Incentives - Knowledge - Knowledge management - Mindset - Time

Fig. 2.3: The perspectives of innovation enablers. The figure is inspired by Johnsson, M. (2017), Innovation Enablers for Innovation Teams – A Review. *Journal of Innovation Management,* 5(3), 75–121.

As you familiarize yourself with each of the innovation enablers described, you will notice that some of them seem very close to each other, even overlapping, so it can be somewhat challenging to separate them at first. Therefore, you must practice recognizing them individually and then understand how their connections depend on the perspective you take. Also, sometimes they are context-dependent, meaning that a situation must be interpreted as a whole, not divorced from its context. Incomplete understanding may lead to misunderstanding. At the end of each innovation enabler described, they are summarized across a few brief points. Table 2.1 summarizes innovation enablers from all three perspectives, in alphabetical order.

Tab. 2.1: The innovation enablers from the organizational, innovation team, and team member perspective.

#	Innovation enabler	Perspective		
		Organization	Innovation team	Team member
1	**Awareness**: the ability to "see" invisible or undiscovered innovation-related opportunities			X
2	**Capabilities**: skills and knowledge needed to work in innovation teams			X
3	**Climate**: an encouraging environment stimulating new innovative initiatives and creativity	X	X	
4	**Collaboration**: functional innovation teams and collaborations internally between departments, and externally with suppliers, customers, and expert networks		X	
5	**Culture**: norms and rules for "how to do here"; Tolerance for initiatives that go wrong	X	X	
6	**Dedication**: the personal commitment to want to participate in an innovation team			X
7	**Economy**: monetary and non-monetary resources	X	X	
8	**Education**: innovation-related competence development in theory and practice		X	
9	**Empowerment**: trust from management to the innovation team to make their own decisions about resources or investments; autonomous work under the responsibility of the members of the innovation team		X	X
10	**Entre-/intrapreneurship**: "doers" who make things happen			X
11	**Human resources**: access to colleagues within the organization who can contribute to the innovation project and who can also share experiences and help avoid bottlenecks		X	
12	**Incentives**: financial and non-monetary rewards as motivators			X
13	**Knowledge**: special knowledge concerning innovation and innovation work; diverse knowledge areas			X
14	**Knowledge management**: knowledge of how to, in practice, use knowledge and fill knowledge gaps concerning innovation projects			X

Tab. 2.1 (continued)

#	Innovation enabler	Perspective		
		Organization	Innovation team	Team member
15	**Management**: encouragement of exploration of new ideas	X		
16	**Mindset**: self-confidence and attitude of the innovation team members – "I can. . .," "I want. . .," "I will. . ."			X
17	**Need**: explicit and clarified customer needs to meet, to explain why the innovation project is required		X	
18	**Processes**: processes, models, and proven innovation methods that guide from idea to established product on the market		X	
19	**Strategy**: structured ways to invest in short- and long-term innovation projects	X		
20	**Time**: time set aside for the innovation project, time for reflection, and time for education and learning throughout the organization	X		

Innovation enablers from an organizational perspective

This section demonstrates six factors that affect an innovation team from an organizational perspective: climate, culture, economics, management, strategy, and time. Among these factors, management gets special attention, as management in many ways determines how the remaining enablers are made possible.

Innovation enablers from the organizational perspective:
- Climate – an encouraging environment stimulating new innovative initiatives and creativity
- Culture – norms and rules for "how to do here." Tolerance for initiatives that go wrong
- Economy – monetary and non-monetary resources
- Management – encouragement of exploration of new ideas
- Strategy – structured ways to invest in short- and long-term innovation projects
- Time – time set aside for the innovation project, time for reflection, and time for education and learning

Climate

From an organizational perspective, the innovation climate stems from working together with innovation within the organization, developed through shared experience of common policies, approaches, and procedures. Climate is generally less stable than culture is, and it can be considered an expression of a culture at a specific moment, a snapshot. Climate refers to human aspects, such as behavior, while culture relates to structures. It has been shown that organizations which create an innovative climate are, in general, financially more favorable than are others. The climate significantly influences employee motivation to be creative, which is a part of the innovation process, as further described in followings sections, and is among the keys to developing an innovative organization.

Nevertheless, an innovative climate is a relatively complex area consisting of various factors, as briefly outlined below. Most of these factors are independent, but with slightly different content and meaning. Most of today's research on innovation climate stems from Göran Ekvall, who already in the 1990s presented ten dimensions for a creative and innovative climate from an organizational perspective. Still, research is ongoing regarding how these factors affect an organization's ability to innovate:

Resources
- Challenge – are employees challenged, emotionally involved and committed?
- Idea time – is there time to reflect before acting?
- Idea support – are there enough resources allocated to try new ideas?

Safety
- Trust – do people feel secure expressing different opinions?
- Playfulness – is the work environment relaxed, and is it okay to have fun?
- Lack of conflicts – are there personal conflicts?
- Dynamics – is the organization dynamic to change?

Curiosity
- Debate – to what extent do people discuss different topics?
- Freedom – are employees free and able to decide their work?
- Risk-taking – is it okay to fail with an initiative?

As stated, a climate is less rooted than culture. As such, by relatively simple means it is possible to change a non-innovative climate into an innovative one. To make a non-innovative culture innovative, though, requires long-term and sustainable work. It does not happen overnight. Since the focus is on innovation teams and how they can work with innovation projects, its climate will also be discussed in the coming sections in this chapter.

Brief summary of climate
- An innovative climate has a positive effect on innovation work and is easier to change than culture.
- An innovative work climate benefits the organization financially.

-   An innovative climate encourages creativity, which is the beginning of innovation work.

Culture

Culture is usually defined by shared values, norms, and knowledge, both conscious and unconscious. Culture does not have to be visible at first glance, but rather, "it is just there" or it "sits in the walls." Within an organization or an innovation team, culture is influenced by members' behavior and treatment, based on their fundamental values, assumptions, and beliefs. An organization's culture is greatly influenced by management when in the recruitment of new staff. To create and encourage a culture for innovation, they should strive to bring in employees with varying knowledge, abilities, backgrounds, interests, and gender. A strong culture ensures that everyone is on the right track and thus plays a vital role in the organization's innovation capacity, which must also be reflected in the various phases of the innovation process; for example, idea generation work differs significantly from development work and market introduction.

A strong culture is nurturing for newcomers to learn, through the culture, how things are done, for example, through internal training or reprimands. Some of the most essential factors in creating an innovative culture are tolerance for mistakes and constant open communication. To some extent, an organization should even encourage individuals to make mistakes, as long as doing so leads to improvement and learning. In organizations where mistakes are punished, employees commonly become passive, which stifles innovation. A positive culture for innovation is based on a complex system of different factors contributing in different ways. In a negative culture, resentment easily rises against new proposals and initiatives that could lead to new products.

Changing a culture requires long-term work. Years of persistent work are to be expected, starting with management acting as role models. Of course, a well-developed plan for change is also necessary. From the perspective of an innovation team, management should communicate to other employees in the organization that it is okay to become involved in an innovation team's work.

Brief summary of culture
-   The culture "sits in the walls" and takes a long time to change – be persistent when aiming for change.
-   Employees influence culture. Keep that in mind when recruiting your next co-worker.
-   Tolerance for failure is an important part of a culture that promotes innovation, as long as it leads to increased learning.

Economy

Economy is usually described as monetary resources, but it can also correspond to what an organization invests in an innovation project (e.g., in terms of time, hardware and software, education, and human resources). Not only is this enabler important for the current or planned innovation project, but also it shows that innovation is valuable for the organization. Here, the difference between large and small organizations is considerable. While small organizations can be agile and entrepreneurial, a large organization can buy what is needed and, thus, more easily than small organizations attract both customers and suppliers. However, this is also a management issue in that management must demonstrate their preparation to invest in innovation projects, which correspond definitionally to certain risks.

Furthermore, investment is necessary to develop capabilities for collaboration and innovation, not only for the creation of technical and non-technical products. One way to make such an investment in an organization is to encourage innovation initiatives that arise not only for example, in R&D. In short, the economy has several dimensions. A reserved budget can lead to faster innovation if it is combined with self-government. However, a budget that does not allow for sufficient time is useless. Work is not done by itself. A solution to lack of time can be to relieve parts of the innovation team members' everyday work to make time for tasks that contribute to the innovation project. Yet another problem is that the focus on innovation work is limited if financial problems occur repeatedly.

Brief summary of economy

  Invest in a reserved innovation budget for long-term survival.
- Combine monetary and non-monetary resources in an innovation budget.
- Invest in combining technical development with non-technical innovation projects, such as organizational development.

Management

To maintain competitiveness, organizations need to innovate continually, which also means that management and leadership must be developed. Some of the driving forces for this development include competitors, threats from new market players, and rapid technological change.

Techniques to accelerate management development include consciously reminding management of the importance of management development, questioning, creating a problem-solving culture, changing the work environment, and building experience with new cultures. This is a challenge for management and forces it to be on its toes to handle scenarios and perspectives with unique difficulties. Generally speaking, it is about creating leadership that allows the low-risk exploration of new ideas without risking the organization's functions or business. Any mental barriers that cause management to reject more radical ideas automatically must also be identified. Too often, management is being rewarded for small, harmless changes rather than for more daring investments and prefer to focus on historical success as a recipe for new success, and do not base their perception of potential success on the current state of affairs and on future trends. By contrast, Innovation usually requires a medium-long- or long-term perspective to be implemented, often entailing several years of work. Therefore, strong determination and perseverance is required, which is linked to stable, sustainable management and access to skilled employees who understand how to stimulate and develop the conditions for collaboration between functions and other organizations and to become more competitive.

Top and middle managers have different roles in innovation work. The top managers are expected to convey and communicate visions and goals in broad terms and to connect middle managers to these goals. Middle managers then translate these into activities according to an innovation process. This process requires a comprehensive portfolio of competencies, such as good knowledge of organizational theory, behavioral knowledge, and negotiation techniques, so the presence of middle managers' is crucial to the eventual result. Changing an organization takes a long time, often 6–10 years, and the most challenging work occurs after the initial enthusiasm has subsided. It has been repeatedly pointed out that managers' and middle managers' convictions are key to creating links between economic, structural, social, and cognitive activities, considered the cornerstones of strategic innovation work.

A formally structured young organization is often less innovative than is an informally structured one, but formalization in an older organization does not necessarily harm innovation work. A flat network-based structure enabling communication and encouraging multifunctional work is among the most successful ways of working. To make it work, however, management must show leadership that encourages employees to work as an innovation team supporting diversity and togetherness, but where there is an opportunity to work independently in the very earliest phases of innovation work. Structures also include the implementation of effective innovation processes that provide an organization with new ideas that can be developed so that the organization can remain competitive. Such processes require internal and external networks to consist of a mix of customers, competitors, and consultants. When this mix is developed and work, its components become important sources of new ideas that can be further developed or stimulate already ongoing initiatives in the organization.

Strategic leadership can be said to be a process linking strategic planning, implementation, and follow-up with recurring learning, competence development, and change. Value creation through optimizing the innovation process has become a subject of increasing interesting at the management level. It enables the creation of products even in the short term; in the longer view, intangible values are generated, such as technical leadership and better market positioning.

Open leadership inspires independent work and influences creativity both individually and organizationally. To achieve that, management must better understand the individual's need for autonomy and structure to be motivated and devoted, as well as to assure employees they will not be punished for mistakes. Furthermore, complex organizational forms must be managed to help the organization develop a structure to stimulate innovation. Mangers have to support flexible and original thinking and act as role models of this thinking. When aiming for radical innovations, management needs to support the abilities and skills of employees in the various phases of the innovation process: that is, to explore and discover new innovative opportunities, to create business plans and business opportunities from what has been identified, and to build the business itself so that the developed innovation can stand on its own two feet. When the management significantly supports an innovation project, it positively affects the project in several ways. Work is conducted more efficiently, for example, idea generation accelerates, products reach the market faster, and the innovation team learns more quickly from various problems and disturbances along the way. Likewise, absent management harms an innovation team's work such that it diminishes the innovation team's ability to complete it. With this knowledge, management can by simple means support the innovation team and increase the pace of development work. Simply put, show appreciation and be interested in what the innovation team does. When the innovation team gets stuck, they need sympathy and emotional support. It helps the team solve problems and get back to work.

An effective leader of an innovative organization must encourage both exploratory and exploitative work and must be able to switch flexibly between different forms of leadership. Encouraging exploration means applying an open leadership style and encouraging people to work in different ways, experiment, and allow for independent thought and activities, as well as promote attempts to challenge established patterns and routines to upset the status quo. However, management must consider whether the organization is mature enough to execute such exploratory work. If there is too much tension in the organization, it may be appropriate to first test such exploration outside the regular organization. Still, project managers must have the required experience to handle this type of two-way leadership. Management must also manage and facilitate the new knowledge created in an innovation project. When top management increases its formal control, which often happens, this increase usually signals that they want more explicit knowledge (i.e., more documented instructions and governing documents). Too much control risks not only destroying the important link between tacit knowledge and explicit knowledge, because it is in the periphery that new knowledge can be created, but it also risks reducing opportunities for knowledge gathering in general and, in the long run, negatively affecting innovation work. One must also be aware that a possible relocation of innovation initiatives can affect the rest of the organization. New ideas arise not only in R&D. They arise everywhere and all the time. An inability to access inspiring employees to collaborate with them has a negative effect for innovation initiatives. Any relocation of innovation work should therefore be temporary, and as soon as possible, it should be reintegrated into regular operations or completely spun off to independent organizations.

A mix of exploratory and exploitative innovation work is necessary. Too much focus on either may be fatal for the business. Being always first introducing products on the market requires enormous marketing resources to break through to a traditional market, but the advantage of this priority is that a significant market share can quickly be seized if the investment is right. To some extent, the market leader can drive the innovation agenda, and others are forced to follow, chasing the market. However, being first is no guarantee of success. The timing must also be right. The trick is to be both first and best. To some extent, being a good runner-up means profiting the hard work of others by following in their wake and saving development costs. As they say, "The second mouse gets the cheese."

However, there are no free rides in innovation work. It requires organizations to be fast and flexible, able to adapt to what competitors invent. The difficulty with being a latecomer to the market is to constantly find unique offerings for things that are already known, and it is easy to end up in a price war. The aim to be first and best translates into simultaneously introducing completely new products and improving existing ones. Consider again the innovation project portfolio. When planning to make both of these investments simultaneously in an organization, managers must allocate both resources and abilities to these entirely different ways of working, which are sometimes contradictory. Exploratory innovation work presupposes risk taking and sees deviations as opportunities, while incremental innovation work strives to prevent risk and deviation. To manage these two components, one must take advantage of entrepreneurs in the organization, because they can often manage risks, innovation, proactivity, and competition more naturally than others. Such people are important for an organization that wants to remain competitive. Fast organizations win over slow organizations, and entrepreneurs are quick. Overall, strategies are needed to plan for a portfolio of innovation projects including a mix of large and risky innovation projects and projects that involve continually evolving products.

Brief summary of management
- Be interested and present, but do not pick at details.
- Strive for a combination of incremental and radical innovation.
- Be persistent. The shift into an innovative organization takes time.

Strategy
Organizations with a conscious innovation strategy perform better than others, particularly when management prioritizes that strategy. An innovation strategy commonly divides into parts, for instance product innovation, process innovation, business system innovation, and resources for research and development for continued competitiveness. Together, these components create opportunities to develop new offers to customers and remain at the forefront of competitors. They are also used to successfully enter new markets, develop new products, and form a suitable product portfolio.

To create a capacity to achieve an innovation strategy, management must consciously stimulate learning by increasing knowledge of how to explore new and unexplored areas, for example new technology, businesses, or markets. When it comes to making this happen at the operational and management level, cooperation is often better than competition, because investments can then have a more significant effect. No matter which market area we aim for, the focus must always be on the end market. It is possible, of course, to aim for a local or global market, but it is almost impossible to first invest in one and then do the same thing in the other, because customers behave very differently. The copy-paste doesn't automatically succeed. Rather, even moving a business idea from one city to a nearby city in the same country can be quite challenging.

Therefore, new market-specific factors in the expansion plan must be considered. For example, Sweden is considered a test market regarding technology and design. Sweden is attractive in this role because Swedish people are seen as being aware of trends, they travel often, and they handle the English language quite well. They are also not very numerous, which limits marketing expenses. However, it doesn't always play out well. Swedish people also tend to be set on their traditions. In Umeå, a city in the Nordic area of Sweden, McDonald's is famous for being put out of business shortly after trying to establish its famous burgers. The reason is that citizens were used to use cutlery, even for hamburgers. When McDonald's didn't make an exception to this customer request, it didn't take long for their location to go out of business. Shortly after, the local franchisee, MAX, won the "hamburger war", of course providing cutlery to those who wanted it. Probably unknown to McDonald's at the point of market entry, but not to MAX, was that people south of Umeå don't use cutlery, but from Umeå and north, they do. Another example, the German grocer franchisee, Lidl, thought that a copy-paste of how cashiers operate in other places would also work in Sweden. The Lidl way was for the customer to place groceries on a very long conveyor belt, back into the shopping cart after being registered at the checkout and, after payment, into grocery bags at separate packing desks. Customers were furious about the logistic solution at the cashier, which to a large extent were the opposite of what they were used to in other grocery stores. It didn't take too long for Lidl to correct the mistake. The lesson learned is to do the homework before expanding businesses in unknown areas.

As an organization approaches collaboration with its customers, partners, and competitors, the strategic work of value creation and organizational design changes. Today, being competitive is very much about the ability to absorb new knowledge, no matter its source. It is not enough to have a well-developed strategy to learn new knowledge, however. The experience must also be spread and communicated efficiently and naturally throughout the organization to be understood and applied in the employees' daily work.

Brief summary of strategy
- Develop an innovation strategy – it pays off.
- Cooperation through mutual complement often yields better results than does competition.
- Be careful using copy-paste strategies – they can be costly.

Time
Time is frequently discussed in innovation work. Time is necessary for the actual work to, for example, obtain information about the market and to meet end-users, potential customers, suppliers, and more. Meaning, time is needed for things other than product development as well, including time for reflection on the knowledge generated by the flow of information and time to engage important networks. Further, time is needed to attend exhibitions of personal interest for inspiration outside the business, as it can turn out fruitful. Today, front-loading is often discussed as key to successful innovation work, which means that at the beginning of an innovation project, much time should be spent to understand what problems to solve. The more time spent to define, frame, and understand the underlying problem, the greater the chances of achieving creative results. In any case, management must show its commitment by investing time and money to encourage the development and implementation of new ideas and processes, without overburdening people with too many or too varied projects. As a team member, everyone needs to know how much time must be spent on the innovation team's projects – at least 10–15 percent, is a guideline for most organizations that consciously engage their employees in innovation work. However, adding innovation work to someone fully occupied already will not drive the work forward but rather cause stress and underperformance.

Brief summary of time
- Invest time to engage networks, frontloading and inspiration – it pays off.
- Set aside time that really exists – do not place innovation projects on top of all other work.
- At least 10–15 percent work time or more is reasonable for a member of an innovation team.

Innovation enablers from the innovation team's perspective
In this section, the focus shifts slightly to innovation-enabling factors from the perspective of the innovation team. From this perspective, it appears as one unit, surrounded by the organization's different departments and overall context. Here, we find nine other conditions:
- Climate – an encouraging environment stimulating new innovative initiatives and creativity

- Collaboration – functional innovation teams and collaborations internally between departments, and externally with suppliers, customers, and expert networks
- Culture – norms and rules for "how to do here"; tolerance for initiatives that go wrong
- Economy – monetary and non-monetary resources
- Education – innovation-related competence development in theory and practice
- Empowerment – trust from management to the innovation team to make their own decisions about resources or investments; autonomous work under the responsibility of the members of the innovation team
- Human resources – access to colleagues within an organization who can contribute to the innovation project and who can also share experiences and help avoid bottlenecks
- Need – explicit and clarified customer needs to meet, to explain why the innovation project is required
- Processes – processes, models, and proven innovation methods that guide from idea to established product on the market

Climate

Climate, as known from the organizational perspective recurs here, but from the perspective of the innovation team. That is, team members need empowerment, room for innovative work, and the confidence to share ideas with other team members. Further, the innovation team needs leadership that promotes internal and external networking with other teams and customers, people with good initiatives, confidence in other innovation team members, and the involvement of people from other projects. The main difference concerns leadership, where an innovation team should lead itself, collaboratively. Shared leadership is difficult to achieve (as detailed in chapter three). Furthermore, the climate in an innovation team must also be allowed to have different conditions than other projects. Management should preferably be more of a service department than a monitoring authority, leaving the team to work in peace, with the time to listen and discuss in a relaxed way. On the other hand, the team members have a great responsibility to get involved in the innovation project on their own. Tasks are created by and performed by the innovation team itself and its network, not least through collaboration with other departments within the organization. Hence, it is critical for management to understand the importance of the team's access to resources through human capital. Each innovation team member determines their degree of involvement and is responsible for getting involved in the work – those who do not get involved risk negatively impacting the project with delays.

In addition to all the organizational factors that affect an innovative work climate, the innovation team itself shapes how the climate is to be developed by believing that they can achieve excellence in their work and feeling that they can solve all problems that may arise. As the innovation team will be relatively small, with only a few members, it has substantial opportunity to influence the development of the climate. However, doing so requires the team need to be introduced, at an early stage, to what an innovative climate is and which factors are decisive. In this work, the facilitator plays an important role (further described in chapter three), but more about that function a bit later in this and chapter three. Establishing an innovative climate is largely based on management believing in the innovation team and themselves acting as role models, supporting ideas, and being committed to the innovation team's work.

Brief summary of climate
- Innovation teams need the freedom to control and organize themselves.
- The members of the innovation team are accountable for tasks and how the climate develops.
- The members of the innovation team encourage shared leadership and lead together as a team.

Collaboration
Collaboration, instead of competition, usually leads to increased value. From an innovation perspective, collaborations in both the short and long term can lead to innovations if the team is open to new impressions and new ways of thinking. And it is just as important that innovation teams be able to collaborate both internally and externally. In general, building good relationships takes a long time, but a good relationship can be quickly destroyed if either party begins misbehaving. This is because collaborations are social relationships built through interaction between people, where open communication and information flow are the necessary tools. Communication is an oft-used concept and a tool for knowledge exchange between individuals. In order to function as well as possible, it must be straightforward and advance the work in the desired direction, towards intermediate goals, objectives, and visions that everyone understands and can stand behind.

Multifunctional, including multidisciplinary, work such as internal collaboration in an organization not only saves time and money, but also improves production and processes. Further, it improves soft values, such as teamwork, communication, and employee involvement. Multifunctional work depends on an open and cooperative culture, however, with participatory management and employees who share information and new ideas. This culture requires, for example, the allowance of overlaps between different departments' participating a project, so that information can be efficiently shared and adapted. At the individual level, the team member needs to feel that they have a specialty or expertise of some kind, that the team's members have something in common around which to build the expertise (such as a project), that team members share an understanding of and are driven by the benefits of differences between individuals, and that members be able to use methods that further strengthen collaboration.

The old expression "customer in the center," or "customer-centered design," is still valid, but innovation work today must include more groups to collaborate with, which means involving end-users, end-customers, suppliers, expert networks, partners, and competitors for those who want to stretch innovativeness even further. Having representatives or team members in direct contact with all these groups creates a more comprehensive picture of what needs to be developed. At the same time, the network of stakeholders risks becoming too extensive, with too many different expectations that must be met.

Collaborating with users is not easy. Preferably, collaboration should occur with end-users who have an impact on other end-users, who can influence the end-customers. In some cases, the end-user and end-customer is the same person. To elaborate, one particularly interesting group of users are "extreme end-users." These users do not merely use products to their breaking point, but adapt and modify products by removing, adding, and combining them with other components and products to deliver functions intended to suit their extreme perspective and area of use. Although extreme users tend to have excessive demands and may therefore represent a limited market, they can be a source of inspiration for new ideas that give rise to new products. Therefore, the innovation team must identify the proper end-user relating to the original problem to solve, chose carefully, and initiate collaboration.

Meeting customers' explicit and unspoken needs by studying their behavior prompts better market understanding. It is essential to understand the difference between one customer and another, however. What is identified as a customer may sell to another customer, and so on. It is important to understand the entire chain of customers to the end-customer. The end-customer makes the final purchasing decision, and the choice of purchase will affect the producing companies in the contract manufacturing industry. For example, substantial conversion occurs among contract manufacturers who manufacture mechanical drivelines and gearboxes for the car industry by the end-customers (i.e., car buyers, now buying more and more electric cars). This high conversion rate leads to mechanical drivelines and gearboxes are not needed in the same way as they are for combustion-engine-powered vehicles. If contract manufacturers do not keep track of this trend, they risk facing a scenario similar to that of the financial crisis.

While the end-customer makes the crucial purchase decision, the decision may well be based on pressure faced by the end-user, which provides another aspect to understand. An example of this is the pressure employees exert when it is time for new work tools, such as new company vehicles. In one case, management in transportation organizations was offered a favorable deal on a brand of vehicles, but they ended up buying another brand – for the reason that the entire staff refused to drive what was offered, threatening to quit on the spot. Another example is our sweet children who, applying great pressure, can move the purchase decision of a product to a completely different product that still has the same function. For example, clothes or new cell phones tend to be sensitive in that matter. In general, the benefits of customer involvement are faster development and feedback on product proposals. However, customers do not always know what they need, as they may not always be up to date in terms of technical or functional competences. Therefore, customer involvement fits in different places in the innovation process. In incremental development, customer involvement fits best early in the process, while it fits better late in more radical innovation projects.

Many have objected that it is risky to involve end-users and end-customers in development work, arguing that critical information can leak to competitors. Sure, it's a risk. But there are even more significant business risks in not involving them, and customer involvement does not necessarily entail meeting the end-customers in person. Making observations at a distance, important information can be collected to develop ideas and concepts, which can then be presented in future product proposals and thus garner buy signals. An easy to grasp example is "Print on demand." The manuscript is ready, but will not be printed until it is ordered, reducing the publisher's risk. More closely related to innovation are exhibitions in which concepts are shown to garner reactions from the market. Depending on the response, future products have elements of what was shown at the fair. Another example is small start-ups offering concepts and prototypes on various internet platforms where end-customers can pre-order a product without it being available at the time of the order. When a certain number of products has been sold, the product is manufactured. The same phenomenon exists in the real estate industry, where a property developer shows future apartments or houses. Customers are required to pay a down-payment before the home is finally designed and built. An economist might call this "cash management" or "risk minimization." No customers – no production. Regardless of product focus, customers need to be studied to capture critical elements in need of resolution and to understand the market in which the product is available.

The suppliers' knowledge of new technology is essential, and it is accessed through collaborations. Such collaboration is especially important for large organizations to work with suppliers, as they are not usually as entrepreneurial as smaller organizations are. Being attentive to what is offered by suppliers can play out well. It is not uncommon to be offered "shelf heaters" that the supplier would like to get rid of, for instance, and an everyday example seen in clothing stores nowadays is "mid-season sales," where the stores have understood that inventories not sold by a specific date must be sold at a significantly reduced price to be sold at all. As a customer, this time presents an opportunity to get a good deal. On the other hand, the season to feel comfortable with the clothes bought at a bargain may be short. "Mid-season" deals are obvious, while "shelf heaters" are perhaps not. Considering a potential short season, it will be interesting to see how the car industry plans to clean out its warehouses as the complete halt of sales of combustion engine vehicles is close to reality. They are already banned in an increasing number of large cities. However, technology trading at the component level or material suppliers may not be short-term in their trading. Still, they are affected by commodity prices and exchange rates, which affect how much profit margin the same product provides when selling. So, to stay up to date on what suppliers offer, get familiarized with their technology development and future plans by attending trade fairs, joining discussion groups, attending seminars, and the like.

Networking with experts is always relevant to innovation work. In practice, this means participating in business networks, conferences, and courses sharing experiences and lessons learned. The advantages of the networks include increased information flow, which stimulates an innovative climate and increases know-how. Another advantage is to learn to hear the difference between discussions and sales pitches. Sometimes, "round table conversations" – which are basically good for the participants to discuss a given topic from their different perspectives – are in practice an exercise in "listen-to-me -because-I-have-right-conversation." Not so stimulating.

Collaborating with strategic partners on a long-term basis may seem obvious, but it is worth pointing out that collaborations with universities can lead to competitive advantages and sustainable innovative results, which may not be initially obvious. The academy can sometimes be perceived as cumbersome and somewhat slow to collaborate with, but it opens fantastic opportunities for organizations to get involved in student work in the slightly shorter term, as well as research in the longer term. In student projects, it is possible to relatively easily get many different conceptual proposals for solutions to a clear and delimited problem, for example help with visualizations, business plans, market research, design proposals, and much, much more. Student work can jump-start a project and inspire further development by an innovation team or other parts of an organization.

Research collaborations are a bit different. There, both the organization and the academy need to find an intersection where each parties' problems can be explored to create long-term values for both parties. Actively participating in research provides an advantage that may not be completely obvious at first. It is easy to think that reading the most recent published scientific publications will give the biggest knowledge advantages compared to others in the same industry. This notion overlooks something, though: what is presented as the "latest in research" is a report based on material that may be several years old. Most research is conducted through research grants from various funders through calls, where an application usually takes several months to write. This is because organizations must be involved, and the university must ensure the quality of the project proposal before it is sent to the funder for evaluation. Subsequently, the application must be processed and reviewed by experts, which also takes several months and may mean a year of waiting for information on whether the research can even start. If the message is positive, the research begins, data is collected for the question posed, then analyzed, and its results are discussed. By this point, another year or two may have passed since the project idea was conceived. The next step is to write the article itself, which will hopefully be published in a scientific journal. The writing is relatively fast, but then it can take from a month to several years before the results are published. So, what is presented as new on the radio or in the daily press has been known for a long time by the organization involved in the research, and having such knowledge at that early stage can be a competitive advantage. Those involved in the research know its results when they arise. This knowledge can be shaped into, for example, new competitive products, working methods, or processes.

It can also be valuable to join networks in other contexts, seeing them from your perspective. This experience increases opportunities for disruptive innovations. Two organizations that differ in business areas are likely to find existing opportunities, merging their core competencies into new products. However, they must complete one other, not being too different, which complicates collaboration and, therefore, inhibits innovation. Lasting collaborations rely on the parties having the right attitude, respecting each other, communicating positively, and having a strong will to work together. Contracts and agreements are a manner of confirming collaboration. However, before reaching the point where a contract is written, "no-strings-attached" collaboration is often a fruitful, which is to say, collaboration without ties or direct agreements that regulate it. Of course, normal decency, business acumen and business agreements apply. The advantage is that it is possible for collaborators to learn from each other and to subsequently increase their ability to innovate. To establish cooperation at all, it is wise not to discuss overly detailed agreements at the beginning, as this undoubtedly suppresses the desire for innovation. At the same time, overall agreements are necessary to create trust and demonstrate seriousness in the face of innovation work.

Collaborating with competitors to increase creativity, learning, and innovation, is unconventional. Before initiating a collaboration with another organization within the same business area, intellectual property rights (IPR) (e.g., patents and other copyright assets), should be reviewed to ensure no conflicts occurs on that point, at least. Sometimes there is unjustified concern about getting rid of intellectual property rights while at the same time as there is an underestimation of the benefits of exchanging experiences. Yet, don't be naive: Know-how is stolen or a source for inspiration all the time. One example of competitors collaborating is clusters of organizations. For example, organizations in the same business in the manufacturing industry can be delivering the same component to the same customer, particularly where the customer requires volumes that no one organization can manage to produce, but together they can. As they collaborate, they can meet the customer's needs and reduce their risks regarding heavy investments in machinery and personnel. From the customer's perspective, this arrangement reduces the risk regarding downtime, as two suppliers deliver independently.

Brief summary of collaboration
- Collaboration may lead to innovation, so find areas/competence that complement each other. Consider the IPR and that it is individuals who collaborate – not the name of the organization or brands. There must be a match.

- In innovation work, collaborations with end-users, customers, and suppliers are essential for positive results. Collaboration with competitors is also a way to innovation.
- Innovation team members should be able to collaborate within the team but also to create collaborations internal and external to the organization, preferably with the academy for inspiration and for access to early research results.

Culture
Like the climate, the innovation team's culture is also affected by the factors that come from the organizational perspective. In this context, the significant difference is that it relates to a newly formed innovation team, and then there are all the prerequisites to create a culture that promotes innovation work right from the start. As mentioned earlier, culture is more robust than climate. Therefore, it is crucial that bad behavior does not settle in the working atmosphere. As a result, choice of team members becomes essential. One of the most important key factors for a positive culture in the innovation team is tolerance for everyone making mistakes from time to time and an openness to bringing in temporary expertise. When this is to be translated into practice, the degree of openness will directly show how easy it is for new temporary members to join the innovation team and to support their expertise. Another key factor is that communication works within the innovation team. Through effective communication, any errors can be corrected and corrected more easily and quickly. Unfortunately, organizations sometimes tend to "darken" errors known in the early stages and send them on to the next person, who unknowingly continues the development work according to the prevailing conditions. The result is guaranteed to be an end product that either does not pass the final tests before delivery or comes back with a complaint. In the worst case, the customer becomes so irritated that they choose another supplier next time.

Creating a culture that detects and corrects faults but at the same time works quickly with various deliveries is always profitable. The 80–20 percent rule is a functional approach in this context, and it has two meanings. The first meaning is that when 20 percent of the project is completed, 80 percent of the future production costs for the product have been determined. As the project continues, changes become increasingly expensive to implement. The second meaning regards performing a job in three steps: First, conduct about 80 percent of a job, and then start something else for a while. Then come back and do 80 percent of the remaining 20 percent, and then break again for other work. The third time, complete the job. The advantage of interrupting the job to do other things is partly getting time for reflection, to allow problem-solving in the back of the mind, and partly getting time to brainstorm ideas with colleagues, which also gives rise to new solutions.

From the innovation team's perspective, the kick-off is the first opportunity for the culture to be created, as is further explored in chapter three. However, during the kick-off, the focus is very consciously on creating a dialogue about what expectations, rules of conduct, and norms should apply to this particular innovation team. It is absolutely necessary that the innovation team itself be allowed to develop their way of working with guidance from a knowledgeable person who trains the innovation team initially – the innovation facilitator (also described in chapter three).

Brief summary of culture
-   Be careful in choosing members of the innovation team, as they will set the culture.
-   Permission and understanding of the errors that occur from time to time are success factors for a positive, innovative culture, which requires open communication.
-   Make it easy for new members to understand the innovation team's norms and values. It makes the innovation team's work more efficient.

Economy
Economy, as mentioned in the section on the organization's perspective, has many dimensions. An earmarked budget and time set aside can, in combination with empowerment, lead to rapid innovation. Monetary resources (money) are necessary, to a certain level, for the creation of stability in the innovation team. It is essential to pay for, for example, components or consultants without having to unnecessarily involve people in the project. Lack of money often leads to an unnecessary amount of time and energy seeking financing solutions. It does not have to be a disaster for the team that is creative and willing to enter into collaborations or agreements and thereby exchange services. On the other hand, unlimited money often reduces creativity, carrying a risk that the developed product will be insufficiently optimized. One way to avoid this outcome is to set small intermediate goals for new and continued financing. This model is to some extent similar to a stage-gate model, which is traditionally not so innovative (more on that later in this chapter: The innovation process – Agile work for faster results). However, it is possible to form a hybrid model with short pauses in the work, even if it remains agile and flexible. Each sub-stage then has a budget for the innovation team to stick to. The working method can be useful from the perspective of risk management. The dilemma from an innovation perspective is the risk of getting stuck in specific solutions that are financed and "delivered," preventing further changes later despite the possibility of better solutions.

Brief summary of economy
-   Money, time, and empowerment in combination are positive for innovation.
-   Money is important, but unlimited access to money may decrease creativity.
-   Lack of money can be solved through collaborations.

Education

Highly innovative organizations create and maintain an environment in which they are constantly updated with new knowledge and practical skills. They also learn to leverage mistakes to generate new ideas and develop innovations. Training or education is related directly to the chances to discover new innovation opportunities. Therefore, education has become a tool to develop human capital and knowledge of how to handle the innovation process and the associated uncertainty. Specific innovation training has been developed over decades to include practical skills, from the identification of new opportunities for product development and the release of a profitable product into the market. As innovation work has evolved from being, in principle, exclusively an area of engineering or technology to becoming interdisciplinary and multifunctional, related education has also been successfully developed in the same direction, with a well-integrated business focus.

The Internet has allowed more people to share their knowledge, no matter their location. There are basically no limitations to how many people can access the same material. It also makes education accessible that is suitable for varied learning methods, which is good because we all have slightly different ways of absorbing knowledge. With new opportunities, new demands are also placed on teaching and learning. Significant challenges including avoiding information fatigue or information overload through confronting too much information, which then becomes difficult to absorb.

Despite the technical development, innovation knowledge and education are mainly about non-technical skills, such as creativity in problem identification and problem solving, critical thinking, contextual understanding, information seeking, conclusion drawing, self-motivation, concept descriptions, and presentation techniques. Other skills to practice include the ability to developing ideal systems based on imagination and abstract thinking, to reduce existing components in existing systems, or to generate new purposes for an already existing product. In general, learning is about setting aside time for education and about wanting to learn. The greatest threats are not devoting enough time, preparing poorly, and not being genuinely interested. Indeed, there are techniques for advanced knowledge learning. Soon (hopefully?), it may be possible to download new knowledge and skills a little faster, just as in *The Lawnmower Man*, *Johnny Mnemonic*, or *The Matrix*. Until then, traditional "practice makes perfect" applies.

Brief summary of education
- Education in innovation management and leadership is necessary in this context for the same reasons that engineers, economists, or lawyers are educated and further trained in theirs. Take advantage of technology in training. Physical meetings may be unnecessary.
- Innovation is not only something technical. It is multifunctional and multidisciplinary.
- To benefit from education, the desire to educate and enough time is necessary.

Empowerment

Innovation teams allowed to work independently have greater control over their work situations. This allowance helps team members to use their energy to be creative around a common interest, in itself enabling innovation opportunities to be discovered and seized faster than would otherwise be the case. Suppose this independence is combined with supportive and committed leadership that provides the team the freedom to make and take responsibility for their own decisions. In that case, great opportunities for innovation emerge. By contrast, too much autonomy or too much independence can also have adverse effects on performance. Therefore, a balance between strategic and operational autonomy needs to be developed in an organization, where employees can be responsible for how the processes are handled, but not necessarily have decision-making power over strategic product areas. Too much room for self-government on the innovation team can easily reduce focus. The opposite leads to too rigid processes.

Empowering innovation teams means the management and sponsor trust the innovation team to plan and decide which tasks are to be performed to achieve the goal. If this prioritization of trust is new, managers may find it challenging to let go of control and stand in the position of spectator. To practice, keep the first innovation project small, with a short timeframe, with minimal risks. Learning through practice is key.

If this is the first time the organization has created an innovation team, it can be challenging to know how to work independently and take responsibility for any completely new tasks that are part of the innovation process, as well as to establish collaboration with completely new partners. From a management perspective, they must feel confident that the innovation team is doing what is expected. From the perspective of the innovation team, it is mainly about being humble before the task and seeking support from experts in areas not currently being mastered. Another dimension that arises when a team is unfamiliar with empowerment is that the team doesn't dare to drive the work. Those who have worked in an organization where the boss is the law struggle to ignore that habit when control is loosened. It's easy to be a world champion from the TV couch. Many of us can attest to that. It is just as easy to have the best tips in the coffee room about how innovation work should be managed or executed. So, when given the opportunity, it is advisable to gear up, get together in the team, prepare, and embrace the adventure.

Brief summary of empowerment
- Independent and self-directed work stimulates creativity.
- Too little autonomy inhibits decision-making, but too much reduces focus on the task.
- Seize the opportunity to empowerment when it arises.

Human resources

Many argue that human resources (i.e., employees and their competence in an organization) are among the important resources and key factors for an innovative organization. This is because employees with their knowledge and competence are involved in all innovation activities. Unfortunately, this level of involvement is not always the case in practice, but it is not uncommon that innovation work is dedicated or isolated to various special departments (e.g., development departments). The advantages of involving more employees are that they perform better and can gain a better understanding of the market. They can thus create more unique solutions to better suit the target group. Another advantage of involving employees outside the development department relates to commitment. Clearly informing employees about ongoing innovation projects allows them to more easily get involved and contribute to the innovation work. We have all heard the glamorous stories of lone successful innovators, but these stories do not reflect reality. There are always more people in the background who have contributed with competence in some way. If it is not family, partners, friends, cofounders, or employees, it is suppliers or others with a market connection of some kind who have been involved and contributed to the success.

Other than data, innovative organizations make decisions based on their human resources, where the ability to respond to the ever-changing market situation lies with employees' intellectual capacity. Employees who are competitive in the market have the confidence and ability to push their limits to achieve new skills in new areas. To this end, an organization must strive to attract people with the right skills by developing and retaining creative people and actively identifying, recruiting, training, educating, paying attention to, and encouraging innovative employees. Knowledge is generally an asset that must be continually maintained to remain. Innovation-related knowledge is no exception. It must be practiced and continuously developed. Otherwise, methods of working soon become antiquated and inefficient.

Certain courageous organizations deliberately employ people who stay in neither the comfort zone nor the middle lane. These people explore on their own, push things forward. They challenge structures and routines. However, a challenge with hiring such employees is that they can cause turbulence within an organization. From an innovation perspective, they are necessary not to end up in the status quo. However, this work must be done purposefully and include both management and other employees at all levels and areas within an organization, as they can cause much turbulence on their way to change the established. The people in the organization, together with the active participation of management, must understand that staff with different competencies should be available for different parts of the innovation work. As mentioned in the introduction, innovation work comprises all the work required to develop an idea for the market. Tasks that at first glance do not belong to innovation work can be absolutely critical; for example, consider competence in understanding market need, market analysis, material expertise, business modeling, supply chain, prototype, production, presentation, and so on. In this context, people who understand their knowledge in an area can contribute to the entire innovation project being developed better, which is a distinct success factor.

From an innovation team's perspective, entrepreneurial and driven people are a prerequisite for getting things done. One of the challenges in practical work with people with similar characteristics is that sometimes they cannot work together. The same can apply to people who are each entrepreneurial in their fields. Therefore, everyone must agree on what is important to prioritize at the moment and to cooperate. Therefore, from the perspective of the innovation team, it is important to access all talented employees in different departments.

Brief summary of human resources
-   The employees in an organization need accurate knowledge to innovate, but they also need to have the power and will to make a difference.
-   Access to employees from different parts of the organization is central to the innovation team's success.
-   The more people who can be involved in innovation work, the better for the organization as a whole. For the innovation team, it is essential that as many people as possible are aware of ongoing innovation initiatives.

Need
It has long been pointed out that organizations need to innovate. If new ideas are not developed and implemented, the business dies out. We have seen many examples of this. Mentioned to this day as examples of radical failures are companies such as Facit, a Swedish typewriter company, or Atari, an American arcade game company. In Atari's case, the company got such a bad reputation from its investment in the game version of the movie ET that the whole company collapsed. The game was perceived as too complicated for the target group, which led to it flopping and the share plummeting. Even today, ET is said to be one of history's biggest game fiascos. What is not often discussed is that Atari was in the middle of a platform change when it came to gaming technology, and Nintendo, which was developed at about the same time, took over most of the market with a better gaming experience. A similar situation occurred for Facit, which happened to be in the middle of the technology shift from analog to digital typewriters and collaborated with a Japanese partner. The company that would later become Sharp started its own sales operations without Facit's participation, which then had no market product of its own to sell and disappeared from the market. Interestingly though, Atari has risen from the dead. They have adopted the new technology with blockchains, launched their own cryptocurrency, ATRI (yes, the Atari token is spelled this way), and are building an active place in the metaverse for arcade games.

Rubik's cube, on the other hand, is variously mentioned as a success, but at the same time serves as a reminder of how important it is to think ahead in product development. The cube came from nowhere, as it seemed anyway, and sold in fantastic editions. It was developed as a mathematical problem and was patented around 1975 (i.e., almost five years before it broke through). The cube had no stated target group, and it is said that it took over a month for the mathematics genius and inventor Erno Rubik to solve it. Anyway, the cube became a success thanks to a driven marketer, and soon everyone wanted to have a cube. One hundred fifty million cubes were sold over three years in the early 1980s, a third of which were original. The market then died completely, and no one any longer wanted the cube. The problem was that it had been too good. When a person solved the cube, it was completed. There was no next level or more to do, except for doing it faster or blind. No possible product development could meet customers' needs, even if the Snake was a brave attempt to create more or less difficult challenging figures, it was not as successful as the cube. It took almost 30 years until the cube was relaunched, then in different variants with several lines and sides to solve.

Only a few remember Ericsson, the cell phone company and competitor to Nokia and Motorola at the time. First they lost the market to Nokia because they refused making phones looking like "soaps." Later they had the opportunity to collaborate with Apple on the iPhone but declined because they judged that the technology was substandard. The rest is history. Kodak made the same mistake with digitized photo technology. A Kodak employee even invented the digital camera, but the inventor had to hide his new camera because management did not believe in the technology. Nowadays, the catchy phrase "Kodak-moment" has dual meanings. It is not only about a nice photo shooting spot but also about radical mistakes missing market opportunities. Even though the electric car was invented close to one hundred years ago, Tesla (the automotive company) is mentioned as the cocky startup that came from nowhere and indirectly forced the intensive electric car conversion of todays. Tesla, first treated as a freak by its competitors, is now (at the time of writing this book) worth more than several of the biggest car manufacturers together.

However, it's easy to make the right choices in hindsight. The vast majority of us cannot easily know which organizations will make catastrophic mistakes with respect to revolutionary technology today. We are in the middle of change at the same time as we must understand it, alongside the future and the coming trends. Watch some documentaries to get a perspective on the present from a retro perspective. It is interesting. However, be careful. Examining the successful businesses of the past only teaches us about history and says very little about future success.

One of the reasons for the significant problems that many of these companies suffered during the financial crisis 2008–2009, causing mass unemployment, turned out to be that they lacked their own products to sell and lacked knowledge of how to develop new products, returning us to unspoken needs (see the previous section in this chapter about collaboration). For customers, such a need is one they have without even understanding it. These needs can be discovered by observing and studying how people behave or how things work in an organization. As soon as an unaddressed need has been identified, it can be developed into a business opportunity where core values and the target market are determined. Simultaneously, the organization's other goals and expectations must be considered. As such, applied research is significant because under controlled conditions, it is possible to test different hypotheses and drive development, learning, and knowledge dissemination on parallel tracks. This process benefits both the organization involved in the research and the society that receives some of the developed knowledge.

A practical dilemma is that new products can be perceived as cannibals in their organization; that is, new products compete with already established products that sell well and provide good margins. This has happened many times, such as in the music industry, where technology shifts have replaced each other regularly. Here, the advent of digitalization enabled the transition, although not entirely without resistance, to go from vinyl to CD and to streaming, soon replacing the physical product with a service, without the need for storage media for music. Some claim people will own nothing in the future. Instead, they will lease or subscribe to services of all kinds, which opens up service development for those aware of market changes.

Brief summary of need
– Engage networks. Believing you know everything about your market may cause serious problems.
– Dare to challenge customers with new and unexpected solutions to an identified, but perhaps unexpressed or not fully understood, need.
– Be prepared to adjust your product to new customer expectations quickly.

Processes
Over time, the innovation process has evolved from step-by-step development in silos to collaboration in iterative cycles. Iterative work in this context means that the same or similar work is repeated at different times in the innovation work depending on the outcome and possible changes in conditions. Nowadays, the goal is to establish interaction with customers and suppliers, both internally and externally, for example to explore technical opportunities, to build customer understanding and create a holistic understanding of the networks, and to co-develop new offers that create new value.

The general picture of the innovation process includes idea generation, development, launch, and value creation. In innovation teams without previous experience, a preparation phase is also proposed before the innovation project formally starts. The phases do not occur as isolated activities but based on their contextual conditions and vary by innovation strategy, organization, and network.

In truly innovative organizations, ideas come from anyone in the organization. These ideas are most commonly evaluated before they are further developed, to ensure that the same work is not conducted elsewhere in the organization. However, the dilemma with idea evaluation in the early phases is that it can be too easy to dismiss excellent ideas too early, inhibiting creativity and self-confidence. On the other hand, the advantage of early evaluation of ideas is that new initiatives can be consolidated and grow larger and stronger, while wasting resources on duplicating work can be avoided.

Methods have also been developed to apply innovation processes in practice. In one sense, it is about navigating between factors that enable and hinder innovation work to identifying new opportunities and to develop new goals to reach. In another, it is about the desired level of novelty. For small changes, to redesign something that already exists or create something entirely new requires different methods for a successful result.

The practical innovation work can be divided into different phases. Depending on which book is read, the innovation process is presented in between two and seven phases or more, which differ in the richness of their detail and their scopes in each phase. Studying the processes on a more holistic level, though, you will notice three clear phases with a distinct difference. In the first phase of the innovation process, the opportunities and ideas are in the focus, and in the later phase, development and implementation are in focus, which is also when the financial risks are greatest. Then follows another phase to identify and analyze values created through the work. One method to later avoid mistakes is to make them early in the first phases and then to learn from them. Fail fast – fail forward. In short, practical innovation work is about making mistakes quickly and cheaply early in the development of ideas and concepts.

The fail fast approach can be described in seven steps:
– Determine what characterizes success and failure,
– find the facts instead of making assumptions,
– be quick and make mistakes fast,
– continue making mistakes but do it cheaply through simple function prototypes and concept models,
– limit uncertainty factors,
– build a culture that celebrates smart mistakes and encourages new faults without repeating the same mistakes several times, and
– note and make available what has been learned through mistakes.

A similar approach is common in software development, testing solutions in fast iterations. An important tool in this work is visual design, which bridges knowledge to support innovation at its most abstract. For example, CAD and additive manufacturing methods such as 3D printers and 3D milling cutters are used to visualize and create artifacts to be touched, felt, and tested in natural environments before further development decisions are made. All of this is done to reduce financial risks in the innovation work and to speed the work towards the market. However, avoid introducing CAD and CAE tools too early, because their richness of detail inhibits the fast iterative process that, for example, simple sketches on a whiteboard allow. As the idea work approaches design solutions, CAD and CAE are superior, since they can now be used in practice for simulation and computational support.

Brief summary of processes
- On a holistic level, the innovation process divides into three phases: the creative phase; the implementation phase, where the product is developed and established on the market; and the third phase, value generation. Choose methods for each phase that best suit your idea; however, remember "cheap and fast."
- By setting a clear but open goal early in the process, it is easier to achieve results.
- In the early phase, use simple sketches. Then, use more advanced tools such as CAD and CAE in the later phases.

Innovation enablers from the innovation team's members' perspective
The factors that affect the innovation team from the team members' perspective are presented here. The individual's different competencies become prominent, alongside their ability to manage their knowledge and skills. These two aspects play an important role when a new innovation team is formed. The theoretical knowledge that a person has is important in this context. At least as important is for a member to be able to translate knowledge into actions based on their role in an innovation team. Here, ten factors enable the innovation team's work from the member's perspective, as explained. Certain factors are described from an organizational perspective because it is often organizational conditions and management decisions that can influence team members' practical work.

Innovation enablers from the innovation team's member's perspective:
- Awareness – the ability to "see" invisible or undiscovered innovation-related opportunities
- Capabilities – skills and knowledge needed to work in innovation teams
- Dedication – the personal commitment to want to participate in an innovation team
- Empowerment – trust from management in the innovation team to make their own decisions about resources or investments; autonomous work under the responsibility of the members of the innovation team
- Entre-/intrapreneurship – "doers" who make things happen
- Incentives – financial and non-monetary rewards as motivators
- Knowledge – special knowledge concerning innovation and innovation work
- Knowledge management – knowledge of how to, in practice, use knowledge and fill knowledge gaps concerning innovation projects
- Mindset – self-confidence and attitude of the innovation team members; "I can . . .," "I want. . .," "I will. . ."
- Time – time set aside for the innovation project, for reflection, and for education and learning throughout the organization

Awareness

An organization's success rests mainly on its ability to attend to what occurs outside the organization, where constant reflection is a key to successful innovation, alongside discussion and reflection on unconventional trends.

When it comes to discovering new innovation opportunities, attention to customers' experience of value is important because it requires a focus on benefits and cost drivers, which can spark innovation. This work considers knowledge of which tools and methods to use for what purpose, as they are different. Different results are produced by different tools, which might include lateral, metaphorical and positive thinking, association exercises, interpretive dreams, pattern mapping, or work about untapped or undiscovered markets. This wide variation means the tools must be chosen carefully. Consider a comparison with a home toolbox. Different tools are needed to hang a painting than to paint a wall or fix a flat tire. The more training and practice with the tools, the better the results.

Essentially, attention to innovation opportunities comes from the interaction of three components. The first is entrepreneurship, including attention to institutionalization, knowledge development, risk-taking, and the development of market-driven innovation culture. The second is knowledge and experience within and outside the organization, meaning knowledge of new markets, customers, and expertise. Last is access to the necessary technologies and competence.

The ability to detect opportunities relies on cognitive behavior and social constructivism, where the individual can detect patterns and simultaneously compare them with the environment and apply a trial-and-error mentality to build knowledge, which are two of the keys to innovation. The great thing is that these abilities can be learned, so everyone in an organization can contribute to innovation work if they receive education in it. An easy way to train employees is to ask them to pay attention to something specific. In a first exercise, it may be counting red lights on the way to and from work. Depending on what products are produced at the organization, a second suggested exercise is to count the places/situations where the products are used. Then, when people notice that they can consciously see things, they can soon imagine their organization's products in new contexts and situations where they do not exist today. Another way to apply this insight is to study how small entrepreneurial organizations work to learn how to reach the market.

As the cognitive ability to "see" opportunities increases, greater and more numerous opportunities are likely to be detected. The success of the Ford Mustang in the 1960s is a fantastic example. This super success was possible thanks to the catastrophic failure of a previous car model, the Ford Edsel, which is, to this day, some call it the greatest car fiasco of all time. In the development of the Edsel, many things were made by the "innovation book"; however, many were not. Simply put, expectations were not aligned to changes in the market situation. The average American was estimated to buy a new car every year or every second year. The Edsel was designed to fit the average Joe, meaning that success was assumed to be guaranteed. Everyone would want the Edsel. The ones who have seen the Simpson's show, the American adult animated show, when Homer becomes a car designer on behalf of his rich cousin, knows what came out. If you haven't seen it, browse the Internet for "Homer designs a car," and you will find a short clip of the episode. Well, the Edsel wasn't that bad, but timing and expectations were unsynchronized. Meanwhile, the interest in cheap sports cars had grown. Here, thanks to the huge investment in the development of the production system around the Edsel, the infrastructure was ready to produce the Ford Mustang, and the rest is history. However, the success of the Mustang would probably not have been possible if people at Ford had not been aware of the direction in which the market was developing and the fact that the Mustang could be produced in the existing production process.

Brief summary of awareness
– Awareness of what is happening in the market is important; foremost, the value customers perceive in a product and trends about users' behavioral changes.
– The ability to pay attention to innovation opportunities is about being present in the moment and being able to think laterally.
– The ability to pay attention to innovation opportunities can be trained – i.e., everyone can participate.

Capabilities
Capability can be explained as having the ability to "execute a particular job." In the context of innovation, capabilities relate variously to the different parts of the innovation process. It is insufficient to be able to make a good plan. The activities must also be carried out, because it is about getting things done to reach the market. Furthermore, skills and knowledge are necessary in specific areas unique to each industry. It is of essence to not forget that non-technical capabilities are as important as technical capabilities from the perspective of innovation. Technology continues to be considered a success factor in that technology development constitutes large parts or subsystems of new products and services that are developed. Still, technological development can be absolutely useless if no one can develop business cases around it.

The capability to handle technology also includes developing processes and systems, which relates to the non-technical capabilities for implementing new methods and processes and for establishing knowledge based on proven methods. In this area, the personal qualities that promote innovation work are considered: namely, understanding complexity, having high energy and self-confidence, and being able to make independent assessments and deal with contradictions. There are positive connections between innovation and intelligence, knowledge, curiosity, dissent, risk-taking, and willingness to pursue projects in goals.

Other important capabilities of the team members', which are rarely talked about, include awareness of strengths and ability to highlight them without bragging, but above all to be aware of shortcomings in certain areas, then to invite people who can limit or eliminate these shortcomings. It may be just enough to know where the right technical competence is and have the ability to involve it at the right time. What managers must consider, is when downsizing a company by cutting staff, a company is at significant risk of losing expertise, negatively affecting innovation work. Some of these potential problems can be solved by, for example, increased external collaboration.

Brief summary of capabilities
- In innovation work, non-technical and technical abilities are equally important.
- Individuals on the team must be able to make independent assessments, have self-confidence, master abstract thinking and deal with contradictions. To cope with this, intelligent employees are required who have the knowledge, interest, curiosity, and willingness to take risks.
- Cutting staff creates the risk of a significant loss of capabilities in the organization and the innovation team.

Dedication
Organizations comprising committed and entrepreneurial employees are known for solving problems and bringing solutions to the market faster than their competitors. However, in view of the individual, his or her motivation to engage must balance being bored due to not having a sufficiently challenging job and not having control because there is too much to do.

The driving force that makes an individual do anything at all is said to come from three different directions. Here, a distinction is made between external, internal, and relationship-driven driving forces. That is, something outside the individual creates the driving force, that the power comes from the individual himself, or in relation with other individuals. When a person is motivated by internal factors, it is mainly about confirmation from others through feedback and recognition for something they have done that has been appreciated, which yields the best results in the long run. Although it is known that external driving forces such as rewards in the form of bonuses lack a long-term effect on individuals' general driving forces, this is how companies usually reward their employees for a job well done. In fact, it is not at all certain that this will make anyone more passionate about their work, which can eventually hamper creativity and innovation.

The driving forces that come from within the individual are most associated with a genuine interest in the work, where the work itself is the reward. They do not come from external pressure. Admittedly, a certain amount of pressure can positively affect the work environment, but only if it is perceived as being caused by the situation and therefore causes something to be given higher priority than normal.

Relationship-driven motivation, which comes from the perception of creating value when working together with others. When two or more parties feel committed to a task, they happily put in the work needed to drive the process forward, which is often necessary for innovation work because it is often associated with uncertain outcomes.

A relatively easy way to create engagement is to reduce the number of projects in which an employee is involved. Anyone claiming to be good at multitasking has probably not tried to do fewer things more focused and careful until completed. Shockingly to some, the result is that the work goes faster and is done better. Working on several projects is one thing, but working on several things at the same time is not at all effective. The multitasker often has the illusion of being productive, while others instead experience him or her as sloppy, absent, careless, and forgetful. There are certainly exceptions. Pay attention to this matter before recruiting to the innovation team any employees who seem committed, but are involved in so many projects that they can't do a good job anywhere.

Brief summary of dedication
- External drivers include, for example, monetary rewards and bonuses, which represents a short-term commitment.
- Internal driving forces such as recognition, the work itself, and personal interest create longer-term commitment than do external driving forces.
- Create commitment by reducing the number of projects in which employees are involved.

Empowerment
As stated earlier, empowerment is about the opportunity to work independently with various tasks, increasing motivation, self-confidence, and sense of responsibility. It also means being able and self-disciplined enough to put yourself to work to get something done.

It may sound strange, but working independently can be very difficult for the individual employee who is unused to it. Many employees want the opportunity to plan their work but need the trust from management to do so and, sometimes, support in planning the work. Therefore, it may be appropriate for management and the employee to have a dialogue about which deliveries are prioritized and when they should be made. Employees are often enough capable to decide for themselves when some tasks are to be done. The same applies to innovation work. For the innovation team, it can be good to discuss when certain tasks should be performed, then via the convener, agree with the sponsor and management to create consensus on expectations. The problem with empowerment of the individual team member is usually uncertainty about tasks to complete or lack knowledge of how to perform them. The solution here is to have a close dialogue and collaboration with the facilitator, whose job is partly to help guide the innovation process and its forthcoming tasks. If empowerment is asked for and permitted, the individuals also have a responsibility to the management, the innovation team, and themselves to use the opportunity and to make the best out of it.

Brief summary of empowerment
- Planning and carrying out work yourself requires self-discipline and the ability to get things done without anyone monitoring.
- To facilitate self-planned work, agree with colleagues and management on priorities and deliveries.
- Empowerment commits to management, sponsor, innovation team, and its members.

Entre-/intrapreneurship
Entrepreneurial and intrapreneurial characteristics have positive effects on a sustainable innovation system in an organization. What distinguishes people who have it is that they are opportunity-driven, take risks, overcome obstacles and, if necessary, break norms, rules, standards, and procedures. Furthermore, they do not wait for opportunities to emerge. They create or discover the opportunities themselves.

Even if entre-/intrapreneurs challenge both management and established regulations, which can be perceived as offensive, management should support such behavior and provide the freedom to create new opportunities within the given frameworks. Otherwise, the risk is that they apply to other workplaces where their skills are taken advantage of. The challenge for an organization is how to best take advantage of such a driving force that is difficult to control. From an innovation perspective, it is fantastic. From a structural perspective, considering order and control, it can be a short-term disaster.

Nevertheless, a very well-known car brand in the premium class has consciously employed people who have run their own companies as entrepreneurs and consultants of various kinds. It does this to deliberately challenge their organization and create energy for important development and to change established processes and working methods. The employments usually do not last long as the employee is unhappy after a while and finds other employment. In the short time that these former entrepreneurs are employed, though, both parties face a win–win situation. In this case, the company gets fresh ideas that advance the organization and create valuable change, and the employee gets some time for peace and quiet.

Brief summary of entre-/intrapreneurship
–   Entrepreneurs have positive effects on an organization's innovation work.
–   Entrepreneurs create opportunities – they do not wait for something to be
    served.
–   Management needs to encourage entrepreneurs even if they are perceived as
    problematic to the organization.

Incentives
Creating a fair economic model for incentives or rewards for innovation is difficult.
Some even claim that it is impossible. There are examples of both positive and negative effects of such initiatives. A strong piece of advice is as follows: Be careful and
think twice. Part of the difficulty in making a fair incentive model lies in the fact that
innovation work is complex. In a quick review of the innovation process, the difficulty lies in knowing who has contributed to the innovation. The time from idea to
market can range from a few months to decades. Should the person/persons who
hatched the first idea receive the reward? Or the person/persons who built on this
idea and then contributed to an improved idea, which in turn led to a model that
showed that the idea was possible to develop? Or maybe the one/those who could
develop the model into a working prototype? Or the one/those who managed to get a
patent on the invention? Or is it perhaps the person/persons who could build a func-
tioning production for the product? Or maybe the one/those who designed the business model? Or the person/persons who sold the first product or service and thereby
brought the product to market? Such questions have no easy resolution.

Some organizations set up a panel or a board of people to decide which ideas to
advance, and it works relatively well. Notably, employees differ in their abilities to
present ideas, however, and without having received any guidance or training in
how ideas are presented, an employee can present good ideas that are voted down
due to a sub-optimal presentation, which is unfortunate. One way to overcome this
problem is to initiate training programs in idea presentation and to practice the
ability to present ideas. Alternatively, let the person who hatched the idea collaborate with someone who can present the idea.

Unfortunately, there are many bad examples of organizations that have given
monetary rewards to idea owners whose ideas reach the market. The intention has
been good, but the effects have been bad. From a short-term perspective, the idea
owner is motivated to work a little extra while others involved do not understand
why they should not receive the reward, so they do not fully engage. Other examples
of adverse effects have been related to corruption. Members of a panel or board have
voted for ideas for further development against shares in the upcoming reward that
they negotiated with the idea owner, "under the table." Such behavior is not good for
the organization, partly because it may become a breeding ground for fraud but also
because the organization may invest considerable resources in development projects

that may have low chances of establishing in the market. Other disadvantages of monetary rewards are that they foster a willingness to receive compensation for each work step performed. They reward employees to go for the low-hanging fruit because it provides the easiest and fastest return. As the pet says, no treat, no tricks.

Innovative organizations stimulate employees' internal driving forces, while less innovative organizations often offer monetary bonuses. The advantages of rewarding the inner driving forces are that it stimulates the tolerance for mistakes, empowerment, and feedback on work conducted, as well as the feeling of control.

Competitions of various kinds are a popular way of trying to attract initiatives for innovation projects. However, there must be clear criteria and rules that guide the work and any rewards. The problem with prize competitions is that those who do not win anything can feel exploited if they discover that parts of their proposals are further developed into new products by others. For instance, suppliers compete in procurements when everyone already knows in advance who will win. Another problem is that a jury may be forced to choose a winner from the entries submitted even though no idea has been good enough. However, On the other hand, competitions encouraging collaboration have positive team effects and can create a positive climate and a positive culture in a workplace. For some employees, it is an incentive to work in a self-governing innovation team where they feel that management provides space for their initiatives that benefit the organization's future development.

However, there are also positive examples of monetary rewards, where the best are associated with the effects achieved and not the work itself. Long-term incentives have entirely different outcomes than do short-term incentives, where short-term incentives provide incremental innovations and long-term incentives favor radical innovations. Does it really matter? Yes, it does. As mentioned in the introduction, innovation is necessary for an organization's long-term survival. An investment of 10 percent radical innovations, in the long run, returns 70 percent of the organization's revenues. To then invest in exclusively incremental innovations, which can feel right because it provides a return in a short time, is risky over time. Since long-term incentives provide radical innovations, it is natural to wonder how this knowledge can translate into something concrete. It has been shown that offers of co-ownership or return from IPR are successful, as are shares in the company. In this way, the perspective is shifted from short-term to long-term effects.

Brief summary of incentives
- Think carefully before reward systems are initiated as a stimulus for innovation work. It is very easy to create a structure that has negative effects.
- More innovative organizations strive to reward employees' inner driving forces, while less innovative organizations use monetary rewards.

–   Monetary rewards for individuals easily create internal problems in the form of cooperation resistance and jealousy. For monetary rewards, choose long-term commitment as co-ownership or shares.

Knowledge

Having sufficient knowledge of innovation has become increasingly important. It has become essential for knowledge-intensive organizations specialized in non-repeatable activities, which has led to knowledge becoming one of the strategically most important resources for successful innovation in the increasing knowledge-based competition. To succeed, competence is also required when hiring employees who will participate in innovation projects.

The organization's knowledge is developed when common sense, knowledge creation, and decision-making connect. With the addition of a conscious and frequent flow of information that binds this together even tighter, innovations may be created. However, employees must be trained and educated before they can positively impact the innovation process. They need to be able to use their knowledge in relevant ways, because knowledge in itself does not generate new values.

A practical way to use knowledge is to focus on how different stakeholders change through the different phases of an innovation project. Knowing each stakeholder's perspectives, their main interests, and how they are perceived by each other at a certain point in time leads to positive commitment and increased understanding, stimulating positive outcomes from the innovation work. Another way to use knowledge is to connect different members in a multifunctional innovation team. However, knowledge gaps that are too large must be avoided through constant information exchange and, for example, time set aside for presentations on different areas of specialization.

Knowledge networks require direct and close interaction between individuals with relevant knowledge and expertise, which the social network structure must enable. Tacit knowledge (i.e., knowledge that can be difficult to explain) is usually called know-how, and it is experienced or learned from others. As compared to explicit knowledge, which is knowledge in a visual format (e.g., instructions), tacit knowledge is more difficult to absorb and takes much longer to learn. Despite the general understanding that interactive learning is part of the core of innovation knowledge, though, tacit knowledge is so embedded in the individual that it may not even be aware of its importance and significance, which complicates learning and the spread of important knowledge in the organization.

From the team member's perspective, it is central to have the ability to understand where to gain access to tacit knowledge in the organization and that the organization also understands how to support the team member. A key activity here is to acquire tacit knowledge from people who are not necessarily employed by the organization but who still have valuable knowledge for innovation work. In that work, customers, suppliers, and competitors are common sources of knowledge.

The team member's ability to transform collected tacit knowledge into his or her own tacit knowledge and then use it constructively returns value to the organization. This knowledge transformation process is achieved by sharing knowledge with others, preferably executed through meetings. Initially, the meetings need to be frequent and relatively intense to build mutual trust, which is a key factor in getting the team to establish. Once the personal relationship is established, distance meetings are much easier. However, thanks to Covid-19, online meetings have become the new normal for many people, making relationship building reasonably easy despite different geographical locations. This topic will be further detailed in chapter five, which focuses on global innovation teams.

To be competitive in the long run, the answer is not to rely on the administration or management of already gained knowledge or keeping the status quo. Perseverance requires the ability and experience to generate new knowledge constantly, alongside the willingness of the organization to develop its knowledge. Certain methods to achieve this have been mentioned earlier (e.g., active participation in academic research) in connection to establishing collaboration. If, for example, an innovation team is involved in research, it has direct access also to tacit knowledge that gets generated, as described above. It can transform that knowledge into new products or organizational benefits long before that knowledge becomes known to others.

Brief summary of knowledge
–   Knowledge of innovation requires training – practical and recurrent training with innovation-savvy people.
–   Recruiting employees for innovation requires knowledge of innovation.
–   Participating in research projects provides access to entirely new knowledge before others.

Knowledge management
Knowledge management is precisely what it sounds like – knowledge of how to use knowledge practically. Organizations with well-developed knowledge management are generally more innovative than are other organizations. They are more competitive and more profitable, and a well-developed knowledge management strategy is among an organization's most important success factors.

Generally speaking, knowledge management has two components, the overall and the practical. At the overall level, knowledge management is about understanding tools and methods for learning, such as knowing how to learn from customers and establishing tools that measure the effects of work to identify knowledge gaps to be filled through training and recruitment. At the practical level, it is about being able to perform the work and understand the results. In a practical context, it means a team member's capacity to consciously manage the creation, transfer, preservation, and utilization of an organization's implicit and explicit knowledge assets to promote an organization's interests. This capacity includes, of course, IPR, but also human capital, structural capital, and relational assets, all of which are uniquely knowledge-based. Other areas of innovation-related knowledge management are knowledge of process management skills, the ability to build competence and adapt the work to the different phases of the innovation process, and the ability to detect new innovation opportunities in existing products (e.g., through conceptualization, evaluation, and so-called re-innovation).

The balance between exploiting existing knowledge and creating new knowledge significantly influences innovation outcomes. Here, management is decisive in determining how the conditions to apply knowledge management are established. An important tool is the combination of quality work with knowledge management and consciously creating slack in the organization, so that there is room for inspiration and reflection. That is to consciously ensure that employees are not fully booked with projects, for example, sparing some time for people to dig deeper into their personal areas of interest for new lessons.

Large and small organizations also differ in knowledge management, where smaller organizations generally turn to external networks to deal with their innovation challenges, while large organizations try to mimic the smaller ones by creating smaller project-based units. The advantage of smaller units in a large organization is that they can more easily detect and meet competitors' offers, as a small unit can work with more agility.

Effective knowledge management also leads to organizational learning, the basis of innovation at the organizational level. The most competitive organizations can learn to learn, that is, to incorporate learning processes and knowledge building in the daily work and focus on transforming silent knowledge into explicit knowledge. It also minimizes the risk of organizations becoming too dependent on individuals, which can have almost catastrophic consequences if one person quits and takes all knowledge to the new organization. Therefore, methods must be established to disseminate knowledge through the organization to become part of the culture, where knowledge flows in and around all the nooks and crannies of the organization.

Brief summary of knowledge management
- Knowledge management means the knowledge to manage and exercise knowledge in theory and practice.
- More often than large organizations, small ones use external networks to increase access to knowledge, learning from those networks.
- Managing innovation-related knowledge also means establishing methods for more people to learn about innovation, and for more people to learn to exercise their knowledge.

Mindset
Innovation is associated with risk and uncertainty, primarily of a financial nature. A positive outcome is far from guaranteed, and uncertainties arise from innovation work being perceived as unstructured. People generally deal with risk and insecurity in their daily tasks, but whether this is deemed dangerous or necessary to avoid is highly personal. How people choose to interpret the meaning of risk and uncertainty shapes the result of the innovation work, both individually and collectively. For instance, people positive to risk and uncertainty in innovation contexts rarely use these concepts but instead talk about opportunities. Prior experience is usually used to analyze the potential effect of a specific risk or uncertainty, which then can lead to creative solutions to avoid or minimize the identified risk or uncertainty. However, because risk assessment is subjective, the solution does not become more creative than the sum of experience of the people who have been involved in creating the solution. That is, when seeking innovative solutions, people with a positive attitude towards innovation are needed to move forward and not be limited to present conditions.

However, if employees think innovatively all the time, the risk is to get caught up in a constant exploration, where the work never begins. This kind of risk can also arise from employees feeling insecure, lacking self-confidence, or not wanting to make fools of themselves, which may reflect the organization's lack of tolerance for mistakes. Without room to test ideas that may not last, employees become reluctant to show their ideas before they are "ready" – which they never will become without sufficient room. To avoid such stalling, the organization needs to clearly communicate that it is okay to try and share ideas under progress.

Innovation work is a highly sophisticated and cognitive process. One of the key insights is that it begins with profound observations, investigations, and understanding of the problem that is about to be solved. Success in this work requires effort seeking value to be created. Here, a positive attitude and encouraging atmosphere are quite helpful, where small achievements are continuously celebrated. A major accomplishment is not needed to celebrate success, and it is more a reminder that it is the ongoing work that drives the innovation project forward. The occasion may be, for example, the completion of a field study, a certain number of interviews, or the testing of a concept model, which is thus celebrated together. Learning experiences worth celebrating should be highlighted. It is just as important to learn things that do not work well or as expected when innovation work is carried out. Storytelling is a good tool to motivate employees and to build team spirit, as is having a playful atmosphere where humor is a feature of everyday work.

The art of creating self-confidence has a more significant effect for innovation work than one can imagine. With strong self-confidence comes a greater eagerness to pursue ideas and better utilization of cognitive resources, which positively influences the innovation climate. This is built up through positive feedback on completed work. Interestingly, it applies even if the work itself was mediocre, given the expectation –

through positive feedback, self-confidence and an ability to work creatively and in a solution-oriented manner is strengthened. The results are noticeable both individually and in team tasks, mainly through increased initiative and commitment that extends beyond what the job description formally stipulates. Successful innovation teams are characterized by trust, vision, the pursuit of perfection, security in belonging to the innovation team, and support for innovative initiatives.

However, innovation is an art form in which the individual wins over the status quo, which is challenging. Most people naturally want to preserve what they know, even if the present situation is weak. The argument is that it might get even worse, and from that perspective, it is better to stay in an unpleasant situation rather than trying something new. Change always wins eventually, however. The innovation work itself requires that many questions are asked and new skills are learned, with adaption, collaboration, and a strong belief in great results. To align these requirements, the individual must be willing to perform all these activities, a variable strongly influenced by the prevailing culture of the organization.

Brief summary of mindset
- A positive attitude is crucial for innovation work, "I can. . .," "I want. . .," "I will. . ."
- Positive feedback build self-confidence, which is positive for innovation work. Communicate that ideas are okay to present as potential innovation projects, regardless of their status.
- Celebrate small work victories and highlight learning as positive results. Provide positive feedback: It strengthens self-confidence.

Time
Time is regularly discussed in innovation work from at least two perspectives. First, time can be included as a component of the product, as such. That is, time is saved by removing a step in the manufacturing process or moving an assembly plant closer to the final destination of the product to avoid long transport times. In advertisements, "saving time to spend on more valuable things to do" is many times the main argument on behalf of new products. In process development, time-saving is a significant goal and result, and the focus is therefore on how to simplify or eliminate steps. Seeing time as a product is therefore valuable for team members to understand. The second perspective regards time to carry out the innovation work itself. In an innovation project, the team members should have an average of at least 10–15 percent of their work to it. In some periods, more time is needed, and in other periods less time. At the beginning of the innovation project, more time is definitely required, as in-depth work is needed to understand the problem to solve and to set the scope of the project's forthcoming solution. If possible, devote as much time as possible to the innovation project, as the more time spent, the faster the

results arrive, and the fewer projects you are involved in, the greater commitment. Too little time may result in frustration and low priority, which is not optimal for positive progress.

To promote an environment in which innovation is developed, there must be time to engage, process, and reflect on all the information that flows through a workplace. Understandably, a designer needs time to develop a solution. Yet, when a designer spends extra time understanding the problem to be solved, more creative solutions emerge.

Work-free time is a topic touched on in many contexts. New ideas are born or created in the gap between two tasks, as is well known. When a person is at mental rest, good job-related ideas come (e.g., on the bus, at the training session, in the shower, or when browsing a newspaper). The time for "no-work" on working hours is underestimated. Not being constantly fully overloaded with work tasks presents an opportunity for new ideas to sprout and grow strong. Anyone who thinks that some free surfing is a waste of time needs to rethink, so long as it does not put people at risk or disrupt production. Where should new input come from if it is not part of the job to get inspiration from more than the ordinary work team or the coffee table? The slack opens potential space for new ideas, which can be channeled into existing problems in the organization.

Brief summary of time
- Time can be used as part of value creation in a new product.
- With a lot of time to spend in the initial phases to understand the problem, good conditions are created for more creative proposals.
- In the space between tasks, as well as in leisure time, ideas arise more easily. Slack is not equal to waste of time.

The innovation enablers affect innovation teams' work

The above-described factors distinctly influence innovation work. In a slight oversimplification, there are only two modes for an innovation project: in development/progress or not. If an innovation project stagnates for a longer period of time, it will most likely die by itself. Therefore, attend actively to work to ensure that the above-mentioned factors are addressed for an innovation team in its work.

Regarding incentives, an enabler of the work of innovation teams, giving the project legitimacy signals to the rest of the organization that management is behind the innovation project. One of the easiest ways to do so is to recognize the innovation team's effort by constantly following it in meetings and letting them discuss the innovation project with visitors. Such acknowledgment stimulates the internal driving forces of the innovation team members, strengthening the innovation team and the work environment.

In practical work, the different enablers are not equally important for the innovation teams and their sponsor. It may be obvious, but the innovation team's sponsor tends to focus more on the enablers that influence the innovation teams from an organizational perspective at the beginning of the innovation project. Culture, climate, and a positive attitude are among the three most essential enablers in the initial phases of the innovation process, from the sponsor's perspective. As the innovation team emerges and the project develops, the sponsor's focus shifts to maintaining a positive attitude and commitment to the innovation team. The innovation team, for its part, focuses mainly on factors that affect their work more directly, especially time, economic factors, and the engagement of members in the work.

The presented factors aren't considered important merely by the innovation teams. They affect the results of their work as well, as seen in Tab. 2.2. If an innovation team is asked why they are not advancing, the answer is usually that they lack time and resources in terms of competence and economy. However, this lack is most likely only part of the truth. Beneath the surface is more to find. The experience of lack of time and resources is also often associated with other aspects, such as lack of collaboration, dedication, entrepreneurship, knowledge, knowledge management, and mindset. Suppose the team feels it lack trust to enter collaborations. In that case, the sponsor needs to be involved in solving the problem together with the convener (and possibly the facilitator).

The problem is that projects risk dying if they do not get these factors right, but it has also been shown that when projects have stalled and then regained their dedication, collaboration, and mindset, projects can take off and be developed again. Still, it is difficult to correct a problem with an unknown cause, for the reason it is difficult to understand what you do not know. In this work, the facilitator has a particularly important function, as he or she can highlight a problem and propose actions to solve the same.

To conclude, an innovation team should be built on people dedicated and able to solve potential issues arising in a project and know its boundaries.

Tab. 2.2: Innovation enablers effect on an innovation project.

Innovation enabler's effect in an innovation project	
Most positive effect on an innovation project	**Most negative effect on an innovation project**
Dedication	Dedication
Mindset	Human resources
Collaboration	Mindset
Knowledge management	Collaboration
Entrepreneurship	Time

Organizational structures and innovation teams

This section focuses on how different organizations are structured, as the structure itself either stimulates or discourages innovative initiatives, greatly affecting how successful innovation teams can be.

Industrial or post-industrial structure affect innovation capabilities

Based on existing organizational theories, significant differences undoubtedly exist in different organizations' structures. In general, there are two extremes: the industrial or post-industrial organizational structure. The industrial structure is the classic structure with clear hierarchies, standardizations, centralization, and various specialized departments, where each department does its part and interacts very little with other departments. Silos and lines are common concepts used to describe that kind of organization. Frankly, the operation is quite like an assembly line on which everyone has a specific role and does nothing outside that role to avoid changes and disruptions. From an innovation perspective, development is divided into, for example, R&D or the development department, and the remaining departments are support functions. Once a new product is developed, the rest of the organization tries to sell and deliver it. The advantage is that an employee can be very focused on its particular area of work without having to care so much about what is happening in other places in the organization. The disadvantage is that the structure does not promote collaboration. Rather it contributes to a lack of understanding of how everything in the organization connects, troubling the holistic view of the business. In practical terms, the individual lacks knowledge of how different competencies can complement each other. All too often, subsystems developed in different departments do not fit together very well because of poor communication during the development work. Other negative effects may include that products are developed with a strong technological focus and little or no involvement of end-users or end-customers. As a result, the product is not received with open arms.

The post-industrial structure, unlike the industrial one, is decentralized. It is based on diversification and has no particular structure between departments. The organization is innovative in itself and encourages change and development initiatives, which can spur any place in the organization. In the extreme, there is neither management nor middle management. Work tasks are distributed, and decisions are made in consensus. Here, some argue that consensus is the worst way to make decisions, as it may take a long time to agree on everything. On the other hand, some say that joint decisions spur motivation and a feeling of belonging. To solve the problem of endless discussion, though, the innovation team is created with few people, all being experts in various fields, which eases decision making (as further discussed in chapter three).

Innovation teams in the post-industrial structure

From an organizational perspective, an innovation team is best suited to an organization that either has a post-industrial structure or at least strives to have it. The post-industrial structure encourages initiatives more readily than does an industrial structure, as the approach is to not get stuck in given structures and hierarchies. Employees are allowed to take responsibility and initiatives from what is best suited to the given situation. This approach may present great challenges for management and middle managers, since the work is not about controlling employees but about creating the conditions for employees to take innovative initiatives. Doing so requires not only the innovation team to be trained, but management as well. So, before an innovation team can be formed, management must accept that the forthcoming innovation team will not follow established rules and procedures in their work to develop the next generation of products.

Innovation teams in the industrial structure

However, innovation teams are also ideal for organizations that, on the surface, can be perceived as rigid and challenging to develop, such as government agencies, public services or institutes (e.g., schools and healthcare), and producing industries. The only difference with these types of organizations is which goal to achieve and, thus, what composition of individuals should be included in the innovation team. The existence of laws and regulations that may seem to hinder innovation for any of these organizations is not unique. They exists for all organizations, to some extent. Regulations can serve as guidelines to inspire new solutions. Of course, regulations may be outdated, and therefore should be challenged with new proposals, which is an argument for authorities to continue to develop and renew laws and regulations to meet today's and tomorrow's challenges. To make the change happen, there must be a willingness to develop the organization's various products to become better, faster, more efficient, or perhaps more modern, to fit in the context of operation. Nursing, education, the social insurance agency, the public employment service, and so on can therefore develop both new products and private businesses. For example, clearly authorities must work on innovation to develop new investigation, monitoring, control, or follow-up functions to execute their mission or only to improve the working situation on the site. The challenges here, for example, often lie in keep pace with the development of criminal activities and future crime and in writing laws to cover emergent crime. One example of this problem is that drug manufacturers can slightly change substances, such that they are making not-yet-illegal drugs.

The first innovation project

The first time an innovation team is created, it may be wise to limit the innovation task to a small and manageable project. An appropriate first project can involve 6–12 months of work. It is long enough to provide perspective on the work and room for reflection and unexpected solutions as the work progresses. At the same time, it is clear enough to complete in a reasonable timeframe, which makes it plannable. Be specific in what problem or problem area to work on. Or at least the direction of innovation focus. The advantages are several: members are encouraged to trust management, it is easy to follow the development of the project, members have better oversight, an unwanted result is not catastrophic, completions come faster, and lessons come faster to the organization.

Brief summary of organizational structures and innovation teams
- Organizations applying a post-industrial structure are more innovative than other organizations.
- A post-industrial structure is recognized by, for example, decentralization, collaboration between departments, and low barriers for initiatives.
- Keep the first project small to learn about the processes and build self-confidence.

The innovation process – Agile work for faster results

This section introduces the innovation process and its phases. It mainly regards how agile innovation work can be conducted. To be able to navigate their organization and to move forward with the project, agility will eventually become a priority for an innovation team, given the accelerating pace of innovation.

Innovation work – Not fuzzy nor difficult, but more complex

The notion that innovation work is fuzzy, ambiguous, or just for the "smart ones" is outdated. Nothing could be more wrong. It's neither unclear nor difficult at all. It is as concrete and structured as any other work, and there are well-developed methods and tools for different tasks. "It's easy when you know how to do it," I've heard someone say. It is well said. To get there, however, practice is necessary.

    Teresa Amabile, a prominent researcher, says that innovation work consists of two parts: creativity and implementation. Simplistically explained, a new product is conceptually created and then developed and sold on the market. However, being creative is a surprisingly small part of innovation. Edison might have said that genius is 1 percent inspiration and 99 percent perspiration. Maybe it should be "persistence" or "perseverance," but in any case, the idea all is accurate. The inventor of the Global Positioning System (GPS) and the color graphic display, Håkan Lans, stated that the creative phase is about 3–5 percent of the entire work. A successful serial entrepreneur I met stated that, when the product is finalized and ready to be launched on the market, about 20 percent of the innovation work is completed. The rest is about business development and marketing activities. With that, all arguments about innovation being fuzzy are firmly dismissed. All there is to it is to roll up the sleeves and get the job done.

The innovation process – From rigid to agile and flexible

Over time, the innovation process has evolved from being slow and rigid to becoming more flexible and integrated with the organization's context. Modern research and proven methods advocate this flexibility and integration, but as mentioned at the outset, it is of great importance that newly formed innovation teams receive education on how agile innovation work is executed. Presently, various innovation processes are flourishing, divided into more or less detailed phases. In principle, it does not matter which innovation process is chosen, as long as there is room to act innovatively at every phase, it allows iterative work, and close cooperation with potential end-users and end-customers is applied. The following section exemplifies an agile innovation process in four phases, followed by a brief explanation of how an agile innovation work can be executed in practice. See it as inspiration for what it might look like. Feel free to use it if it suits your purpose. The rookie mistakes are to control everything, down to each small detail, to feel that everything should be "right" before the work can continue, or to suppose that the influences of those who will use and pay for the upcoming product are irrelevant.

Work fast without cutting corners

Although work is conducted quickly and flexibly, this speed and flexibility should not be misunderstood as working carelessly. Do not cut corners. Agile work is primarily about solving tasks in the order in which they appear and finding ways past unforeseen obstacles. However, certain problems should definitely be avoided. The most important thing is not to decide too early on the solution, a common mistake for inexperienced innovation teams. Another important thing is not to lock yourself away somewhere and develop the solution to perfection in isolation. When the product is eventually completed (if ever), there will probably be a shocking experience when the customers do not understand the new solution and therefore do not buy it. The same problem arises in organizations that do not consider impressions from their upcoming customers and end-users during the development of the product. It is not necessary to ask customers or end-users personally what they think, as they do not always know what is best – but it is essential to understand current trends to predict future needs, affecting how a new product should be developed.

The innovation process in four phases

Traditionally, the innovation processes divide into three steps, regardless of how many steps are described: the idea phase, the development phase, and the value creation phase. Hence, it begins with creative work reflecting the desired direction of the organization. Once the ideas and concepts have been created, reviewed, and evaluated, one or several are developed and launched on the market. Finally, the values created by the work are collected, including both monetary values from possible sales and values based on experience and other non-monetary considerations, which can then constitute structural capital for future innovation projects. Subsequently, it all begins again, based on insights, learnings, and experiences.

Linked to the group development process, one phase that has not yet been discussed is the preparation phase, which adds a phase to the innovation process, as seen in Fig. 2.4. As the focus is on high-performing innovation teams, specifically preparing team members for the upcoming work, the innovation process is strongly advised to be extended with this initial work. Since the initial ideation work represents a small portion of the total work to get a new product on the market, it is well worth investing in time to prepare to increase the chances that the created innovation groups become innovation teams.

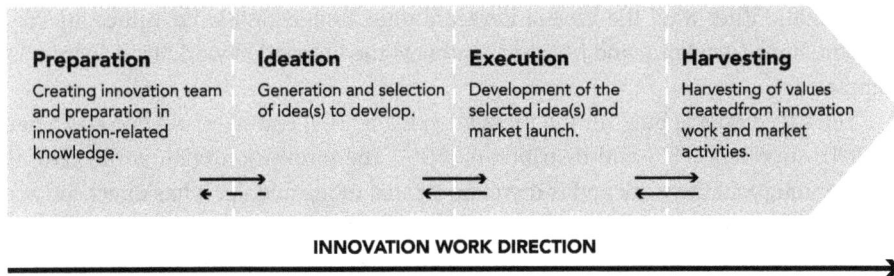

Preparation	Ideation	Execution	Harvesting
Creating innovation team and preparation in innovation-related knowledge.	Generation and selection of idea(s) to develop.	Development of the selected idea(s) and market launch.	Harvesting of values createdfrom innovation work and market activities.

INNOVATION WORK DIRECTION

Fig. 2.4: The innovation process. The figure is inspired by Johnsson, M. (2018), The innovation facilitator: characteristics and importance for innovation teams. *Journal of Innovation Management*, 6(2), 12–44.

The process is otherwise the same as any other innovation processes, with one important difference. The preparatory work is not recommended to be an iterative process in the sense that the innovation team wanders between the preparation phase and the idea phase. The innovation team is created once. In case of emergency, however, this work is redone, accounting for the difference between the preparation phase and the other phases. The figure is schematic and illustrates the workflow with a start and a work direction. The work of agile innovation is anything but linear. It is iterative and circular. Those who have tried a traditional stage-gate method and then work agilely usually do not want to go back. Agile work engages and encourages new ideas and initiatives, where action and entrepreneurship are in focus. Waiting and inaction do not propel a project. Progress is key.

The Raft model – An agile and iterative innovation process

The model described in the following, called the Raft model, is developed in an innovation context in that it originates from innovation advice for private idea owners and companies. The Raft model got its name from river rafting, where you paddle by rubber boat down flowing rapids, a great experience. Rafting is exciting and challenging, but it can also be risky if you are careless. It requires both the ability to navigate the swirls and rocks and the determination to paddle vigorously down high-cliff waterfalls. The reward when you eventually come down to still water is great, including the joy. It's so fun that you want to do it again, immediately. That's what innovation has become for me, which inspires the Raft model.

The model consists of a triangle of four fields, as seen in Fig. 2.5, which provides a holistic overview of the entire innovation process and the business model. Suppose the product under development is not to be sold in the sense that it generates monetary revenues. In that case, the business model mindset can still be used, because the innovation team is responsible for reaching the market, which can be internal as well as external. Either way, the innovation team must understand what values are created and how, for whom, and by whom and how the innovation work itself should be completed.

The Raft model is built on the innovation team ("I"), end-user and end-customer ("U/C"), suppliers ("S") and distributors ("D"). The innovation team is the central player throughout the work and is therefore located in the middle. It has direct contact with the actors in each field. The end-user is the person who will use the developed product or service, and may be, for example, a private individual or an employee of a company. The end-customer is a private individual or a person in an organization who pays for the product or service to solve a need or who decides to implement something that may be free of charge. This person can be an end-user at the same time. Therefore, the innovation team must understand the similarities and differences between the two. The field of suppliers enfolds access to the necessary skills and components to design, develop, and produce the forthcoming solution to be accepted by end-users and end-customers. Both competence and components can be found internally in the organization or through external suppliers or consultants. Finally, distributors, a link in the classic "value chain," are where the product is sold or delivered, namely through middlemen to reach the end-customers and users. Frequently, an organization's customers are in this field, in which case they form the target group for the innovation project. Many people make the mistake of only looking after these customers' needs and failing to investigate the end-user's and the end-customer's needs, that is, the customer's customer (or those even further steps away). Consequently, there are a range of users and customers to investigate to identify end-users and end-customer and figure out their relations to each other.

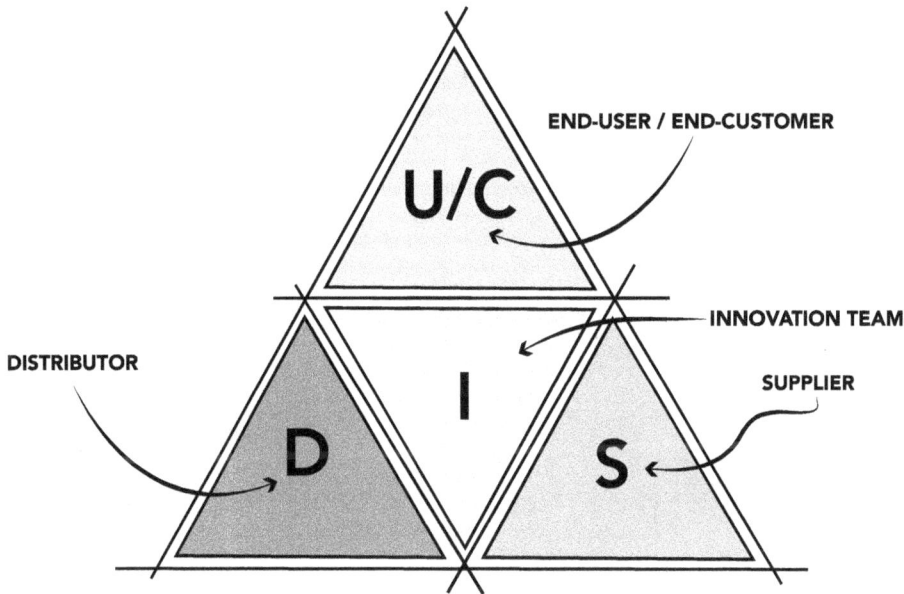

Fig. 2.5: The Raft model. The figure is inspired by Johnsson, M. (2009), *Sälj skinnet innan björnen är skjuten.*

The work process, as illustrated in Fig. 2.6, is that the innovation team, based on direction designated from management, starts with careful problem identification without trying to develop potential solutions, then formulates the project goals to be achieved. Once these are conceptualized, end-users and end-customers are identified. Then, to identify the problem to solve and to verify it through carefully chosen interaction methods. This work aims to clarify the different requirements of these actors, which will later become a specification of what the upcoming product should offer.

In the work collecting information from end-users and end-customers, "needs," "wants," and things "nice to have" are separated. The specified requirements are then used to identify all the suppliers needed to complete the product. It is important here to understand what drives a purchase or a buy-in. Sometimes, the "wants" drive the purchase, not common sense. Consider the introduction of the iPhone. The phone itself was not initially very good, to be honest, as noticed earlier. It had a very nice design, though, and the opportunity to fill every person's need for functionality through its various apps, which no other phone could offer. This information about what drives a purchase is collected from potential end-users and end-customers. In the Raft model, suppliers can be both internal and external and can correspond to both competence and components. As the requirements are understood, the work begins by simple sketches and prototypes, followed by increasingly advanced prototypes detailing functionality, about all of which end-users and end-customers are involved through the provision of feedback.

During this work, it is important to identify which possible regulatory requirements and certificates must be met. In parallel with this work, the value chain is mapped to explain how the forthcoming product will be delivered to reach the end-user. Understanding how this is done for a competitive product makes it possible to create new competitive advantages through original thinking. If necessary, this investigation should include how procurements are conducted and what companies are established that provide similar solutions. It can sometimes be easier to try to enter a collaboration than to win a procurement.

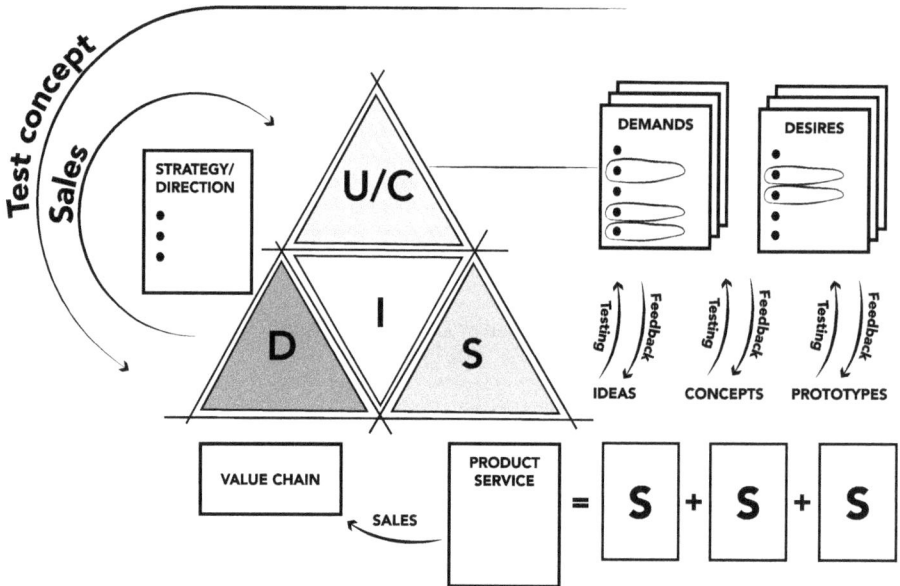

Fig. 2.6: The figure illustrates the Raft model and how the innovation team interacts with end-users, end-customers, suppliers, and distributors in the innovation work. The figure is inspired by Johnsson, M. (2009), *Sälj skinnet innan björnen är skjuten*.

The innovation team is formed in the preparation phase (Fig. 2.4). This phase sets strategic direction for the innovation project. As noted earlier, if it is the first time an innovation team is assembled in this way, it should preferably be assigned a relatively easy task with a short development time. To create engagement throughout the project, the innovation team needs room to find new solutions along the way. In my opinion, this is one of the most significant differences between product development and innovation work: Product development usually rests on a clear project plan, where very few surprises are expected in working towards the goal, which might be a few percentage points less production cost or better performance of some kind. By contrast, innovation work means that the goal can be as obvious as for product development, but that there is room to find completely new and unexpected solutions on the way towards the final product.

It is up to the innovation team to thoroughly investigate the cause of the problem to be solved. This investigation is completed by the innovation team identifying end-users and end-customers and conducting appropriate field studies to find the root of the problem. Many different tools and methods to conduct field studies and need identification are available freely online or in numerous books. A tip is to spend a few hours investigating what is out there and create a toolbox that matches the assignment. Keep in mind to choose tools carefully, as results will vary. Based on the information collected, the innovation team can determine the most important needs and requirements that must be met for the future product or service. The total product or service often consists of several different components from different suppliers, internal and external. External suppliers are overwhelmingly interested in helping to develop a product or service. As well as advocating close collaboration with end-users and end-customers, collaboration with external suppliers is important unless all the skills and components required are already in-house in the organization. The most important question for the innovation team to answer is whether the problem they working on as a whole can be solved. The next step is to test prototypes and concepts on end-users and end-customers to collect feedback, followed by further adjustments and tests. However, do not try to solve all the problems that arise. Keep some news for future products in the product lifecycle, considering the innovation project portfolio mentioned in the introduction. It is vital to get to the market as quickly as possible, while ideas are fresh. Another argument for saving some ideas for future products is that research shows that successful market establishment is done through an initially simple solution, gradually developed as users and end-customers embrace the new product.

Depending on the goal, for example, being an active part of the value chain or receiving income from a licensing agreement, there are several alternative approaches. When each actor finds the idea attractive from their perspective, there is a good chance the idea will reach the market. The work can be facilitated if the innovation team, in their interaction with the various actors, constantly ponders the key questions: "What's in it for me?" and "What's in it for them?" Today's value chain does not look like it did a few years ago. Today, companies are not as loyal to their value chain as before, meaning that they more often try to get closer to the end-customer by skipping a middle-man or two, if possible. In practice, companies may sell to both retailer relations and end-customers through their own shops or online. However, remaining loyal when it comes to discounts and special deals is vital for long-term customer relations. Stepping too hard on someone's toes will produce a reaction. The important thing is to have cost coverage, regardless of which routes are taken.

Some people find it risky to involve end-users and end-customers early in their work because of the risk of losing ideas and of the news becoming public too early, giving competitors the opportunity to get ahead of the market. However, many of these problems can be prevented, for example, through contracts with those who are involved. Successful innovation projects are based on collaborations of various kinds. It is in this spirit that the Raft model has been developed. The innovation team should not focus on developing the idea in physical form until they have discovered what end-users and end-customers think – look at crowd-funding pages where conceptual products are available. The products are not produced until a critical mass of customers have registered to purchase them. This scenario is no different from those in other industries, such as the real estate industry, where customers sign up for a newly produced apartment or villa before it is built, where the purchase is based solely on a prospectus. The same applies to district heating or internet connection. When a certain number of households have signed up to join, the excavator comes to ensure the connection is possible. From an innovation perspective, it is about having a comprehensive strategy to handle innovation work. Anyone who has learned agile innovation work based on what is to be developed will be at the forefront of what the market will demand or as a quick follower, if it is their focus. As the Raft model works, it can be seen as an ecosystem for the innovation project, where all actors involved must gain some value. If any of these elements falls away, the project will most likely not successfully reach the market.

Brief summary of the innovation process
– Innovation processes vary in content and layout. To get going - select one and adjust to your preferences.
– Work structured to ensure input from end-users, end-customers, suppliers, and distributors – there is no fuzziness here.
– Agile innovation work is fast as passing obstacles are embedded in the methodology.

The innovation facilitator – Stimulating successful learning

Previous sections have demonstrated factors affecting the work of the innovation team, the organizational type best suited for innovation teams, and possible structure for the innovation process. As noted, each part is quite simple to grasp, but put together, the process becomes relatively complex, which is why the innovation facilitator (facilitator) has a central role in the formation of new innovation teams. Therefore, the facilitator is a key component in the process of creating high-performing innovation teams (as highlighted in Fig. 2.7). Although the facilitator has been mentioned already in the introduction and on certain occasions in previous sections, there is new focus here on the facilitator's role and the knowledge and experiences they must possess.

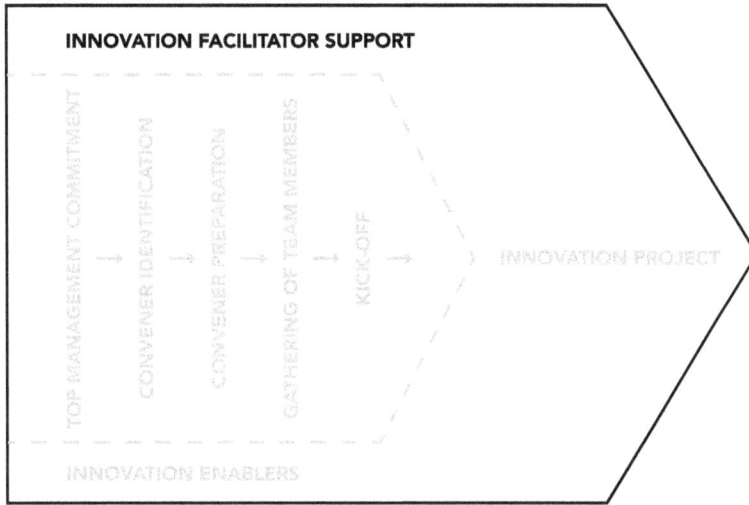

Fig. 2.7: The innovation facilitator support, as part of the creating high-performing innovation team model.

The innovation facilitator – When and how to support the innovation team

The starting point is that the organization aiming to assemble an innovation team for the first time should develop new products and learn how to handle innovation work and the group dynamic process simultaneously. Here, the facilitator is particularly important. The alternative is to engage a consultant or other external expert to act as project manager and to ensure that the project is completed on time and successfully. This option is excellent if the goal is to produce new products. However, if the organization wants to learn how the work was done to be able to repeat it on its own and strengthen its innovation capacity, then that approach is reprehensible. The moment the consultant leaves the organization, the knowledge also tends to dissapear. The facilitator, on the contrary, supports the innovation team by providing knowledge about the innovation opportunities and the innovation process, as mentioned in previous chapters, and by guiding and coaching the innovation team during the ongoing project. The advantages are that the innovation team learns much faster by performing tasks themselves and inviting and engaging employees and other experts to various tasks. Simultaneously, however, there needs to be an understanding that this method also means that the newly formed innovation team must be given the space to make and learn from mistakes.

The facilitator's skills and experience

As mentioned, the facilitator has a key role in creating new innovation teams, and his or her skills and experiences are crucial in the outcome. A study of the facilitator's role showed that they should have a deep knowledge of innovation, how to apply it, and group dynamics in both theory and practice. A facilitator can be an internal or an external person. The most important thing is that the facilitator allows the innovation team to execute the project independently, to avoid adversely affecting learning.

A compilation of competencies and experience shows that a facilitator in this context needs to be able to do as follows:
- Provide hands-on and situational advice,
- steer back innovation teams that lose focus or stray,
- encourage the innovation team to "break or stretch established rules,"
- assure the innovation team that agile innovation work is acceptable,
- provide feedback to the innovation teams on whether they are on the right track,
- be available as support when the innovation team needs it,
- highlight end-user focus early in the process,
- highlight the entrepreneurial spirit of the innovation team,
- assure the innovation team that uncertainty is okay,
- create the confidence to involve expertise outside the innovation team if necessary,
- build confidence in the innovation team to do things its members usually do not do,
- challenge the innovation team, if necessary,
- coach and facilitate in a way that is appreciated by the innovation team,
- communicate in a way that is appreciated by the innovation team,
- give the innovation team room for self-determination,
- encourage the innovation team to push their boundaries,
- recognize the innovation team for their work,
- give the innovation team feedback on their work,
- guide in the innovation process,
- listen to what the innovation team has to say,
- do not outshine the innovation team,
- do not take the lead of the innovation team's work,
- do not take credit for the innovation team's work,
- do not strive to standardize all innovation teams,
- have practical experience from innovation work,
- provide an understanding of the benefits of temporary networks,
- create confidence in the way innovation teams choose to work,
- help to select the right people for innovation the innovation team,
- support innovation teams without disturbing them, and
- believe in the work of innovation teams.

The facilitator is ready to step in

The facilitator's involvement in the team varies in the different phases of the innovation process, as illustrated in Fig. 2.8. In the pre-phase the facilitator plays a crucial role in the preparation work when the innovation team is formed. However, the facilitator's job starts during the conversations with the management and sponsor of the future innovation team, with an explanation of how the work will be done in practical terms. That is, the facilitator's role is to identify team members and get them into independent work in the idea phase, where innovation opportunities are identified, and at the beginning of the development phase, where the ideas begin to materialize. During this work, the facilitator has a high presence because these phases are most abstract and thus most complicated if the team members have little experience dealing with uncertainties and open-ended requirement specifications. In the latter phases of the innovation process, the facilitator's presence will decline to a form of back-office.

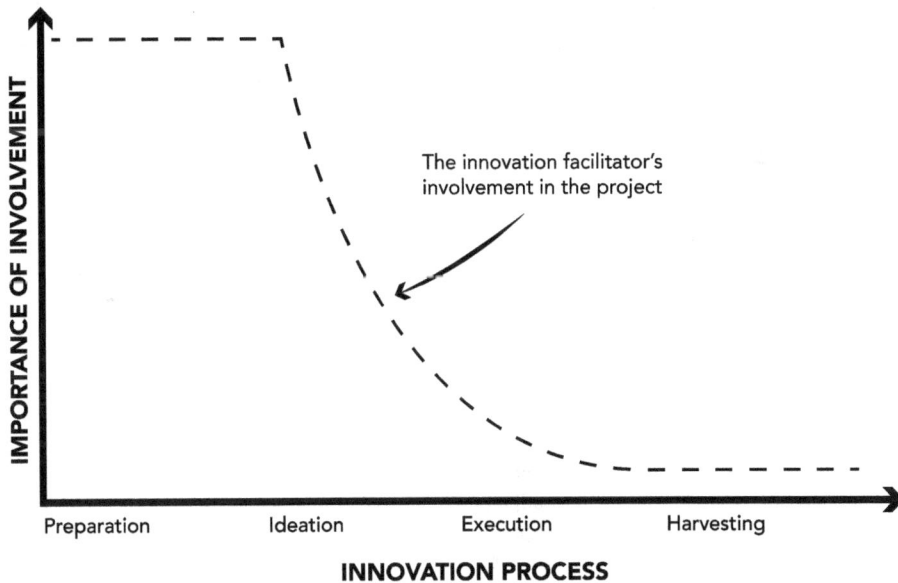

Fig. 2.8: The facilitator's involvement in the innovation team's project. The figure is inspired by Johnsson, M. (2018), The innovation facilitator: characteristics and importance for innovation teams. *Journal of Innovation Management*, 6(2), 12–44).

As with the factors that enable the work of innovation teams, the different characteristics and skills of the facilitator fulfil different functions at different times, and can therefore also be seen as enablers for the innovation teams to begin their work. In the preparation phase, the facilitator has to support the management and the formation of the innovation team by explaining the importance of which members should be invited to the innovation team. Critically, in this phase and the idea phase, the facilitator helps to strengthen the innovation team's confidence and belief in what they do, provides concrete situational advice, and gives quick feedback on development. As projects unfold, it is easy to think the facilitator takes on an increasingly minor role. Instead, the role transitions to remotely following the work of the innovation team and being prepared to quickly come in with advice and tips if the innovation team goes astray without noticing for themselves. Supporting without interfering while challenging the innovation team's choices in development work is a delicate task the facilitator is expected to accomplish. Here, the facilitator needs an ability to believe that the innovation team will cope with the tasks on their own and not take the work over themselves, because that will impede learning. However, if the tasks turn out to be overpowering or too much for some reason, the facilitator can partially assist with these and suggest that the innovation team can then continue with on its own. The facilitator has then shown a possible track, but the innovation team has done it themselves and can feel satisfied with the work, increasing their confidence. If the facilitator has solid knowledge of the innovation process, they can listen to the innovation teams and provide situational advice on actions or next step s to take. Here, it is essential that innovation team receive quick feedback on their work, including both positive comments and suggestions for improvements and future tasks.

Case:

In one case, the innovation team was set up and ready to go. The first task, referring to the Raft model, was for the team to understand the end-users' and end-customers' needs and requirements. Usually, the team members never met these groups of people. Their understanding regarding customer needs was limited to their customer, which had a retail position in the value chain. The information from the company's customers was not first-hand information from the ones buying and using the product once it was developed. Although the team members were very knowledgeable and experienced in their fields of expertise, this challenge became too difficult to handle. To partially solve this dilemma, the facilitator stepped in, conducting a workshop to support the team in figuring out who the end-users and end-customers were. The facilitator then wrote a draft of interview questions for the team to adjust and use when approaching the end-user and end-customer. The input was valuable for the project's progress and the team's learning as the facilitator noticed the problem and showed how to proceed without completing the entire task. The team members were excited about learning a new skill set.

The facilitator supports and guides during challenging situations

The specific difficulties for inexperienced innovation teams who will work agilely are several and not easy to sort out on their own. The facilitator plays an important role. Agile work is sometimes difficult to plan. It can be challenging to understand and interpret the varied needs of end-users, end-customers, suppliers, and distributors, while remaining constantly open to new and unexpected potential solutions during the work. The facilitator helps the innovation team stay focused on the goal and supports them by not getting caught up in details, making decisions, and moving forward, that is, creating trust in the process. The agile innovation work consists of iterative work, as mentioned earlier. In practice, iteration means making decisions and implementing activities, quickly evaluating these, and making new decisions and planning actions based on previous lessons learned. Since uncertainty is inevitable as innovation projects develop, the presence of the factors mentioned above is significant. The alternative is to plan down to the smallest detail, then execute without the slightest deviation. In that case, you are assured that you have done all things right, although not necessarily the right things.

The four areas of expertise of the facilitator
The role of the facilitator is most intense in the first phases of innovation projects, where four areas of expertise have been identified in which the facilitator must be able to manage, train, and advise. The facilitator should support the formation of the innovation team and ensure that they start strong, yet the facilitator should be able to train and advise the innovation team in its development process from group to innovation team, as well as be able to relate these activities at the individual, team, and organization levels. The facilitator should also be able to train and propose activities within the different phases of the innovation process. Finally, they should understand and attend to the factors enabling the work of the innovation team to identify and recall the shortcomings that the innovation team itself cannot understand or discover, based on their current level of knowledge.

Work in three levels
The facilitator's work occurs over three different levels: knowledge, knowledge management and teaching. Knowledge regard specifically innovation-related knowledge, including both a theoretical and practical understanding of how innovation and its various tasks are conducted, as well as knowledge of the different factors that enable innovation work. The second level, knowledge management, regards the ability to transform knowledge into relevant advice and to guide an innovation team according to their advice. Here, knowledge management concerns providing timely, situational advice – both as feedback on already completed work and as advice on upcoming activities. Finally, teaching requires an ability to advise and provide feedback that the innovation team can understand and turn into their own knowledge. In this work, the facilitator needs to be able to adapt and vary its communication to create genuine commitment among team members.

Brief summary of the innovation facilitator
– The facilitator is a support function to the innovation team, sponsor, and management.
– The facilitator's involvement is (when required) essential in forming the innovation team and the first parts of the innovation process – ready to step in for nudging or some practical work.
– The facilitator must master the innovation enablers, the group development- and innovation process, and teach the newly formed innovation team about the just mentioned.

Summary

Chapter two has introduced four areas that all affect innovation team in different ways: innovation enablers (i.e., factors enabling the work of the innovation team); the structure of innovative and non-innovative organizations; agile innovation work and the practical work process; and the facilitator, a support function when the team is formed and then continuously during the innovation project.

Since the innovation team does not exist as an isolated entity but is located in an organization and consists of team members, innovation enablers consist of factors within these three perspectives – the perspective of the organizational, innovation team and that of the team member. Certain of the factors are relatively similar and overlap, so training is necessary to distinguish them, but also a context that gives meaning to the content.

From an organizational perspective, the factors affect the innovation team more comprehensively, while those from the innovation team's perspective affect the work more directly. The factors from the team members' perspective influence the work in that it is about the team members' knowledge and abilities to do the practical work.

All innovation enablers affect innovation work divergently and have varied impacts on different phases of the innovation work.

Of the factors that enable the work of an innovation team, some have a greater impact than others. One is that management prioritizes innovation teams as a way of working and at the same time communicates this priority publicly, to avoid organizational misunderstanding. Innovation teams suffering from a lack of commitment, entrepreneurship, human capital, knowledge, positive mindset, knowledge management, collaboration, or time will most likely lose momentum in the innovation project. By focusing on increasing team members' commitment and mindset and initiating new collaborations, however.

The organization's structure affects innovation work and can be described as non-innovative or innovative organizational structures in its extremes (i.e., industrial or post-industrial structures). In the industrial organizational structure, employees divide into "silos" and conduct their work without direct cooperation with other departments. Innovation work is completed by an R&D or development department, and the remaining departments become different support functions. In the post-industrial structure, employees collaborate between departments and have a responsibility to freely control their work based on what is best for the organization at the moment. Innovation teams are best suited to organizations that have post-industrial structure or strive towards it.

Innovation work is not fuzzier nor more difficult than other tasks, but it differs significantly from other work processes. The abstract phase that people, in general, find fuzzy is considered to be so largely because of their lack of familiarity with such work. Therefore, training in abstract thinking and handling uncertainties help increase the locus of control. In this context, working agilely means working flexibly and solving problems as they arise. The overall message is that doing the right things is more important than doing things right (i.e., without carelessness), which means quickly and cheaply prototyping your way towards viable solutions with a significant focus and the presence of end-users and end-customers. In parallel, knowledge of how to produce and deliver to customers is developed through close cooperation with suppliers and distributors.

An innovation facilitator (facilitator) helps to create the innovation team, together with its sponsor. The main task of the facilitator is to train and support the innovation team during their innovation projects. However, unlike other types of training, this training occurs primarily through the convener as the innovation project develops. The reasons are two. The first is that it takes too long first to learn innovation work and then start an innovation project. Learning from practical work is much faster. The second is that the innovation team should learn in-depth how innovation work is done, which does not happen with innovation consultants as project managers.

The facilitator needs to have certain qualities and skills to succeed in their mission. One such quality is deep knowledge of innovation management and practical experience with innovation work and group development. In addition, the facilitator must be able to support the innovation team without disrupting their work and to steer the innovation team on the right track if it strays from its main goal. A newly formed innovation team can easily unconsciously steer back towards known processes and patterns because of old habits, and the facilitator must watch for this tendency.

What characterizes a suitable facilitator is that they master the agile innovation process and the innovation enablers, creating innovation teams and acting as advisor during ongoing innovation projects. They serve these functions primarily through their theoretical and practical knowledge of innovation management and its various tasks, alongside their abilities to transform knowledge into relevant advice, to guide an innovation team according to their advice, and to educate, advise, and give feedback in ways the innovation team can understand.

Questions for reflections and discussions

Innovation enablers – Factors that enable innovation team's work

Below, some reflection and discussion questions summarize the essence of the section on the innovation enablers, the organizational structure, the agile innovation process and the facilitator. They appear in alphabetical order and are equally important to discuss. None of the questions have a "yes" or "no"' answer, with the idea, of course, that the questions will initiate discussion and that the areas that are not so clearly developed or polished can begin to form. As well, the questions serve as a reflection on the current situation, and they can be used to look forward and to ground the preliminary work. Then they can also be used for monitoring activities.

The questions below are asked from the three perspectives on innovation enablers: those of the organization, team, and team member. They also have an ongoing impact on how an innovation project is developed. For this reason, the questions have been asked partly based on how the organization and management can support the innovation team's work, partly with the perspective of the innovation team in mind, and partly considering how the team member can contribute to the work. This approach creates an understanding of the innovation team as a whole.

Feel free to use the questions as support for management meetings and planning for future innovation initiatives and follow-up discussions with the innovation team. Since an innovation team consists of team members, their reflections on the issues should also feature in the discussions. They can also be applied to identify suitable team members by touching upon how team members can contribute to different innovation opportunities.

The organizational/management perspective questions are asked from a "we, in our organizational-perspective." Notably, these questions can be answered by management, the innovation team, and the individual team members. In discussion of the same question from different perspectives, as suggested here, different answers may emerge that be in tension, or gaps in understanding may be revealed. Such cases can be further discussed to develop joint conclusions and common understandings and knowledge. Involve expertise to learn about specific areas if necessary.

Awareness – The ability to "see" invisible or undiscovered innovation-related opportunities

Organization/management
- How do we, in our organization, ensure that our innovation teams and other employees are trained in the ability to pay attention to changes in the market or to discover new product needs to develop solutions for, not only at work but also in their spare time so that it stimulates innovation work?

Innovation team
- How do we, in our innovation team, ensure that we train and develop our ability to discover new needs to satisfy?

Team member
- How do I, as a team member, train and develop my ability to discover new needs to satisfy?

Capabilities – The skills and knowledge needed to work in innovation teams
Organization/management
- How do we, in our organization, match non-technical with technical capabilities in our innovation teams?
- How do we, in our organization, teach, train and strengthen our innovation teams' members and other employees' innovation-related capabilities?
- How do we, in our organization, avoid losing essential competencies related to innovation work in the event of layoffs?

Innovation team
- How do we, in our innovation team, ensure a well-balanced mix of capabilities for the innovation project?
- How do we, in our innovation team, teach, train and strengthen our innovation-related capabilities?
- How do we, in our innovation team, notice that we may lack necessary capacity for the innovation project?

Team member
- How do I, as a team member, develop my abilities to align with the development of the innovation project?
- How do I, as a team member, help draw attention to the innovation team that someone/some abilities must be added to the innovation project?

Climate – An encouraging environment stimulating new innovative initiatives and creativity
Organization/management
- In our organization, what does an innovative working climate mean, and how does it affect the work of an innovation team?

- How do we, in our organization, develop and maintain an innovative working climate?
- How do we, in our organization, ensure that an innovation team can maintain an innovative working climate?
- How do we, in our organization, ensure that an innovation team can create the conditions for self-government?

Innovation team
- What does an innovative working climate mean in our innovation team?
- How do we, in the innovation team, develop and maintain an innovative working climate?
- How do we, in the innovation team, create the conditions for self-government?

Team member
- How do I, as a team member, help develop and maintain an innovative working climate?
- How do I, as a team member, contribute to creating conditions for self-government?

Collaboration – Functional innovation teams and collaborations internally between departments, and externally with suppliers, customers, and expert networks
Organization/management
- How do we, in our organization, ensure that an innovation team can establish the collaborations they need for their innovation project?

Innovation team
- How do we, in the innovation team, establish collaboration with end-users, suppliers and different customers in the value chain?
- How do we, in the innovation team, establish collaboration with other organizations and external networks?
- How do we, in the innovation team, establish collaboration with student projects for increased inspiration for an ongoing innovation project?
- How do we, in the innovation team, establish collaboration with researchers to develop new knowledge about advanced issues?

Team member
- How do I, as a team member, connect and establish collaboration with needed partners for the innovation project?

Culture – Norms and rules for "how to do here," tolerance for initiatives that go wrong

Organization/management
- In our organization, what does an innovative culture mean, and how does it affect the work of an innovation team?
- How do we, in our organization, ensure that an innovation team can maintain an innovative culture?

Innovation team
- In our innovation team, what does an innovative culture mean?
- How do we, in the innovation team, work to develop and maintain an innovative culture in the future?
- How do we, in the innovation team, ensure that new or temporary team members can easily understand and feel included in our culture?
- How do we, in the innovation team, build a culture that allows mistakes?

Team member
- How do I, as a team member, help develop and maintain an innovative culture?
- How do I, as a team member, contribute so new or temporary team members can easily understand and feel included in our culture?
- How do I, as a team member, learn from my or others' mistakes and not make others feel bad for their mistakes?

Dedication – The personal commitment to want to participate in an innovation team

Organization/management
- How do we, in our organization, create a willingness among our staff to engage with the innovation team's projects?

Innovation team
- On what is our commitment to the innovation team based?
- What do we, as an innovation team, want to prove?
- What are we, as an innovation team, driven by?
- How do we, as an innovation team, ensure that we maintain our commitment to reaching the goal even when things are not going as planned?

Team member
- As a team member, what is my commitment based on?
- As a team member, what do I want to prove?
- As a team member, what am I driven by?
- How do I, as a team member, maintain my commitment throughout the innovation project?
- How do I, as a team member, help other team members maintain their commitment throughout the innovation project?

Economy – Monetary and non-monetary resources
Organization/management
- In our organization, what are the investments for long-term innovation projects, and how is it reflected in the innovation team?
- How do we, in our organization, ensure that the innovation team has sufficient finances to run the project all the way?
- What can non-monetary resources be in our organization when it comes to innovation projects, and how do we secure these resources for the innovation team?
- What milestones in the innovation project are critical to achieving continued funding, and how should they be prioritized?
- How do we, in our organization, encourage the innovation team to collaborate creatively if the economy demands it?

Innovation team
- How do we, in the innovation team, ensure that we have enough finances to run the project all the way?
- How do we, in the innovation team, deal with any lack of finances?
- What non-monetary resources are important for the progress of the innovation project, and how do we in the innovation team ensure that they are acquired?
- What milestones in the innovation project are critical to achieving continued funding, and how should they be prioritized?
- How can we create creative collaborations as a consequence of lack of money?

Team member
- How do I, as a team member, help secure the economy of the innovation project?
- How do I, as a team member, help acquire non-monetary resources if necessary?
- How do I, as a team member, help achieve important milestones in the innovation project?

Education – Innovation-related competence development in theory and practice
Organization/management
- How do we, in our organization, ensure that we train innovation teams about innovation management and continuously train it?
- How do we, in our organization, utilize distance learning so that our innovation teams and other employees can be trained at the same time?
- How do we, in our organization, create a commitment to and desire to learn about innovation management?

Innovation team
- How do we, in the innovation team, continuously educate ourselves in innovation management and other relevant training for the innovation project?
- How do we, in the innovation team, find out what training we need to handle the forthcoming innovation work?

Team member
- How do I, as a team member, find out what training I need to handle the forthcoming innovation work?
- How do I, as a team member, stay engaged and continuously develop my theoretical and practical knowledge of innovation work?
- How do I, as a team member, set aside time to prepare for upcoming training sessions?

Empowerment – Trust from management to the innovation team to make their own decisions about resources or investments; autonomous work under the responsibility of the members of the innovation team
Organization/management
- How do we, in our organization, encourage innovation team members and other employees towards empowerment and self-government?
- How do we, in our organization, ensure that the innovation team members and other employees take responsibility to empower themselves and make the best of self-government?

Innovation team
- How do we, in our innovation team, ensure that we create a good level of empowerment and self-government to promote creativity without losing focus on the task?

- How do we, in our innovation team, communicate our expectations of responsibility, decision-making, and implementation to the management to meet their expectations?
- How do we, in our innovation team, communicate our progress to management to feel confident that we can manage the responsibility we have been assigned?

Team member
- How do I, as a team member, demonstrate that I take responsibility for the empowerment and self-government of the innovation team?
- How do I, as a team member, communicate that I take responsibility for the empowerment and self-government of the innovation team?

Entre-/intrapreneurship – Doers that make things happen
Organization/management
- How do we, in our organization, encourage employees to become more entrepreneurial?
- How do we, in our organization, encourage entrepreneurs to join us, if only for a short period?

Innovation team
- How do we, in the innovation team, commit to working entrepreneurially?
- How do we, as an innovation team, engage entrepreneurial people in our innovation team for the innovation project if necessary?

Team member
- How do I, as a team member, ensure to working entrepreneurially?
- How do I, as a team member, develop my entrepreneurial skills if necessary?

Human resources – Access to colleagues within the organization who can contribute to the innovation project and who can also share experiences and help avoid bottlenecks
Organization/management
- How do we, in our organization, ensure that the innovation team can create collaboration between departments?
- How can we, in our organization, help the innovation team spread information about ongoing innovation projects to enable employees to more easily contribute knowledge and resources?

Innovation team
- How do we, in the innovation team, create opportunities for collaboration between departments?
- How can we, in the innovation team, disseminate information about ongoing projects to make it easier for employees to contribute knowledge and resources?

Team member
- How do I, as a team member, help involve people in the innovation project if necessary?
- How do I, as a team member, actively disseminate information about our innovation project?

Incentives – Financial and non-monetary rewards as motivators

Organization/management
- What does the reward system look like in our organization?
- What effects can be expected from the existing/non-existing reward system?
- How do we, in our organization, reward the internal driving forces of the innovator team members and other employees?
- How can we, in our organization, arrange a reward structure that stimulates both in the short and long term?
- How do we, in our organization, stimulate positive feedback to the innovation team members and other employees?

Innovation team
- How do we, in our innovation team, want to be rewarded for our work?
- How do we, in our innovation team, ensure that we don't get greedy?
- How do we, in our innovation team, stimulate positive feedback between each other?

Team member
- How do I, as a team member, contribute to the innovation team being rewarded in the way we deserve?
- How do I, as a team member, make sure I'm not greedy?
- How do I, as a team member, give feedback to my colleagues in the innovation team?

Knowledge – Special knowledge concerning innovation and innovation work
Organization/management
- How do we, in our organization, ensure that the members of the innovation team and other employees can develop their innovation-related knowledge?
- How do we, in our organization, leverage the innovation team members' tacit knowledge of innovation work so that other co-workers can benefit from it?
- How do we, in our organization, ensure that the innovation team can communicate and share knowledge with the team, in the rest of the organization, and across other networks?

Innovation team
- How do we, in the innovation team, continuously develop our theoretical and practical knowledge of innovation work?
- How do we, in the innovation team, share knowledge and learning experiences in the team, the rest of the organization, and other networks?

Team member
- How do I, as a team member, set aside time to develop my theoretical and practical knowledge of innovation work continuously?
- How do I, as a team member, share knowledge with the team, the rest of the organization, and other networks?

Knowledge management – Knowledge of how to, in practice, use knowledge and fill knowledge gaps concerning innovation projects
Organization/management
- How do we, in our organization, ensure the development and practice of innovation-related knowledge management in our innovation teams and other employees?
- How do we, in our organization, make sure to teach our innovation teams and other employees to develop experience about how to apply innovation-related knowledge management?
- How do we, in our organization, support our innovation teams and other employees to develop knowledge management through external networks?

Innovation team
- How do we, in the innovation team, ensure the development of innovation-related knowledge management?
- How do we, in the innovation team, ensure to apply the innovation-related knowledge we have achieved?

Team member
- How do I, as a team member, develop and apply innovation-related knowledge?
- How do I, as a team member, make sure to practice the elements of the innovation work I feel unsure about?

Management – Encouragement of exploration of new ideas
Organization/management
- How does our organization's management plan for long-term innovation-related activities, and how do those activities affect an innovation team's work?
- How do we, in our organization, ensure that the managers of innovation teams do not feel left out or threatened in their new function of supporting instead of managing?
- How does our organization's management handle incremental and radical innovation investments, and how does that handling affect an innovation team's work?
- How do we, in our organization, ensure that management shows interest in an innovation team's practical work?

Innovation team
- How do we, in the innovation team, ensure that management does not feel left out or threatened in their new function of supporting instead of managing?
- How do we, in our innovation team, act to keep the management interested in our work?

Team member
- How should I, as a team member, act upon management as a support function to not create unnecessary tension or hurt feelings?
- How do I, as a team member, contribute to keeping the management interested in our work?

**Mindset – Self-confidence and attitude of the innovation team members.
"I can. . .," "I want. . .," "I will. . ."**
Organization/management
– How do we, in our organization, stimulate a positive attitude for the innovation team members and other employees?
– How do we, in our organization, encourage the innovation team and other employees to celebrate small work victories in ongoing innovation work?

Innovation team
– How do we, in the innovation team, maintain a positive attitude towards the innovation project and its development, and against each other in the innovation team?
– How do we, in the innovation team, maintain a positive attitude towards each other in the innovation team?

Team member
– How do I, as a team member, do to have a positive attitude towards the innovation project?
– How do I, as a team member, do to have a positive attitude towards other members?

**Needs – Explicit and clarified needs to meet – Needs that explain why
the innovation project is needed**
Organization/management
– How do we, in our organization, help the innovation team to identify existing and future needs to develop products for?
– How do we, in our organization, ensure that the innovation team can require the right skills and equipment to meet future needs?

Innovation team
– What do we, in the innovation team, do to identify existing and future needs to develop products to?
– How will needs/problems change in the future, and how can that be addressed?
– What would a competitor have done to solve the same needs/problems?
– How do we, in the innovation team, ensure we have the right skills and are rightly equipped to meet future needs?

Team member
- How do I, as a team member, contribute, identify, and verify current and future needs to develop products for?
- How do I, as a team member, search for appropriate skills if necessary to strengthen the innovation team?

Processes – Processes, models, and proven innovation methods that guide ideas to become established products on the market
Organization/management
- How do we, in our organization, ensure that the innovation team has access to appropriate processes and methods for their innovation project?

Innovation team
- How do we, in the innovation team, ensure that we have suitable processes to use for our work?
- How do we, in the innovation team, apply design thinking and user-centered design to find relevant information about the problem to solve.
- How do we, in the innovation team, use simple tools at the beginning of the innovation work and more advanced tools, such as CAD and CAE later, for fast and iterative work?
- What criteria do we use to evaluate ideas, concepts, prototypes, and so on for potential future work?
- How do we, in the innovation team, use the mindset of a potential competitor to solve the identified problem?

Team member
- How do I, as a team member, actively learn and practice suitable innovation tools for agile, iterative, and flexible innovation work?
- How do I, as a team member, do to think like a competitor?

Strategy – Organizations with clear innovation strategies are more successful than others
Organization/management
- How do we, in our organization, define innovation?
- If there is no clear description: Write a two-sentence formulation in which the first sentence describes what innovation means to us, and the second sentence describes how we will work with innovation in our organization.
- What is our innovation strategy?

- If there is no clear description, begin with the definition as above and continue with a short description on how to implement innovation in our organization on a generic level, formulated similarly as other formulations on strategies.
- How do we, in our organization, communicate the innovation strategy to the innovation team and the rest of the organization?
- How do we, in our organization, collaborate with other organizations on a strategic level?

Innovation team
- How will we, in the innovation team, work to have the innovation strategy as a guidance for our innovation project?

Team member
- How do I, as a team member, show that I understand what the organization's innovation strategy means for the innovation project, and thus my work?

Time – Time set aside for the innovation project, time for reflection, and time for education and learning
Organization/management
- How much time do we, in the organization, allocate for innovation teams to work on the innovation projects?
- Is this time enough to reach the expected goals?
- If yes, we will get the desired results, but what would happen if we allocated even more time or other resources?
- If not, how do we make more time for the innovation teams?
- How do we, in our organization, encourage the innovation team to spend more time in the initial phases of the innovation project to really understand the problem to be solved?
- How do we, in our organization, ensure that the innovation teams spend enough time on the innovation project assigned, not being disturbed by other work or projects (multitasking) to the extent that it affects the innovation project negatively?
- How do we, in our organization, support our innovation teams and other employees with time for reflection?
- How do we, in our organization, support our innovation teams and other employees with time for work on personal interests, which may be useful for the organization in the future?

Innovation team
- How do we, in the innovation team, ensure that we prioritize work on the innovation project for which we have allocated time?
- How do we, in the innovation team, ensure to allocate enough time in the first exploratory phase of the innovation process?
- How do we, in the innovation team, ensure to prioritize time for recurring reflection during the innovation project?
- How do we, in our innovation team, find ways to work on the innovation project in the case of insufficient time allocated by management?

Team member
- How do I, as a team member, prioritize time for innovation work?
- How do I, as a team member, avoid negative multitasking such as fragmented tasks or being involved in too many projects?
- How do I, as a team member, approach management in the case of being involved in too many projects, affecting the excepted results negatively?

The innovation enabler's impact on innovation work

The factors (innovation enablers) demonstrated in the previous section all affect an innovation team's work, so the general question regards how to avoid them affecting the innovation team negatively.

Organization/management
- How do we, in our organization, ensure our innovation teams strive to have the innovation enablers met during start-up and ongoing innovation projects?
- How do we, in our organization, allocate resources to innovation enablers not fulfilled?

Innovation team
- How do we, in the innovation team, support innovation enablers at an acceptable level?
- How do we, in the innovation team, prioritize innovation enablers that are not secured?

Team member
- How do I, as a team member, pay attention to whether the innovation project is negatively affected by any innovation enablers?

- How do I, as a team member, contribute to realizing innovation enablers that are not secured?

Organizational structures and innovation teams

The structure of the organization affects how innovation work can be carried out. As mentioned earlier, all organizations benefit from innovation in the long term. However, If the owner of the organization plans for an exit or retirement in the near future, heavy investments in innovation actions may not be profitable.

Organization/management
- How do we, in our organization, evolve towards and maintain a post-industrial structure to promote innovation work?
- How do we, in our organization, involve more and more employees in innovation work of various kinds?

Innovation team
- How do we, in the innovation team, utilize most of the opportunity to run an innovation project ourselves?

Team member
- How do I, as a team member, contribute to making the results of the innovation project as good as possible?

The innovation process

The innovation process has evolved from gradually developing a product, to working agilely and flexibly, to increasing the speed of development, where most of the work is neither creative nor abstract.

Organization/management
- How do we, in our organization, communicate that innovation work is neither fuzzy nor for the "smart ones"?
- What do we do, in our organization, to feel confident that the innovation team is "doing what they are supposed to"?
- What do we do, in our organization, to feel confident that agile innovation work delivers to the quality standard we expect?

Innovation team
- How do we, in the innovation team, embrace an agile way of working?
- How do we, in the innovation team, track parallel projects in the innovation project?
- How do we, in the innovation team, relate to sudden changes in conditions regarding expected outcomes or goals to reach?

Team member
- How do I, as a team member, work quickly, iteratively, and in constant evaluation of what other team members and I create in the innovation project?

The facilitator – Stimuli for successful learning

As mentioned, the facilitator is critical to the innovation team's forthcoming work. Different competencies and skills affect the innovation team's learning and the outcome of their first innovation project. The facilitator's role is to support the innovation team to get the most out of the project.

Organization/management
- How do we, in our organization, ensure that innovation teams have access to a facilitator during the time the innovation team develops and learns about innovation work?
- How do we, in our organization, ensure that the facilitator has the skills to support an innovation team?

Innovation team
- How do we, in the innovation team, relate to the facilitator's advice, objections and feedback to suggested, planned and conducted activities?
- How do we, in the innovation team, stay positive about conducting new activities we haven't done before?

Team member
- How do I, as a team member, stay open-minded and at the same time critical of the facilitator's advice, objections and feedback to suggested, planned and conducted activities?
- How do I, as a team member, dare to conduct activities that the facilitator might suggest but that I feel uncomfortable doing due to uncertainty?
- How do I, as a team member, learn as much as I can from the facilitator's experience?

3 Creating high-performing innovation teams in five steps

This chapter focuses on how to create an innovation team, in practice. It builds upon the previous chapters, whose focus was to demonstrate the building blocks and foundations of what the innovation team needs to know about and handle in its upcoming work (e.g., knowledge of the innovation process and the factors that enable the work of the innovation team). Particular focus was placed on the facilitator, a focal point that recurs in this chapter, as the innovation team forms. In this chapter, the focus is more on what steps to take (as illustrated in Fig. 3.1, including which members should be part of a new innovation team and the success factors in getting the innovation team to take off. The process is based on step-by-step work that is not nearly as iterative as the innovation process. The work is both top-down and bottom-up, so management's consent is crucial. However, it is equally important for employees to want to do the job.

In this chapter, you will learn more about the high-performing innovation team process's five steps:
- Top management commitment – ensure management's commitment and support
- Convener identification – identify a convener of the forthcoming innovation team
- Convener preparation – prepare the convener for the upcoming work
- Gathering of team members – identify the best fit people
- Kick-off – the official start of the innovation project

In the list of what steps to take to form an innovation team, notice that the innovation team is not formed until point four. This may seem a late stage, but generally, creating a successful innovation team is about good preparation – kind of like when wallpapering a wall or removing rust on an old classic car. If the new, fine wallpaper is carelessly glued on the wall without fixing old damage with filling and sanding, the overall impression is not likely to be good. New paint on a rusty car will return rust almost momentarily. In short, cheating on the steps will not yield the desired result, and it may not be that fun. Accordingly, moving back to the creation of the innovation team, the preparations are about ensuring that management believes in and supports the creation of the innovation team, as the work assembling an ideal innovation team may not be the same as assembling other teams. In addition, group dynamic problems must be avoided, which are all too common when new groups are formed to work together. The aim is to create an innovation team that consciously develops together, feeling joint ownership and leadership of the innovation project. As such, the innovation team should have a convener instead of a project manager. As noticed in the introduction. This work process for

https://doi.org/10.1515/9783110731934-003

creating high-performance innovation teams is called the HIT process, or high-performing innovation team process.

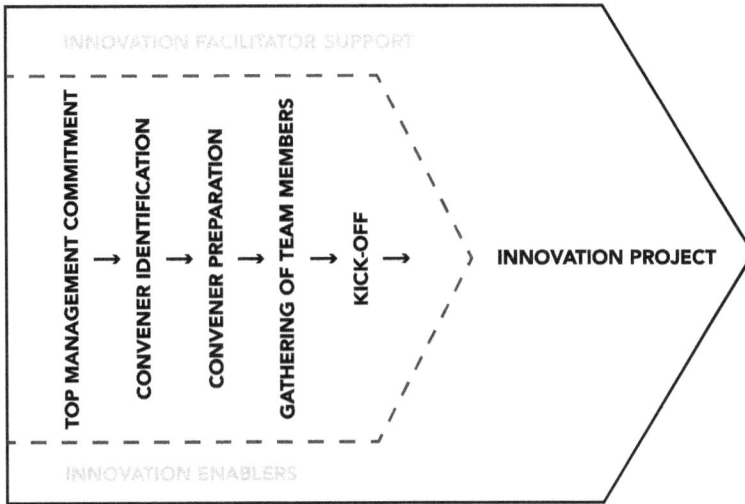

Fig. 3.1: The HIT process, as part of the creating high-performing innovation team model.

Now, it's time to get into the different steps of the process. First, put down the book, take some time to stretch the legs and get a cup of coffee or a favorite beverage. On the way back, bring a pen and paper or a tablet to take notes on and to collect your thoughts. If you've not yet been inspired, this chapter may take you there. At the same time, equip yourself with patience. Things take time, as they say. Do not rush through the process, and the result will be so much better. The most important element of the process it is to create commitment. Most people don't find being forced to do some-thing to be engaging. Therefore, if you are initiating this process in an organization or working as a facilitator or convener, be responsive and flexible in portraying things. Let those who are involved shape their understanding of what is presented, at the same time as you develop a common overall picture. Remember, each participant and stakeholder will consider, "What's in it for me?" Expect to repeat the same presenta-tion many times but in different contexts, and recognize that different perspectives are required to consider. The commitment will come as people are appropriately intro-duced, given that they have a fundamental interest in the topic and have had enough time to process what has been presented. Let it take time, but don't let it slip peoples' minds. After a few days or weeks, make a schedule to follow up on the people in-volved, to take the next step. Push ahead, involve and engage but don't push through: That's the difference.

Step 1 – Top management commitment

In the first step, the focus will be on management explaining why it's a good idea not rush to step four, where the innovation team is formed. Here, the focus is on engaging management and getting their full support, which is crucial for the future of the innovation team.

Management is crucial for long-term success

To be clear, management support is crucial in establishing innovation teams as part of an organization. Initiating such work and then leaving it to its fate is likely to damage future innovation initiatives. The alternative, not to make this kind of work official, only creates grounds for self-organization working "under the radar," "pet projects," or "skunkworks," where enthusiasts develop ideas without management's knowledge. The problem with these projects are they steal attention, and may not even align with the organization's objectives or strategy. Frankly, it is theft of organizational resources. This phenomenon should not be mixed up with corporation labs, such as Google X, Apple Labs, or Amazon Lab126. Here, people are employed to create disruptive solutions.

Develop understanding on innovation and innovation teams

One of the greatest challenges with this first step is to convince management that some of the work is to be able to deal with uncertainty and that innovation work is an investment and not a risk per se. In many cases, managers dislike risk and spend many of their working hours minimizing it. Since innovation work does not guarantee successful results in the short turn, the term "innovation project" seldom results in standing ovations among those not convinced of its need for survival. On the other hand, the argument that the opposite eventually leads to termination is not noticed as long as the approaching disaster is not yet visible. This problem is particularly significant in organizations with a large turnover of people in management. Without a long-term approach, it is easy to get caught up in cost-cutting, leaving little room for investments in innovation initiatives.

Therefore, the first step is to ensure that management takes responsibility for the project. In doing so, the following questions can be used to study and discuss the management's approach to innovation in your organization:

- Does management support innovation efforts by allocating both financial and human resources?
- Does management make realistic assessments of market expectations closely linked to end-users to capture their expectations accurately?

- Does management ensure that innovation projects receive the necessary support from all parts and levels of the organization?
- Does management ensure a structured system or method to assess potential innovations before significant investments are initiated?
- Does management encourage employees to take risks within reasonable limits if at the same time it means taking advantage of learning from any mistakes and not seeing mistakes and not successful initiatives as failures?
- Does management work actively to ensure that the organization maintains its open and permissive structure to allow employees to engage between department boundaries or work actively to develop the structure in this direction?

The sponsor – key person on an important mission

In addition to management's pivotal function, the future innovation team's sponsor has one as well. In this case, the sponsor is a person who supports the team in their work without directly interfering in what they do. The sponsor also acts as a communication channel between the innovation team and management and other department managers or those involved outside the reach of the innovation team. The sponsor will smooth the innovation team's upcoming work, as they sometimes need access to skills they lack, which may exist elsewhere in the organization. In those moments, the sponsor can act as a door opener. The sponsor has a further task, perhaps the most important, which is seemingly relatively unappreciated: namely, to be accountable for a potentially discontinued innovation project without necessarily blaming the innovation team and its performance, as well as to give credit to the innovation team for their successes and not take all the credit for themselves. To make this function work, the sponsor must be as convinced as management is that innovation teams work agilely suit the organization's development.

Be patient, it takes time

If management is inexperienced in innovation work, it is worth bearing in mind that it often takes up to six months to understand why innovation work has value for the organization and to start implementing innovational activities such as trying out, evaluating, and adapting different innovation processes to suit the organization and rewarding employees for various innovative initiatives. To succeed in changing an organization and to become more innovative, management must ensure accurate and accessible information and time for employees to digest it, turning it into their own knowledge. To create a sense of control for management, they can point out a strategic direction with areas to develop instead of ordering innovations. This is a perfect place for the innovation teams to start working for the first time.

To learn the methodology, start small

One way to start implementing the process of creating innovation teams is to initiate one or two pilot projects to demonstrate the benefits of innovation team work and build a pool of knowledgeable employees who can pass the message on in the organization. Also, pilot projects allow room to learn from any mistakes made. Admittedly, some have argued that pilot projects are excuses used to shut down initiatives without being questioned. Instead, think in the same way as when advocating for the innovation model. Think of prototypes that develop iteratively towards fully functional solutions. With this mindset, a pilot for an innovation team is a good and concrete way to test, develop, and improve a method under limited and controlled conditions. Strive for the best conditions possible for the pilot, so that the evaluation is fair and so that lessons can be learned.

Empowerment for innovation

An individual's ability to control and manage their work is an important ingredient in the creation of an innovative organization; the same goes for innovation teams. They must be given the space to work independently. Still, it also requires encouragement and active initiatives to ensure that employees feel that they are not making fools of themselves or are being confronted with "this is not how we do things here." Even though empowerment is requested and provided, it can also be difficult to know how far the team and its members' responsibility to empower extends. To ease such difficulties, certain guidelines can be helpful:

- Show the boundaries within which it is okay to develop ideas without getting permission from management or starting a formal project.
- Describe the reasonable level of business risk for how far an initiative can go.
- Structure the organization to encourage it to involve many in new initiatives.
- Define responsibilities in the organization to increase clarity regarding how innovation work can be completed.

Increased space for empowerment, combined with training in problem-solving methods, leads innovation teams to take more responsibility for their activities, which is positive for innovation output. In addition, innovation teams who develop their ability to propose improvements to their work have much greater opportunity to successfully realize the improvements and find more uses for their solutions.

Brief summary of step 1
- Management support is crucial for long term success.
- Plan for a first small project; learn from that and advance.
- Set boundaries and empower the forthcoming innovation team.

Step 2 – Convener identification

Now that management's commitment is established, it's time for step two: to identify a convener to form the innovation team. It's easy to think that a convener is equivalent to a project manager, but this equivalence is false if the aim is to create long-term learning as well, as explained below.

Establish conditions for long-term learning

Just as the innovation processes over time has moved towards becoming cyclical and iterative, so too have the requisite skills of an innovation leader. Previously, innovation work was primarily associated with engineers who developed technical solutions. Still, since innovation work has evolved to be cross-disciplinary and multifunctional, innovation leaders are now required to handle multiple areas. In practice, this expansion of necessary knowledge has led to innovation leadership increasingly being about understanding, managing and leading the innovation process, as well as navigating all the uncertainties constantly affecting the current conditions of an innovation project. In other contexts or projects, it can be good to appoint a chief project manager, project manager, or an external consultant who runs innovation projects and gets things done. None of this is wrong if the main purpose is to quickly get to the finish line. If the intent is to create an innovative organization and learn how to cope with the innovation work without external expertise, then it is wise to reconsider the approach, however. After all, as soon as the consultant leaves the innovation project, most often, everything returns to what was before, and the learning aspect of innovation work is hollowed out.

The convener is not a project manager

To create the conditions for learning and joint ownership of the innovation project, a convener is appointed, who, if needed, is supported in turn by a facilitator (as explained in chapter two). A high-performing innovation team has no project manager. The innovation team leads itself based on what is best at the moment and what benefits the project going forward. The convener is not a project manager but a person who holds together the group that is to become an innovation team, which may sound strange. The identification of the convening person is preferably made by management, together with the facilitator the first time, or times, as it is easy to confuse the convener function with project management. The goal is therefore for the newly formed innovation team to become a self-governing and self-leading innovation team. In this work, the innovation team must be supported in how a team leads itself when new challenges arise on an ongoing basis. Here, the facilitator crucially trains and sometimes coaches team members in abstract problem-solving techniques.

The convener wants change, in collaboration

The role of the convener is preferably assigned to a person who is trusted by their management and colleagues, likes the organization, is proud to work there, and wants to get involved in developing the organization's work. In short, it's an enthusiast who wants to make a difference and can listen to others, share ideas and make knowledge available to others, turn those ideas into action, stimulate others to get involved, and can let other prospective team members take their place and run the project together. The convener should also highlight the team members' competencies and strengthen their self-confidence in moments of mistrust. While the convener will have a slightly larger holistic perspective at the outset and know the innovation processes at a somewhat higher level than the rest of the innovation team, because he or she has recurring conversations with the facilitator, the rest of the members quickly catch up. The search for a convener requires much patience. Find the right person takes time, as does meeting their immediate manager and describing and explaining the work of innovation teams and the role of the convener so that no ambiguity can cause concern to the convener or innovation team in the future work. As a starting point, it can be expected that the convening person needs to have at least 15–20 percent working time available to work with and in the innovation team and during the initial work, sometimes more, to properly integrate the role.

Case:

In one case, a project was initiated by a manager, who was also the project's sponsor. A person volunteered for the convener role, which surprised the manager/sponsor. The person in mind was not known for taking command and initiative in projects and was not very experienced in innovation projects. However, the person was interviewed by the facilitator regarding the role and expectations to fulfill. As the convener in this case would also become a team member with a specific function, the following step (step 4 in the HIT process) was also investigated. Even though the person wasn't the manager/sponsor's first choice, the volunteering person got the job based on the commitment communicated through the interview. The person showed to be a perfect fit for the job and the project's focus. Preparations went excellent, and the team members were swiftly gathered for a kick-off shortly after the interview. As the project progressed, the convener showed persistence and commitment not seen in other projects involved. The lesson learned in this case was that people might possess hidden qualities suitable for innovation team work (in this case as a convener) not shown in everyday work.

Brief summary of step 2
- The convener is not a project manager but aims for joint ownership and leadership.
- The convener channels potential issues with the facilitator, sponsor, and management.
- The convener needs time for their duties and should not be an extra burden.

Step 3 – Convener preparation

In the third step of the HIT process, the focus is on establishing the self-confidence of the convener to start recruiting team members. Here, the facilitator puts much energy into repeatedly explaining and reflecting with the convener. Everything must fall into place to the level that the convener understands the whole project and some overarching details. The details will come as the work emerges. Accordingly, this chapter covers aspects of how the introduction of the convener is conducted and what focus to have. It also affirms that patience is a virtue in the creation of an innovation team.

The role of the innovation facilitator

The preparation of the convener should be executed by a person comparable to a facilitator, that is, a person with both theoretical knowledge and practical experience regarding the formation of innovation teams and innovation work. Once the convener has been appointed, preparations begin with the facilitator during meetings before the innovation team is gathered. In the first meeting, it is appropriate for the facilitator and the convener to get to know each other, before the innovation-related methods and techniques are presented and explained. Of course, naturally the discussions will regard how to do the practical work relatively quickly.

Generally speaking, the facilitator's first role is to slow down the pace. The convener is usually eager to get started and create the innovation team at once. However, to avoid failing before the project has even begun, the convener needs to receive some explanation.

Crash course – this is what to know about

The introduction of the convener is equivalent to a warm-up for the upcoming creation of the innovation team. Without the preparation, there is a risk of the convener getting too much information to absorb the essence of what is to be done in the forthcoming work. The convener needs time to digest the information and room to ask questions before engaging in real deal. However, not all possible scenarios can be prepared for, because innovation work is unpredictable, even if it is structured. In conclusion, the convener receives a crash course in the following subjects:
- The agile innovation process and the importance of not stopping for obstacles
- Team members needing to be selected based on divergence, specialist knowledge, volunteerism, entrepreneurship, and organization development
- Empowerment and joint team responsibility to develop the structure and working practices of the innovation team

- The group development process and what problems usually appear a group emerges towards a team
- Development of joint ownership and leadership
- Change resistance and how to deal with it
- The facilitator's role as a support and coach through the work

Creating the innovation team according to project focus

It is usually appropriate to start by explaining how the agile innovation process works and then alternating with team members to invite, problem-solving techniques, and so forth. Soon, the impression will become that everything is connected, leading to difficulties keeping details separated. However, the innovation process and the innovation team are the core to which all is related. The convener's first task is to define the competencies and functions needed for the team, covering all the parts described in the Raft model (i.e., end-users, end-customers, suppliers, and distributors). Of course, another innovation model can also work – the key is that the mentioned functionalities are covered. Do not involve too many people (more about team size in step 4). Together, the members are responsible to ensure that various activities are carried out in these areas, thereby creating joint ownership and leadership. The main work of the convener is to ensure that the work environment is satisfactory and that decisions are made jointly without spending too much time on endless discussions before decisions are made, as well as to ensure that everyone in the innovation team helps and supports each other even though the work sometimes goes sideways.

Case:

In one case, a convener was introduced, supported by management and the sponsor. The kick-off was smooth, and the project developed according to plan. All of a sudden, the convener signed off and changed jobs, however. It was a surprise for all involved. The remaining team gathered to determine whether the convener should be replaced by a new one with similar skills or if it was an opportunity to add knowledge to the team that better suited the project's current situation. The solution was neither. One of the existing team members stepped forward, asking the team if it was okay to take the convener role. It was okay for all involved, and the work continued with four people. Shortly afterward, the same situation occurred, however: The second convener also signed off for another job. An additional member was requested at this point, as the workload was assessed to be too much for the three reaming persons. The third convener was recruited by the resigning convener and introduced to the project by the facilitator. The project was completed on time. In this case, the lesson learned was that conveners could change jobs unpredictably several times without dramatically affecting progress. The reason was that the team was designed for co-leadership. It was also reflected by the recruitment of team members, who were all self-motived, entrepreneurial, and problem-solving individuals, to mention a few skills they possessed. (But more about that in the following step 4 in the HIT process.)

Unstructured vs. structured processes – sort out potential confusions
Among the most important work of the facilitator during the preparation is to be calm and attentive to how the convener reacts to the different elements of the suggested methods. Commonly, the agile innovation process feels unstructured and difficult to follow in an organization either with structured processes established already or with no processes at all. The confusion can be significant for organizations applying agile project management for product development, as such procedures are rigid. They usually divide into short sprints followed by reconciliations and updated backlogs. Here, there is usually little room for innovation. On the other hand, the agile innovation process, as demonstrated earlier, is also structured, but unexpected outcomes are expected. In the meetings between the facilitator and the proposed convener, it becomes clearer whether the convener has the strength to advocate for a new, or at least different, way of working. Much courage and maturity are required for such work. Therefore, the facilitator's main task at these meetings is to build the necessary self-confidence. The convener must feel that the sponsor and the facilitator, if necessary, can intervene and talk to managers or other employees who need extra explanation as the work progresses.

Clear goals but open-ended results
As mentioned, management should generally direct the development of new products. Still, it should be direction with a goal that can accommodate entirely new solutions, which then become the innovation team's task to solve. If the innovation team is tasked with improving something with a set metric, such as 5 percent lower production cost, 7 percent better performance, or 4 percent lower energy consumption, that's probably the results that will be achieved. Avoid setting the goal too precisely. In the agile way of working, the innovation team will meet and be confronted with all possible stakeholders, and together they potentially can generate unexpected results.

Keep management and sponsor updated during preparations
In the preparatory work, close discussions are held between the innovation team's sponsor and the convener to align their understanding of the direction of the innovation project. Once the work gets underway, the sponsor and or other management persons should not practice micromanagement on the innovation team. Any discussions of the project will preferably be had privately by the convener, the sponsor, and the facilitator. When all ambiguities are worked out, the convener talks to the rest of the innovation team.

Manage change resistance

Innovation is closely associated with change management. Therefore, it also relates to change resistance, as noticed through lively protests and silent indirect resistance from both employees and people in management positions. To avoid group development problems, it is important to plan for those problems before the innovation team is created, beginning as the convener is appointed and continuing through the subsequent steps (i.e., when the convener is introduced and the team members are identified in the organization). Naturally, most people try to preserve what has been and not put themselves at risk. For a convener of a new innovation team, it is not easy to propose new ideas or new ways of working that challenge the familiar. Here, the facilitator must explain how the work will be done in practice. A key ingredient to prevent resistance to change is transparency with all information and availability of information on a platform on which everyone can take part, not only the innovation team but also in the rest of the organization. Through open communication about what the innovation team is currently working on, employees in the organization cannot say that they didn't know what was going on. With open communication, employees also gain the opportunity to get involved and help where needed. Here, once again, the facilitator can notably explain and demonstrate how to leverage the information flow to spread engaging information and to incorporate new opportunities and solutions for the project, not only in what is communicated in the workplace but also in things that are seen or heard in their free time.

If it stops – reboot

If it turns out, for some reason, that the convener does not want to proceed with the work, look for another candidate who can take over before starting the work of the innovation team. If it proves necessary to search for a new convener because the intended person does not like the arrangement, or if the facilitator feels that there is potential misrecruitment, then the need for replacement should not be seen as a failure. Rather, it is simply part of the process. If possible, it is much better to adjust at this early stage than to do it once the innovation project has begun, as doing it at that point may be far more complicated.

Case:

In one case, an intended convener was very interested in creating an innovation team. Management agreed to initiate the project with the person in mind taking the role of convener. The convener was introduced to the group development process and the agile innovation process. However, the following step involving the formation of the innovation team of people from different departments didn't feel right for that person. The work was halted, and a new convener was thus searched for and identified, so the process started over with the introduction. Sad, of course, but it was the right decision for all involved. Moreover, though the kick-off was delayed, the innovation project, as such, did not face any harm, as it had not yet begun. The next potential convener identified completed the process and formed the innovation team, and the innovation project was successful. The lesson learned in this case was that the process allowed the convener to take in the forthcoming work in advance without affecting the project negatively.

Brief summary of step 3
- Preparing the convener is a crash course on both group development- and innovation-related theories and practices.
- The convener must handle open-ended goals, iterative processes, and a lot of uncertainties – and staff a multifunctional team that can handle the same.
- If the convener finds the assignment not suitable for any reason, it is not a failure but just part of the process – reboot and go again.

Step 4 – Gathering the innovation team members

Finally, it's time to put the innovation team together. So far, the team-assembly process has centered on a sweeping review of conditions and preparations. However, the investment in preparation will pay off in the practical work. In this section, the focus is notably more on competence and functionality than on personality characteristics when inviting team members, as well as a clear focus on engaging team members' managers.

Key persons – how to select team members

For some time now, much research has been conducted about how different personality types have different characteristics and abilities, all of which affect how a team can perform its mission. People can be introverts, extroverts, analytics, and so on, and different models have emerged for how this variation of personalities should be described in team contexts. The Big Five is a relatively well-known model for categorizing people according to their abilities and personality traits, organized in five areas describing different characteristics, special skills, and areas of knowledge: conscientiousness (i.e., the degree of a person's tendency to be dependable, organized, reliable, ambitious, hardworking, and preserving); agreeableness (i.e., a person's ability to be helpful, friendly, warm, and cooperative); extraversion (i.e., the person's ability to be sociable, enthusiastic, and optimistic); emotional stability (i.e., a person's ability to be calm, secure, and steady); and openness to experience (i.e., a person's ability to be curious, imaginative, broad-minded, and sophisticated). Out of this process come concepts such as "librarian," "coordinator," "manager," "supervisor," "starter," "finisher," "team worker," and so on, which have been developed to describe different people's strengths and abilities. Another common method of analysis is to color code different personalities with red, yellow, green, or blue color, reflecting whether they are goal-oriented and enterprising, flexible and curious, service-oriented and empathetic, or systematic and methodical in the way of being. However, do not be fooled by the different ways of categorizing people. It is not a measurement of peoples' capabilities and should not be used as a tool to select team members for the innovation team. What can be expected if someone is classified as unsophisticated or unreliable even though they do a fantastic job and is considered an expert in their field of expertise? Further, people act differently in different environments and situations, and are likely to possess a mix of several traits.

For the innovation team, instead of doing personality analyses as described above, look for key people in each area of expertise corresponding to the fields in the Raft model, as illustrated in Fig. 3.2. A key person is a person who has unique knowledge in their field of expertise and is appreciated among his or her colleagues and managers, someone to turn to when you want something done, who likes their job, wants to develop the organization, has established networks and can make them grow, has social abilities, likes to work with others and open to new working methods, and is unafraid to challenge established structures. Based on experience explained what a "key person in an area of competence" is in relation to an upcoming innovation project, it has not taken more than a few seconds to identify a key person in, for example, quality control, document management, packaging technology,

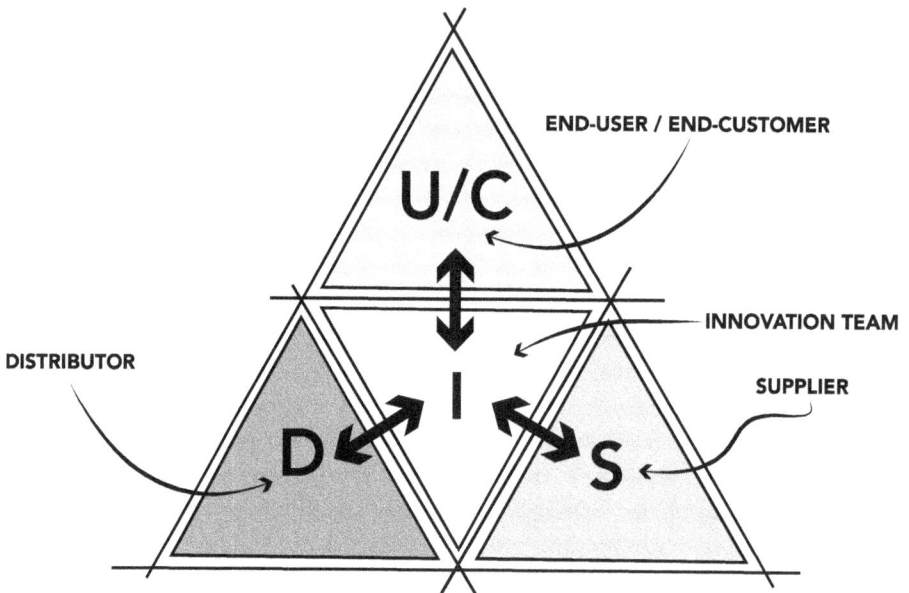

Fig. 3.2: The innovation team members' access to end-users, end-customers, suppliers, and distributors. The figure is inspired by Johnsson, M. (2009), *Sälj skinnet innan björnen är skjuten*.

marketing, systems engineering, logistics planning, foreign sales, and so forth. It doesn't matter what industry is discussed. Everyone knows who the key people are, and they are preferable to recruit to the innovation team. However, remember that the innovation project's direction determines the relevant function and competence criteria. As such, there is no a one-size-fits-all approach. For each new innovation project, a new innovation team must be considered.

Function before personality & multifunctional before homogenous

Since the area of innovation is multidisciplinary in nature, innovation work also becomes multidisciplinary and multifunctional. To make the selection of members a little easier than doing personality tests and the like, one can start from the different fields of the Raft model and determine what functions are to be filled in the team. That is, the innovation team will require members who are part of or at least direct contact with end-users, the end-customer, suppliers, and the distributors. It is the mix of functions that is important in an innovation team. The essential criterion is to select members who can do the job that needs to be done from an individual perspective, but can also contribute to the innovation team's shared goals and assignments. To explain further, if the innovation team is assembled with members who represent only one of the fields in the Raft model (e.g., the supply area) and based on different personality types (e.g., according to the Big Five), the innovation team will still be too homogeneous. This is because the innovation team will lack important expertise on end-users, the end-customers, and the distributors. The same thing occurs if the innovation team is built around one of the other fields in the Raft model. The best results are achieved with divergent expertise through various functions.

As mentioned above, the diversity of skills and access to different networks is among the key factors in members recruitment. But there is also a need for some similarity, meaning similarity to the extent that the members want to work together with other colleagues towards a common goal and be part of the project, want to be present and get involved in the team's tasks, and want the best for the project and the innovation team. Members who are "thrown in" by their manager often lack the genuine commitment required to truly contribute to the best interests of the innovation team.

Case:

In one case, the purpose was to develop a solution to acquire new ideas for the company. For some reason, it is a quite common challenge for companies. In this case, the company was reasonably big and globally established. The first three steps in the HIT process were an easy ride. The management was on board, the sponsor as well, and the convener was introduced to the upcoming work through a couple of meetings. At the meetings, the convener was informed about the concept of multifunctionality, and there were no big issues or unclarities. However, at the kick-off, it turned out that the invited team members all represented the same department but with different functionalities. To conclude, the competence was well-distributed competence-wise, as all members represented diversity, as requested. The work took off with the support of an external innovation facilitator, starting with exploring the problem, following the innovation process. Quite soon, the team found already existing solutions for gathering in-house ideas, so they expanded the scope to develop a solution to gather external ideas for the company. No big deal, or was it? At this point, the team determined that the information they needed must be acquired externally. What became apparent was that the team members had little experience in exploring end-users' and end-customers' requirements regarding the problem to solve. The project stalled. The facilitator advised the team to invite team members representing external communication, as they probably knew about how to collect the information needed. After some investigation, two new members were recruited, and the work took off again, now with new energy and experience of how to conduct advanced investigations into the topic. From that point, the project developed quickly, and a concept was finalized and presented to the management. In total, the core team was seven people, which was in the upper limit of what is recommended (see below in this chapter: The power of small innovation teams). However, they managed to be effective, as the competences were diverse and complemented each other. The lesson was to be crystal clear that multifunctionally in one context is not the same in another context. In this case, the direction of the solution to develop slightly changed, which significantly impacted the team's performance. However, as the competence problems were solved, they could work out a solution.

In another case, however, the situation differed slightly. A problem was detected related to quality issues in the production line. The problem was observed in the welding station, as the parts intended to be welded didn't fit as expected, leading to waste and time delays. However, in an analysis of the problem in more detail to understand what caused problems for the welder, the core problem was located at the cutting station. The pieces were not cut correctly. To find a solution, an innovation team was to be created. Yes, correct. On the scale of incremental–radical innovation, the solution would likely be on the incremental side of the scale. Anyhow, to accomplish that, the manager and sponsor to the upcoming team were introduced to the Raft model and the HIT process by an external facilitator. To sort the areas in the Raft model, considering the context to be fully in-house (i.e., the problem was related to the production line, and the becoming solution was intended to be implemented in-house in the production line as well) all team members in the innovation team would be part of the production line. In addition to the problem, there was an ongoing conflict between the different stations in the production line, partly caused by the problem identified. Therefore, a convener was assigned (i.e., a trustworthy person who could talk to all persons working in the organization). The convener was introduced and prepared for the upcoming work and, in turn, invited team members and involved people covering both the cutting station and the station prior and after to get the full picture of the production line. As the work eventually kicked off in line with the HIT process, a project plan was developed and delivered. Except for solving the problem, the key takeaway for the involved parties was not isolating the problem but involving a wider group of people to build commitment.

The quest for new knowledge

Another thing connecting the members of the innovation team is that they want to develop their innovation management skills and acquire if it does not already exist. For example, they may develop their understanding of abstract thinking so that they can more easily detect the opportunities arising in different contexts, which may not be at all related to the workplace or the problem area in which the innovation team works. These opportunities can appear everywhere at any time, such as when one is shopping, exercising, conversing with a supplier, or perhaps attending a birthday party. Team members must reach a level of innovation-related knowledge to see how seemingly completely irrelevant things can help create new associations and solutions to the innovation team on explicit and implicit problems. That is, the ability to "see the invisible" and discover unspoken possibilities through a well-developed ability for associative thinking. Here, the facilitator is critically responsive to what is said at meetings, reconnecting that to previous meetings or providing suggestions for activities that fit the current question or topic. It happens relatively often that innovation teams discuss different issues where a simple question or comment can help them "see" the possibilities.

Criteria to fulfil by members

So, a Mayer-Briggs investigation, Big Five mapping, or color analysis is unnecessary for the creation of an innovation team. However, all of these theories have select factors in common that are easy to track when the convener is to identify the new team members:

- Team members should like their organization and feel proud to work there.
- Team members should voluntarily want to be part of the development of the organization and its new products and have a positive attitude.
- Team members should be able to see the bigger picture rather than just the department in which they work. They need to understand that all parts of the business connect in one system and that through collaborations, they can create new, more significant products together.
- Team members should be part of or have direct contact with the different areas of the Raft model or similar innovation model (i.e., end-users, end-customers, suppliers, and distributors).
- Team members should be key persons in their respective areas of expertise. That is, ideally they are explicitly good at their work and trust their colleagues and managers; they understand, respect, and value the skills of others as an asset and a complement to their competence. In this way, a team is created to build on each other's knowledge to generate new knowledge that is otherwise difficult to succeed.
- Team members should be organized but flexible and curious, self-motivated, and helpful with great self-confidence, capacity, and entrepreneurial abilities in each area of expertise.
- Team members should find it easy to make new contacts and networks to acquire new skills for the innovation team as the project develops.

- Team members should feel they can handle vast uncertainty and rapid change in an ongoing innovation project. They should be able to embrace new working methods for the development of new products, open and understanding of iterative work, and take in impressions and interpret them as opportunity.
- The team members should promise to navigate (i.e., break/bend/stretch) the organization's stated rules for how development work is done if they counteract agile and flexible work and promise to navigate in and outside the organization to get ahead with the innovation project.

During the introduction, one thing the facilitator puts extra effort into explaining to the convener is how important it is that the "right" people be recruited to the innovation team. One of the points above is that, importantly, members should have a positive mindset and attitude towards the agile work methodology. A negative attitude easily influences the other team members. A single pessimist is enough for the entire innovation team to function poorly. One thing to be sure of in innovation projects is that they will not be straightforward all the time. There will be deviations and unwanted changes that sometimes require new creative solutions to move forward. However, it is part of the work to solve problems and to not worry about that task, so long as the people engaged have a mindset that sees the problems that arise as merely obstacles to overcome on the way to the goal.

Case:

In one case, the innovation team was quite successful in the initial phases of the innovation project. The results came from hard work. Nothing was given for free at any point. However, there was a backlash. The organization had to lay off a lot of people. Even though all team members were allowed to stay at the company, it affected the work anyway because of depressed colleagues who were about to quit their jobs. The work wasn't as fun as it used to be. It was hard to ask for help or support. Anyhow, the team managed to keep up the work even though it was slowed down because of the situation. After some time, the situation improved, and the energy returned to the organization, only to get even worse because of a new series of layoffs. The situation was anything but optimal for a long time for the team. However, they kept on working at the pace they could. It was slow but still progressing. The project was stalled, but never canceled. It was heroic what they did. One of the team members was asked why they continued the project given the situation:

"Because I believe in the product and that it can be profitable for the company."

The story tells us that, thanks to the convener's effort finding dedicated and committed team members, the project progressed even through difficult situations.

Process knowledge before technology skills

As can be seen above, there is very little focus on technical knowledge, which is a common misconception regarding innovation work. In view of the Raft model, the area related to suppliers includes different competencies and resources to develop and realize the information received from end-users and end-customers into a production-ready solution, which can involve several technical and non-technical components that cooperate. It also includes design, text design, packaging, logistics, and so forth (i.e., all knowledge and components needed to complete a product). As such, a member in the innovation team that represents only one of the fields cannot know everything. Instead, they should understand what must be done and the connections to the target group and market channels, as well as have the ability to involve and engage the right skills when required. Further, it means the innovation team can be temporarily strengthened with various experts for certain specific tasks or some time.

The power of small innovation teams

The size of the innovation team should be kept small. An innovation team of four to six members is perfect. As few as three people can work well. Since the innovation team should strive for joint ownership and leadership, there are only advantages with fewer team members. It is easier to make decisions, find meeting times, and create a genuine commitment where no one "freerides" at someone else's expense. It is better to "keep" some empty seats in the innovation team for temporary team members who join for specific tasks than to fill the innovation team completely and, thus, encounter social loafing (i.e., where people do not do their best in a context where other people are conducting the same task). For an innovation team consisting of too many members, the team is most likely not working effectively with its resources.

The case doesn't have to be that team members are consciously not making an effort; it just happens. An example of how individual performance decreases with the number of people involved is the classic tug-of-war experiment from the 1880s, conducted by the German psychologist Max Ringelmann. This experiment led to the concept of the Ringelmann effect. In the experiment, a person managed to pull an average of 63 kilograms. A group of three people managed to pull 160 kilograms, and a group of eight people managed 248 kilograms. Admittedly, more people drew more than one single person, but the individual performance declined by nearly 50 percent when eight people pulled the rope, as compared to a single person, as illustrated in Fig. 3.3. Several different researchers with similar results later conducted the experiments. It was also determined that the eight-people groups did not perform worse because they were out of sync. They simply didn't do as much when more people were involved.

Related studies on responsibility show that the easier it is to remain anonymous, the less responsibility people tend to take. It is often noticeable in the shared kitchen in the workplace or public toilets in everyday life. "Someone else will fix it" – the mentality kicks in. A similar problem occurs in creative work or general meetings: The results don't get better the more people are involved. On the contrary, the overall

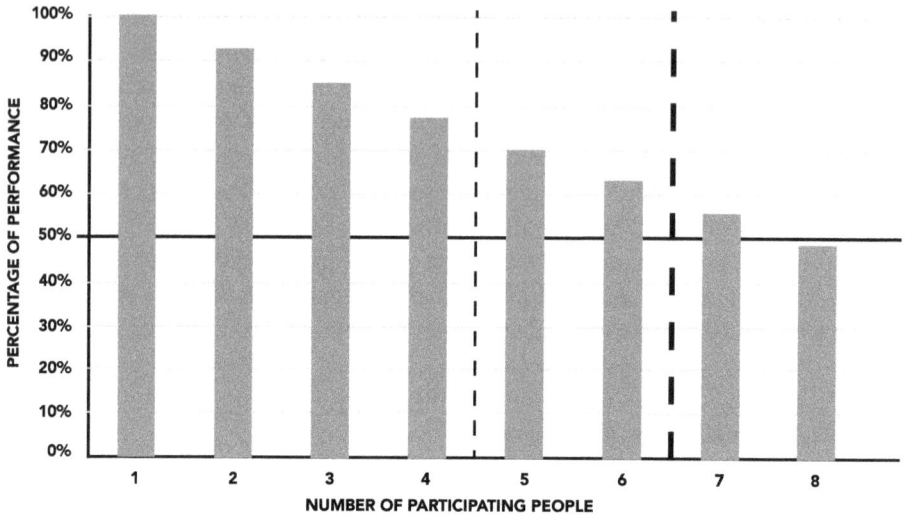

Fig. 3.3: The Ringelmann effect. The figure is inspired by Ringelmann, M., (1913b). Recherches sur les moteurs animes: Travail de rhomme (Research on animate sources of power: The work of man), *Annales de l'Institut National Agronomique*, 2e serie – tome XII, 1–40).

result may decrease with the number of participants. Still, performance decreases dramatically with the number of participants at the individual level, making the work ineffective. This behavior is obvious in groups. In those of more than seven people, the number of participants in discussions decreases, and decision-making takes longer time than with fewer people. Of course, setting an exact limit is difficult, and it depends on who participates, but a reasonable limit to strive for is six to seven people. Following the Ringelmann effect, could a six-person team be as strong as an eight-person team in a tug of war, as illustrated in Fig. 3.4?

As noticed, there are many arguments for keeping the innovation team small. At the same time, though, one of the success factors is that many people are involved in the work. To solve that dilemma, sub-teams with specific tasks are created for the project. With the same arguments as before, these are also created with few participants to establish commitment and pace in work. However, unlike the core innovation team, these sub-teams can be homogeneous in their expertise to quickly build on each other's ideas and create solutions for the innovation project. If necessary, multiple subgroups can be created for similar or adjacent tasks.

Avoiding internal competition in innovation teams

As mentioned on several occasions, innovation teams are based on multifunctionality, where people with different competencies collaborate. In addition to creating a positive dynamic in discussions, this basis has another advantage. Namely, potential

Fig. 3.4: Tug of war. The figure is inspired by Ringelmann, M., (1913b). Recherches sur les moteurs animes: Travail de rhomme (Research on animate sources of power: The work of man), *Annales de l'Institut National Agronomique*, 2e serie – tome XII, 1–40).

internal competition in the innovation team is decreasing, since appointing members according to the "checklist" above means that all members are experts in their field. There will be no discussion or intrigue around who is the best marketer, engineer, designer, and so on. On the other hand, each member has a responsibility to seek answers to the questions that they cannot answer in their area of competence by consulting their colleagues or involving a temporary team member with a unique competence for specific tasks.

Effective communication for success

Another aspect of small and large innovation teams is that the fewer members an innovation team has, the faster and easier it is to share all relevant information. Access to information is essential for successful work. For example, a four-member innovation team has six links between the members. In contrast, a team of ten people has forty-five, complicating communication, as illustrated in Fig. 3.5.

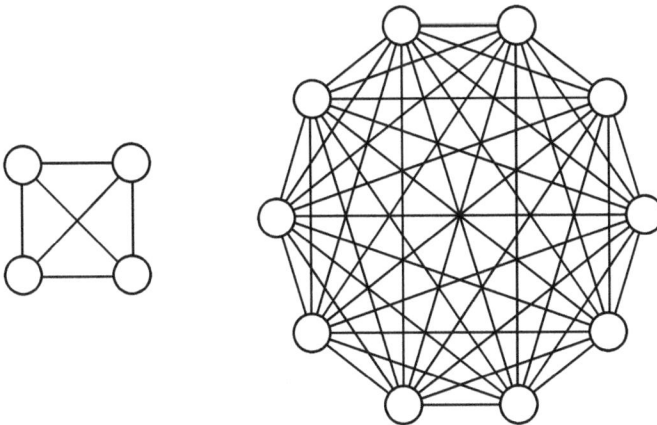

Fig. 3.5: Links between team members; a four-person team has six connections, and a ten-person team has forty-five.

The innovation team – a safe place

One feature that distinguishes a successful innovation team is that members have confidence in each other and each other's competencies. Building trust is a challenge. It must emerge from among the members of the innovation team. The easiest way to do so is to discuss and develop the rules, norms and values that the innovation team should have, then strive to follow them by having everyone be good role models. As said before, all innovation projects will experience challenges, sometimes caused by external events and sometimes by team members not quite following the team's agreed approach. A team member can become overloaded with other tasks or with non-work events that require extra attention. Suppose the problems are caused by a team member who has not been able to deliver what was expected. In that case, the first thought of the remaining members should be, "How can we help?" not attacks and exclusions of the person, thus creating additional problems. Innovation work is about developing the unknown, and with that insight, not all answers can be obvious in advance. If a person is recruited to an innovation team of this type, he or she should feel confident of their place in the team, and not have to worry about being left out, gossiped about, or subjected to other resource-wasting activities. Through helping each other and finding personal solutions, a solid innovation team is created. However, for it to work, even those who become overloaded for some reason must involve the rest of the innovation team before that overload causes problems. The solution is to establish trust to communicate openly. It then becomes easier to help.

Brief summary of step 4
- When finding team members, multifunctionality and key persons within their expertise are in focus.
- Small teams perform better. Instead of allowing the team to involve too many members – establish sub-teams for specific tasks.
- The innovation team should be a safe place – members must help each other to solve potential issues.

Step 5 – Kick-off

Now, in the final step, it's time to start the innovation project, right? The answer is both "yes" and "no": *Yes*, the kick-off is the official start of the innovation project. *No*, the focus of the kick-off is to establish the innovation team and create the foundations for how the team members will work together in the project. The kick-off is devoted to members getting to know each other, sharing expectations, and setting a common goal within the innovation project. Finally, it is to be a joint activity that everyone likes. The practical work of the innovation project begins after the kick-off has been completed, usually with a first meeting, a week after kick-off. Yes, regarding the joint activity, if everyone enjoys climbing trees, go for it.

A final check before take-off

Everything described so far is often relatively new to the convener. So far, the work has focused on understanding the innovation process and how to collect the innovation team. When the innovation project goes live, the facilitator must be calm and help the convener, and potentially the sponsor, to foster thoughts and feelings that the situation is under control, to keep the focus on the upcoming work in the project. The most significant concern usually regards the management's and sponsor's feeling of loss of control of what the innovation team should do when they become self-governing, with the opportunity to take their own initiative and take paths in work that may not have previously been taken in the organization. However, given that team members have been recruited with qualities suitable for this type of work, one can rest assured that things will develop. Therefore, before the actual kick-off, a final check regarding innovation enablers' fulfillment, the kick-off agenda, and so forth is sensible. In that check, the sponsor and the facilitator may offer support, if needed. It can be nice to discuss potential unclarities, and there will be things to discuss that have not yet been contemplated. At the kick-off, the team members will have questions regarding the entire introduction and how the innovation project will affect the daily work. All of which is not easy to answer – but some of the questions can be prepared for, including those of goals, budget, time allocation, and so on (i.e., basically the innovation enablers as discussed in chapter two). Also, a quite common question is asked – "What happens if we don't succeed, will that affect my career negatively?" The answers should be crystal clear: – "Of course not."

Time for action – and for patience

Until now, the work has focused on promoting the working methodologies and recruitment of team members and creating confidence that "everything will go well." So far, the work has taken place in the shadows of the day-to-day operations, and no one has really been disturbed by what has been going on. Despite all the preparations, management and the convener should count on the fact that there remain many uncertainties and questions that the team members will want answered: "How will the work be executed, in practice?"

When explaining forthcoming agile innovation work, text and arrows can be written and drawn on a whiteboard or piece of paper. It's easy to see and understand how all is connected when it is demonstrated. However, theory and practice don't always align. Time is necessary for all involved to develop their understanding and knowledge of what has been explained and what will happen in the future. It also takes time for the innovation team to develop their standards and routines and to develop knowledge about agile innovation work. It should not be forgotten that management, the sponsor, and the convener have a significant head start on the team members' knowledge, as they have had time to digest all information provided by the facilitator. It can take about six months for management to understand the importance of starting change towards an innovative organization. Therefore, the team members also need time to grasp what is occurring, without unreasonable expectations for the innovation team. Learning begins individually and continues as group learning through dialogue and discussions. Following the HIT process, learning related to the innovation team starts with management, moving on to the sponsor, the convener, and finally, the team members.

Keep calm and carry on

At the kick-off, among the main goals is to support the newly formed innovation team in setting its overall plan, formulating project goals, developing the foundation for how the team members will work together and communicate. In other words, the innovation team needs to be allowed to self-organize, and in that work, everyone must commit to everything agreed on. The role of the convener during the kick-off is to create calm, trust, and commitment, which can be achieved by being honest about, for example, budget and human resources so that false hopes are not created. By knowing the limitations in advance, activities can be planned early to resolve potential problems. There must also be no hidden agendas or filters in communication with the facilitator, sponsor, or management persons.

One of the easiest things to get a smooth start is to set up a project number to report time and a joint place to store documents. This information may seem banal, but these two things are the most common new team members are concerned about. The lack of project numbers as a problem may seem strange considering that entrepreneurial members have been recruited. Nonetheless, it is so. If it is considered important, it is easy for the sponsor to solve such an issue.

Learning as an outcome

The innovation team will put great demands on themselves. Failure can be perceived as a personal defeat, which must be avoided. Innovation is about change, and when implementing agile and flexible innovation work by an innovation team that may be inexperienced in such work, it needs support and guidance in the initial phases. Therefore, in the first project, there is every reason to keep ambition at a reasonable level that still shows that the innovation team has achieved something out of the ordinary. With a clear focus and a clear goal with the innovation project, where the innovation team can choose the path and develop suitable solutions, and documented learnings of as part of the project result, they will, through their commitment, ensure that they succeed.

On the kick-off – Activities to prioritize

The focus of the kick-off is not to quickly set a project plan, roll up the sleeves, and get started. Instead, focus on putting the innovation team together properly, quickly creating a team of people who want to work together towards a common goal (i.e., aligning the individuals' potentially different goals and agendas). To succeed, the focus must initially be on the innovation team and not on the project. It's not that the project isn't important, but more importantly, it's getting the innovation team together properly. Going back to the preparatory work, the aim is to create a process consisting of forming, norming, and high-performing, avoiding the phase of conflict (storming). Far too many innovation teams are assembled only for the reason that they have free time that needs to be used, given that they have the right basic knowledge as well. This work, on the contrary, should be done by people who want to participate and who want to get involved. They are specially invited and prepared for what is to come.

The kick-off, led by the facilitator and the convener in collaboration, concludes the preparations conducted and divides into five parts – Introduction, the innovation team, projects goals, structure and ways of working as a team, and next step to take. Below, I suggest how a kick-off can be planned (see Fig. 3.6). The time schedule is intended to work as tentative timeframes, where an experienced facilitator knows to adjust as the team develops and where the discussions take more or less time. One effect of the team being put together with entrepreneurial people is that they tend to be quick to find solutions and are happy to initiate both solution proposals and activities to create solutions already in the kick-off. That initiative is wonderful, but then the point of working innovatively is missed. As a facilitator at the kick-off, the work mainly conveys the importance of not solving the problem yet, although it can be perceived as a waste of time and frustrating for members.

Repetition to align the team

At the beginning of the kick-off, the convener and the facilitator repeat the introduction to the group development process, agile innovation process, and the innovation enablers to track, then explain the goal of the workshop and the initial steps afterward, namely in problem identification. The first part of the introduction may seem exaggerated: Is it really necessary to repeat everything that has been gone through already? By experience, yes, without a doubt. For the simple reason that the more times something is repeated, the more is remembered. Furthermore, team

KICK-OFF AGENDA, EXAMPLE

8:30–9:00	Coffee/tea	14:20 – 14:40	**Coffee/tea with sandwich/fruit/snacks**
9:00–10:00	**Introduction:** The group development process – this is how it works in practice. Agile innovation work – this is how it works in practice.	14:40 – 16:30	**Structure and ways of working: as a team** Meeting structure - activities/structure at our meetings. Rules of conduct in the team – this is how we work and support each other. The blood pact – our joint agreement and commitment to the project.
10:00–10:20	**Coffee/tea with sandwich/fruit/snacks**		
10:20–12:00	**The innovation team:** My expectations for the project – that's what I'm thinking. This project will never fly – and this is why.	16:30 – 17.00	**Next step:** To do – Summary of activities for the next meeting. Next meeting – time and place for the next meeting.
12:00–13:00	**Lunch**		
13:00 – 14:20	**Goals:** Goal formulation – this is what we will achieve with the project.	19:00 –> Late	**Dinner in a pleasant environment**

Fig. 3.6: Example of a kick-off-agenda.

members have probably had time to reflect on what has been said before, and at the kick-off, they can check with the facilitator and the other team members that the most important points are understood the same.

Getting to know each other – professionally and personally

A common misconception is that the innovation team members already know each other. This familiarity is not given in any organization. The kick-off commonly marks the first time that the team members have met. Therefore, everyone must be able to present themselves and reflect on their expectations for the work in the innovation project and on their way of working together. Not only is it good to hear yourself describe what is ahead, but it's also good to hear the other team members describe what they see coming. In this way, everyone can see what skills are available in the team and which may need to be strengthened during the project.

The next step in the get-to-know-each-other process is for each member to describe why they have chosen to join the innovation team and what expectations they have for the work, even though it is full of uncertainty and new ways of working. Additionally, all describe what concerns exist on a personal level towards the project and explain why the project will fail by demonstrating concrete examples. These initial exercises may seem too banal and simple, but they open discussion in a fantastic way, as all members are often thinking about similar things. The most common problems highlighted are that people worry that there will be a lack of time and resources regarding money and competence. There are also concerns that the project will not succeed and, therefore, backfire on a personal level and be a problem in their contacts with colleagues in future projects or career development. Further concerns include that not everyone will do their job as a team member or that the team will generally underperform due to other priorities from managers or the busyness of rescuing other projects. From the eyes of the convener and other team members, sponsors, and facilitators, this is extremely important information as it describes precisely the reality that is at risk of being realized if it is not prevented.

At this part of the kick-off, the final step is to discuss how every point of distrust of the project can be prevented and avoided. Usually, straightforward and concrete solutions arise that everyone can relate to, where some of the problems identified and the solution proposals become tasks for the sponsor to address immediately. Here, there is also relevant information for the convener and facilitator to remind the team of when it is time to conclude and sign the blood pact (further explained later in this chapter – "Swearing the blood pact") at the end of the kick-off.

Setting innovation related goals and sub goals
Formulating a concrete goal to a specific date is always a good start of a project, especially appropriate for innovation projects. The idea that innovation is a fuzzy process is diminished by early talk of what is being created. Innovation is very straightforward, as earlier explained. Setting concrete goals, future tasks will also become concrete. As mentioned, though, the innovation team has probably only received a brief problem description that takes a direction on the desired solutions. How and what the result will be in concrete terms will be up to the innovation team to develop, which will be their first task to complete.

A goal description can read as follows:
- On [date], a concept description should be presented to the management group.
- On [date], a model will be exhibited at the [industry fair] in [city].
- On [date], [the potential customer] will test a working prototype.

Establishing the innovation team – norms and ways of working
What emerges in the discussions about the team members' thoughts on expectations, future problems, and goal formulation will offer a starting point for the next part of the work. With the help of the information, the innovation team's norms and cultural development begins (i.e., how the members should relate to each other in the upcoming work: "What's okay and what's not okay?" "What do we do if . . .?").

Some suggestions on essential topics to discuss and agree to are these:
- How often should we (the innovation team) meet?
- Where/how are we going to meet (in person/online)?
- What are we going to talk about when we meet?

- How to communicate between meetings?
- How long will the meetings be?
- Should everyone be present at the meetings?
- Is it okay to be late for meetings?
- What are valid reasons for deprioritizing a meeting for something else?
- How do we help each other if someone is overloaded with work or for personal reasons?
- How do we relate to mobile phones and emails during meetings?
- How do we document our work?

There are no general answers to these questions. Every innovation team must decide by themselves. However, the more often a new group meets, the faster it is possible to create belonging and become a strong innovation team. On the contrary, the longer the team goes between meetings, the longer it takes to effectively start the work. So, given everything else that team members are expected to do in their professional roles, one meeting a week at the beginning of the project is usually appropriate. The benefits are that the innovation team's norms to develop much faster. Further, the first phase of the innovation process is relatively abstract. Frequent meetings ease the process of clarifying and identifying the problem to be solved. When the work has started with more concrete tasks, meetings usually occur less frequently, every two weeks or less. To think that the innovation team should only meet when they feel they need to, however, is not a suggested way of working. This feeling tends to emerge too rarely, with the risk that the project does not develop fast enough or in the intended direction.

Joint ownership and responsibilities – why it matters
The innovation team lacks a project manager but has a convener, which is important to discuss, so that everyone understands and feels responsible for driving and managing the project together as an innovation team. The convener will indeed have a slightly more significant role in the innovation team (e.g., ensuring that the meetings are set and that there is an agenda). However, all team members are responsible for actively proposing new activities within each area of responsibility and ensuring that everything that is agreed upon is completed and that all material is stored in the document structure that the innovation team creates. At the kick-off, one of the topics to discuss should be how each member intends to be accountable for the development and future of the innovation team. What may seem obvious requires some discussion for everyone to understand that "my way" of working doesn't necessarily have to be the "right way" for the rest of the innovation team. Also, the convener mainly communicates with the sponsor and management regarding progress.

If an external facilitator is involved, the facilitator communicates with the convener about feedback on work conducted and suggestions of coming work, and the convener returns these suggestions to the innovation team. The innovation team thereby feels it is in charge and learns faster.

The innovation team needs an identity

To create a sense of belonging and community more quickly, a name for the innovation team is a relatively easy topic to discuss. Even though it's not easy to agree on a name at the kick-off, the discussion helps the team focus on something that connects members and makes the project official, supporting the innovation team in communicating with others who want to know more. It also gives the work greater legitimacy and creates a kind of confidence that it is serious work. The name can be as simple as a working name for the product to be developed or something that the innovation team strives to achieve. My only tip here is to avoid names that can fuel prejudices about the fuzziness of innovation work or that innovation work is a playhouse or hobby activity. To be considered serious, the work has to be conducted seriously, even if the working methods are playful in spirit.

The innovation team – a safe place

The innovation team should be a safe place for all members. An innovation team solves problems as a team together. It is something that the convener has already talked about in the recruitment of members, but it bears repeating at the kick-off. Everyone must understand the importance of that, no exceptions. No one should talk behind anyone's back, and there should be no pact formations or backstabbing. Suppose something disturbs any of the team members or the innovation project in general. In that case, it should be discussed at one or several meetings until there is a solution everyone agrees upon. Highlight that if someone is overloaded and therefore underperforming, the other team members should first respond, "How can we help," not "how can we replace," the person in question. At the same time, an innovation team is a place to have fun. This work should be fun, creating entirely new things that others will benefit from, and positive energy creates more positive energy. Appreciating and recognizing each other for a good job and celebrating small steps on the journey makes work fun. Big things don't need to be achieved, but small steps deserve a pat on the shoulder and encouragement from the team: for example, if a member has contacted a person who has been challenging to get hold of, or if a part of a field study is completed, or if a draft of a drawing is ready.

Breaking the rules – navigating in the organization

Being a member of an innovation team carries expectations and obligations. One of the most challenging parts, often mistakenly thought to be easy, is making team members feel comfortable breaking potentially established structures and norms when conducting their innovation work. It's easy to sit at the coffee table or be a backseat driver, arguing that things can be done differently: However, doing so is easier said than done, as is revealed when the chance arises. An innovation team doesn't sit around waiting for things to happen. They actively drive and ensure that solutions to problems develop at the pace they need to. In the case of any obstacles along the way, an innovation team finds an alternative path forward. Stig Ottosson describes this excellently in the book *Dynamic Product Development*, where he draws the comparison that innovation work is like running water. It does not stop at the first obstacle. It smoothly rounds the barrier and runs on towards its goal. This fluidity is not about cheating or lowering quality in any way, but about working smartly and efficiently, and quickly engaging the resources needed to get ahead with the work. Put another way, an innovation team navigates their organization to reach the market without stopping for any organizational obstacles.

Swearing the blood pact – let's do this, full throttle

At the end of the kick-off, it's time to swear the blood pact. To this moment, everyone has received important information, also discussing their personal thoughts about the upcoming work and the project's goals. They have considered how to work together and talked about how challenging it is to get something done for real, concluding with "now we have the chance – let's do it." There is only one thing left, other than deciding when to hold the first meeting – swearing the blood pact. It sounds a bit scary, and it is. It's now that every team member truly agrees to the way of working, the goals to achieve, and the innovation team's norms to follow, as well as to navigate the organization. Below is a suggestion for content in a blood pact (see Fig. 3.7). The team is likely to have more things they deem important. In forming the blood pact, it is the facilitator's task to challenge the team and push it to conclude the discussions to generate concrete formulations in written text to agree to, as with any contract. The blood pact is paramount. It is too easy to end the day quickly, thinking that the discussions were clear and everybody will do as discussed, then rush for dinner. The reason to conclude the discussions with signing the blood pact should be stressed. Except that the team should be helpful to each other, respect each other's time, and have fun while working, the promise to navigate the organization is the most critical part of the agreement. Unless the team has the drive to get things done and find new solutions to any problems, the team will struggle to reach their goals.

To make the blood pact clear and visual, consider summarizing it on a whiteboard or a flipchart. When everything is printed, all team members sign with their signature, large and clear. The facilitator, for example, takes a photo of the team next to the blood pact. The picture of the team (hopefully) smiling and showing "thumbs up" is shared among the team, and a copy is stored in the project folder.

Of course, the blood pact imparts nothing more than a moral responsibility. However, it symbolizes that the innovation team members take the agreement seriously and should do their utmost to make the project fly. The purpose of establishing the norms and good will to help each other is among the cornerstones of the innovation team. If the members can't openly discuss topics concerning the innovation team, serious problems can arise. For this reason, everyone "swears the blood pact" in front of each other before the practical innovation work begins. The innovation team is then as ready as it can be to roll up their sleeves and get their hands dirty.

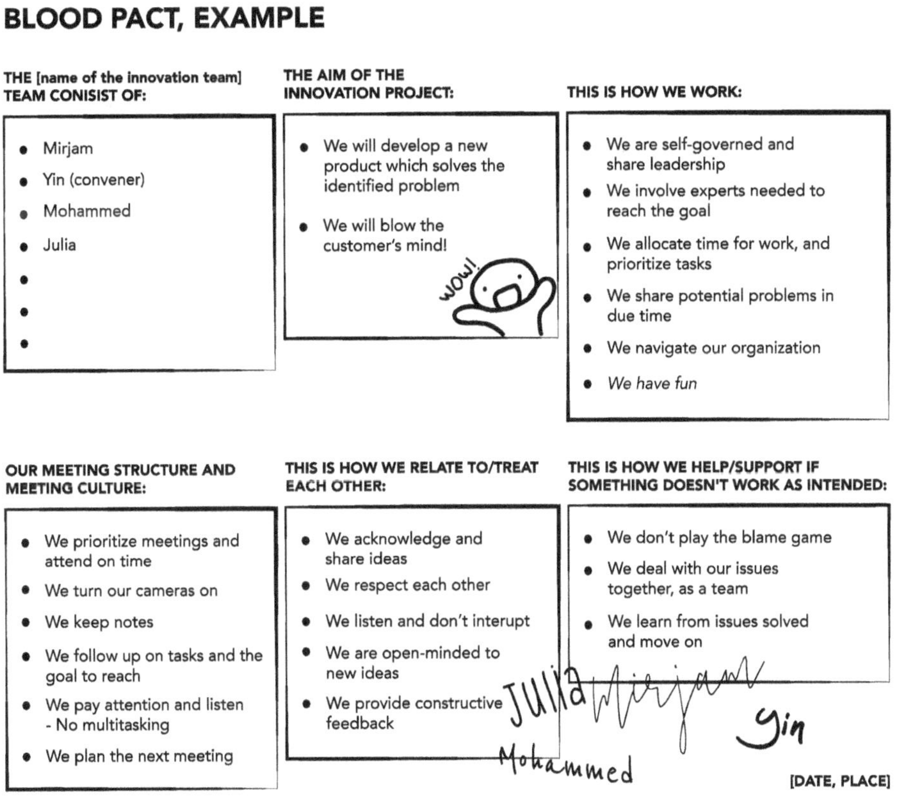

BLOOD PACT, EXAMPLE

THE [name of the innovation team] TEAM CONISIST OF:

- Mirjam
- Yin (convener)
- Mohammed
- Julia
-
-
-

THE AIM OF THE INNOVATION PROJECT:

- We will develop a new product which solves the identified problem
- We will blow the customer's mind!

THIS IS HOW WE WORK:

- We are self-governed and share leadership
- We involve experts needed to reach the goal
- We allocate time for work, and prioritize tasks
- We share potential problems in due time
- We navigate our organization
- We have fun

OUR MEETING STRUCTURE AND MEETING CULTURE:

- We prioritize meetings and attend on time
- We turn our cameras on
- We keep notes
- We follow up on tasks and the goal to reach
- We pay attention and listen - No multitasking
- We plan the next meeting

THIS IS HOW WE RELATE TO/TREAT EACH OTHER:

- We acknowledge and share ideas
- We respect each other
- We listen and don't interupt
- We are open-minded to new ideas
- We provide constructive feedback

THIS IS HOW WE HELP/SUPPORT IF SOMETHING DOESN'T WORK AS INTENDED:

- We don't play the blame game
- We deal with our issues together, as a team
- We learn from issues solved and move on

[DATE, PLACE]

Fig. 3.7: Example of a blood pact.

Case:

In one case, the preparation of the team was working perfectly. Everything was in order, and it was time for kick-off. Imagine: The management was introduced and committed. In conversation with the sponsor, an appropriate convener was identified and prepared for the upcoming work. The team members were invited to the team, and managers accepted their participation. The convener planned and invited the team members to the kick-off. On the kick-off, everything was repeated. The group development process was demonstrated, as well as the agile innovation process and the importance of navigating the organization. The convener did a fantastic job. A team name was suggested, and norms and structure were formulated regarding working and relating to each other. So, finally, in the afternoon when it was time to summarize and sign the blood pact outlined on the flipchart. At this point, one of the team members got cold feet and couldn't agree to the content of the blood pact. The person in question ended up dropping out of the team at the kick-off. Catastrophe? Absolutely, at the time it wasn't funny at all. The energy drained immediately from the room. In another way, it was the best thing that could happen. If the person had remained in the innovation team, it would likely have generated significantly more problems with potential conflicts in the innovation team. In this case, the convener identified a new team member, and the kick-off was reorganized according to the same procedure. The only thing that happened was that the start was postponed, and the new innovation team shot away at full speed.

In another case, the kick-off was completed. Up to a point, the project progressed as planned. After some time, the team lacked commitment from a team member, who stalled the project by not completing the to-do-list in time. Here, on the facilitator's advice, the team met to sort things out. To enlist its inspiration, they put the blood pact (which was written on a flipchart) on the wall to study the agreement they all had signed. They had agreed that the conversational tone should be polite, separating the problem from the person and not kicking out members without significant reason. Then, as a team, they discussed the problem not in terms of the person causing it (i.e., instead how not fulfilled tasks affected the project), and ways to support members facing work overload from other work. A couple of hours later, they had sorted the problems out, and the project took off again, with new energy and committed members. In this case, the lesson was that the signed blood pact, which served as their informal contract, helped the team to focus on a specific problem. Thanks to the members' professional attitude, neither blaming nor trash-talking, the person who caused the problem could feel safe and get the help needed.

After the kick-off

After the kick-off follows detailed and specific work to formulate a project plan with the activities and resources needed to reach the goal. Here, the facilitator will initially have to work hard because inexperienced people in need-finding work often begin generating solutions far too early. Here, it is time to recall, for example, the Raft model or similar models that affirm the need to first address the underlying problem, which is the reason the innovation team has a mission to solve. Once this affirmation is complete and the innovation team clearly understands the problem, proposals for solutions can slowly emerge. How the suggestions are then designed, technically or methodically, remains for the innovation team to solve together with different networks.

Brief summary of step 5
-   When planning for kick-off, make sure to do a final check regarding innova-
    tion enablers and prepare for answering difficult questions asked by the
    team members.
-   The focus on the kick-off is primarily to establish the team, followed by initiat-
    ing the practical work.
-   Concluding the kick-off discussions to a signed "contract," builds commitment,
    belonging, and accountability.

Summary

**This chapter has presented the step-by-step process for creating high-
performance innovation teams**. In point form, it runs as follows:
-   Top management commitment – ensure management's commitment and support
-   Convener identification – identify a convener of the forthcoming innovation
    team
-   Convener preparation – prepare the convener for the upcoming work
-   Gathering of team members – identify the best fit people
-   Kick-off – the official start of the innovation project

The first step is about ensuring the management's commitment and support. Without
management's explicit commitment and to the innovation team's work, they will instead cultivate a culture that encourages "skunkworks." In this part of the work, a
sponsor of the emerging innovation team must be assigned with commitment to and
support of the innovation team. The commitment of management and the sponsor
must be, for example, that the innovation team will be self-organized, navigate the
organization, and collaborate with external partners if necessary. Management should
also point out directions in which they want the emergent innovation team to work or
specify a concrete problem to prioritize without ordering a ready-made solution. This
initial work can take several months to anchor.

The next step is to identify a convener of the becoming innovation team, conducted by the sponsor. It is important to find a person who understands that the
leadership of the innovation team should be co-owned by the members invited to
the team. If the sponsor is inexperienced in this work, an experienced facilitator (internal personnel or external consultant) can be used to support the sponsor. The
role of the convener is to create the innovation team driven by the desire to want to
work together, where it is appreciated and understood that diverse competencies
are good for the team's development and mission.

As a third step, it is time to prepare the convener for the coming work. As in
the previous work with the management and sponsor, the convener may need to
strengthen the self-confidence in the assignment. Here, the facilitator can offer

support by describing specifically, but briefly, the most relevant points to start in the best way possible. The main focus is on the group development process, practical agile innovation work, and the factors promoting innovation work. The convener is also instructed in what type of team members to look for, so that it is possible to develop shared leadership and understanding that the innovation team should not do all the work itself. After a couple of meetings, the convener begins recruiting team members, and after a month or two, should be ready to arrange a kick-off.

The fourth step is to bring together the team members who become the core of the innovation project. The innovation team comprises preferable four to six members. Three members can be workable, but at about seven people, social loafing begins. Strive to gather people with diverse competencies who can trust each other, are key people in their field of knowledge, can rely on the agile innovation process, have the trust of other colleagues, can network, want to share knowledge, want to invite more people to work, want to help each other in case of any problems, want to deliver on time and therefore dare to navigate the organization by stretching established routines and rules, and have received approval from relevant managers to work in the innovation team.

The fifth and final step is to kick-start the innovation project through a kick-off. The goal of the kick-off is to form a innovation team whose members have a strong understanding of each other, establish ways of working together, and set goals to achieve. The most important goal of the kick-off is for all members to feel safe in the team and solemnly promise to work in the way they said they would in concluding the blood pact, the signed "contract" between the team members. One of the most important commitments is to navigate the organizational structure, if necessary, to finish the project on time. In practice, this means that certain rules and routines sometimes may have to be stretched or even broken to move the project forward.

Questions for reflections and discussions

Hopefully, the understanding of how the group development problem may be avoided has increased through the step-by-step process describing how high-performing innovation teams can be created. As the innovation team is about to be formed, the reflection and discussion questions that follow slightly differ from previous ones. Here, the convener significantly influences how the innovation team is created and developed and therefore has some specific questions to consider. The team members have not yet been assigned; however, if a potential team member happens to read the book and wants to become part of an innovation team, there are a few questions to reflect on.

Step 1 – Top management commitment

Organization/management
- How do we, in our organization, ensure that the innovation team receives the support it needs for the innovation project?
- How do we, in our organization, ensure that the rest of the organization supports the innovation team throughout the innovation project?

Potential convener
- How do I, as a potential convener, plan to pay attention that the management provides enough commitment and support, including the innovation enablers?

Potential team member
- How do I, as a potential team member, plan to pay attention that the management provides enough commitment and support, including the innovation enablers?

Step 2 – Convener identification

Organization/management
- How do we, in our organization, affirm that the new innovation team is not run by a project manager but by the convener and the team together?

Potential convener
- How do I, as a potential convener, plan to introduce myself to the management to assign me as convener?

Potential team member
- How do I, as a potential convener, plan to support the arrangement with a convener instead of a project manager?

Step 3 – Convener preparation

Organization/management
- How do we, in our organization, ensure that the convener has enough time to prepare for the task?
- How do we, in our organization, ensure that the innovation project does not become an "extra burden" on daily work once the project gets started?

Convener
- How do I, as a convener, plan to set aside time for preparation, for example, learning the most from the facilitator about group development, the agile innovation process, gathering of team members and preparing for kick-off?

Potential team member
- How do I, as a potential team member, plan to, if possible, support the preparations of the convener?

Step 4 – Gathering the innovation team members

Organization/management
- How do we, in our organization, encourage the convener to invite team members based on multifunctionality who may not have experience in innovation work but who meet all other requirements?
- How do we, in our organization, help the convener explain the process and work of innovation teams and agile innovation work to the managers of intended team members?

Convener
- How do I, as a convener, plan to identify and invite team members best fit for the assignment?
- How do I, as a convener, ensure commitment of the invited team members' managers?

Potential team member
- How do I, as a potential team member, plan to introduce myself to the convener to be invited to the innovation team?
- How do I, as a potential team member, convince my manager(s) I should be part of the innovation team?

Step 5 – Kick-off

Organization/management
- How do we, in our organization, make the innovation team feel confident that management supports the innovation team in the forthcoming work?
- How do we, in our organization, support the convener in the preparation of the kick-off, including answers to challenging questions?

Convener
- How do I, as a convener, plan to prepare for the kick-off, including answers to challenging questions?
- How do I, as a convener, plan not to become a project manager but building a self-govern innovation team?

Potential team member
- How do I, as a potential team member, plan to prepare for the kick-off and the imminent innovation work?
- How do I, as a potential team member, plan to commit to agreements made in the innovation team?

4 The innovation team's continued work

This chapter centers on getting the innovation team going, and certain challenges are highlighted. Once the innovation team is created and the practical innovation work begins, further reading is recommended. Choose a recently published innovation management book where the focus in the early stages is on need-finding and problem identification before the development work begins. Understand the problem that should be solved before starting to build a solution cannot be stressed enough. Field studies are the thing to do. Many have argued that the customers should not be asked about the problem identified. It's said that Henry Ford once stated, "If I had asked customers what they wanted, they would have answered 'faster horses.'" In my opinion, had Ford not understood the problem, he probably would not have developed the assembly line based on inspiration from the butcher business. Correct, the inspiration came from another type of production line. It is not necessary always to ask people directly. They can be observed from a distance or asked indirectly about a problem area without revealing compelling information. However, this is not the place for deep dive, and further reading is recommended if interested in innovation management practices.

In this chapter, you will learn more about the following:
– To develop innovation-related knowledge takes time – be patient, and
– innovation teams and isolation, and how to avoid it.

The development of the innovation team – Things to watch out for

Once the kick-off is finished, the expectations of the team are high. However, there are a few things to bear in mind. The team members are eager to solve the problem, and management wants to see results, a fruitful combination if both parties are patient and work systematically to achieve the results.

Development in stages – The ketchup effect

The innovation team, as such, emerges in stages. In the beginning, its only chance of survival is that the members want to be part of the innovation team and develop the project together. Since the core of the innovation team is built by individuals with diverse competencies and personalities, developing norms and group belonging must be prioritized. Of course, the project should also start with its activities and gradually increase its knowledge about how agile innovation work is conducted. In this process, the innovation team will also dare to discuss the project in

https://doi.org/10.1515/9783110731934-004

their daily work and with people outside the team. After some time, potentially supported by the facilitator, the innovation team will have reached a level of knowledge at which they have learned how to "see" what is not visible, that is, to detect unnoticed opportunities that can be developed into new products. How long this process takes depends on the scope and complexity of the project. Generally speaking, it usually occurs after the problem identification and in the process of choosing which ideas to develop further. Once they start "seeing the possibilities," it's impossible to stop. All of a sudden, there are opportunities everywhere to be developed as new parallel tracks where the best suggestions are merged or into entirely new projects. Enjoy :)

Challenges for newly created innovation teams

Time, or lack of time, is a common cause for a lack of progress in a project. After the kick-off, the team members are usually energized and ready to get going. However, too often, daily work hinders work on the innovation project, draining energy and stalling progress. The reasons are many, all relevant and accurate, such as approaching deadlines in other projects or already planned work activities, travels, meetings, and so on. When you sign up for an innovation team, it is essentially to take responsibility and command over the calendar by allocating time for the innovation project and prioritizing the work planned.

Another too-common problem is that the innovation team isolates itself from the rest of the organization by doing all the work by itself. The team does not talk much about the project with their colleagues, even though that is precisely what is desirable. The reason for this isolation is usually that they have not yet had time to accumulate confidence about their innovation project, meaning that the facilitator needs to step in more actively by pep-talking to suggest concrete activities to conduct.

Yet another reaction is that the organization helps to isolate the innovation team by being skeptical and questioning their work because it does not understand the reasons to change established practices. This resistance can be explained as normal change resistance, preserving traditional working methods, and defending ways of working that are normally topics of trash-talk at coffee break. This conservative response is understandable to some extent. It is in our nature to feel safe in the conditions already known, and preserving the status quo is perceived as better even when it is a bad situation. The argument is one should avoid risking the situation becoming even worse. A facilitator for an innovation team must continually explain and repeat the process, as demonstrated earlier. One of the best pieces of advice to the innovation team is to remain transparent with their work and invite colleagues to participate when the opportunity arises.

Case:

In one case, an innovation team was created. In the preparation work, management confirmed the need for innovation and allocated resources to start the company's innovation journey through an innovation team. A convener was identified and prepared for the upcoming work by an external facilitator. The convener identified team members, and a kick-off was organized. At the kick-off, the team decided to begin planning to identify ideas to explore further, all in line with direction from the management. The team had instructions to work broadly, as long as the target was new products for external customers. Certain potential ideas were identified for further exploration to find potential solutions. In-house meetings were thereby changed to collect information externally from end-users, end-customers, suppliers, and companies in the value chain – all in line with the innovation process. However, a few meetings later, it became clear that the same things were discussed repeatedly. The action lists were also the same. No new information was shared. At the meetings, team members were energized and committed to developing a new product, but in practice, they were fully occupied with daily work and had no time to conduct the work required for the innovation project. The project stalled, and after a few more months, the innovation team was dissolved. The team isolated themselves, believing they should do all work themselves. In this case, time was not allocated, work tasks were not prioritized due to them having too many other things to do, and their colleagues in the organization were not involved in getting the project going.

Summary

This relatively short chapter can be summarized in a few bullets:
- The innovation team emerges stepwise. Let it take some time to develop self-confidence.
- Seeing unnoticed opportunities is a skill that develops as innovation-related knowledge increases. Once the team can detect them, they will see opportunities everywhere.
- A newly created innovation team easily becomes isolated. One reason is that it tends to do all the work itself. Another reason is that the rest of the organization can be skeptical and not want to get involved. To break such isolation, a facilitator must support the team by building self-confidence and suggesting concrete work tasks involving colleagues when they are suitable for the work.

Questions for reflections and discussions

The topics for reflections and discussions assume the innovation team is up and running. Of course, reflecting and discussing in advance makes perfect sense, as it prepares one for later discussions. Here, once again, the three perspectives of the organization/management, the innovation team, and the team members are in focus.

The innovation team's challenges and development

Organization/management
- How do we, in our organization, create a commitment to the innovation team and its project by the rest of the organization?
- How do we, in our organization, encourage the innovation team to involve other colleagues from the rest of the organization in the project?

Innovation team
- How should we, in our innovation team, make colleagues in the organization feel welcome to get involved in the innovation project?

Team member
- How do I, as a team member, develop confidence in handling uncertainty and not knowing everything all the time?
- How do I, as a team member, ensure that my colleagues in the organization don't have to be skeptical about the way we work in the innovations team?

5 Innovation teams in a global setting – Global innovation enablers

One dimension not yet considered is international companies conducting innovation work globally. In that case, innovation team members can be dispersed in various places. To avoid confusion, there are a few things to sort out when discussing global innovation teams, as this chapter aims to do. Working globally, remotely, dispersed, and virtually are substantively different. Subsequently, creating a global innovation team differs from doing so for a co-located innovation team.

In this chapter, you will learn more about the following:
- what a global innovation team is, alongside its benefits,
- factors affecting a global innovation team, and
- how to create a global innovation team.

What is a global innovation team?

A global innovation team is similar to an "ordinary" innovation team. It is intended to conduct innovation work. However, its members are located in different countries or they are dispersed so that they can hardly meet each other except through technical devices, marking the difference between dispersed and remote innovation teams. The latter may be located in in the same building, next city, or similar, where for convenience members meet through technical devices. A virtual innovation team is, by definition, a team meeting online. It may be the same as a dispersed or remote team, meaning they might meet depending on distance between their locations. Distinctively, that is, a global innovation team cannot meet physically without travelling great distances.

The benefits of global innovation teams

Working globally conveys a number of advantages. For example, the company can attract the most talented people, not just those in their location. Furthermore, spanning time zones means that projects don't have to stop – ever. As one person leaves the job in the evening, another team member may pursue the work, which can save incredible amounts of time.

Cross-cultural teams outperform homogenous teams, adding value to global teams if they are made right. There are other aspects to consider. Not traveling long distances has positive effects on performance and on the environment. People who travel usually become less productive, which can affect the work quality negatively, particularly as related to jetlag. Those who have experienced jetlag know that it can

https://doi.org/10.1515/9783110731934-005

be very annoying to wake up in the middle of the night and become very sleepy in the early afternoon. It affects performance. However, performance is also affected by wasted time: for example, in taking the flight to wherever, there is time spent in transit, in ticket/passport control, baggage drops and claims, security checks, customs control, and so on. Some time for work may be available while a person waits in the gate or on the plane, if not disturbed by the boarding ceremony or the cabin service on the plane, that is. Taking a flight for a two-hour meeting easily costs a day's travel, and an overnight as well, depending on the time of the meeting and the travel distance.

From an environmental perspective, it goes without saying that traveling has a negative impact. It doesn't matter whether the energy used is green. It has to be generated from some source that has been produced somehow. Even though the experience of meeting colleagues is great and fantastic results can be seized in companionship, the negative environmental impact will remain. Recently, we were all forced to stop traveling due to the Covid-19 pandemic. To most of us, it came as shock, but as a result, the number of online meetings sky-rocketed. First, meetings were chaotic many times, they suffered technological issues, and people became tired from attending meetings without breaks. Shortly afterward, most people became self-taught virtual meeting ninjas. However, there are a few things to highlight related to global innovation work, which builds on the previous chapter on innovation enablers (i.e., factors enabling the innovation team's work as detailed in chapter two).

Innovation enablers from a global innovation perspective

This chapter builds on chapter two's identification of enablers affecting innovation teams. Here, considering factors affecting global innovation team's work, we add a few nuances to that list, identified through a literature review regarding factor influencing global innovation work. For consistency, these factors are divided into the perspectives of the organization, innovation team, and team members (see Tab. 5.1). The literature specifically identifies that global teams need teaching related to global work to be fully functional, as a result of not meeting each other nor (in most cases) their managers, in person.

Tab. 5.1: The global innovation enablers from different perspectives.

# Global innovation enabler	Perspective		
	Organization	Innovation team	Team member
1 **Collaboration**: functional innovation teams and collaborations internally between departments, and externally with suppliers, customers, and expert networks		X	X
2 **Communication**: formal and informal communication channels dependent on intention and purpose	X	X	X
3 **Culture**: norms and rules for "how to do here"; tolerance for initiatives that go wrong; respect for other's culture	X	X	X
4 **Interaction**: how to build relationships, trust, and social capital			X
5 **Knowledge**: special knowledge concerning innovation and innovation work; diverse knowledge areas			X
6 **Management**: encouragement of exploration of new ideas	X	X	
7 **Sense-making**: ways to make agreements and decisions for progress			X
8 **Technology**: choice of technology to enable, e.g., communication and interaction	X	X	X
9 **Trust**: believe in each other (e.g., to solve tasks)	X	X	X

Innovation enablers in three perspectives – The organization, the team and the team members

Similar to the previously demonstrated innovation enablers in chapter two, several of the factors shown here affect more than one perspective; they overlap and intersect. What is significant regarding the factors is that most of them address the perspective of the team member, followed by those of the team and the organization.

Global innovation enablers from the organizational perspective

This section considers the organizational and management perspective. Although the organization as a whole affects the team indirectly as well (as in the reflective questions at the end of this chapter), five areas from this perspective directly impact the global innovation team, as follows:

- Communication
- Culture
- Management

- Technology
- Trust

Communication
From an organizational perspective, communication is key for successful global innovation work. It is crucial for developing trust and resolving conflicts. Further, it enables
knowledge transfer to reduce knowledge gaps. However, time zones must be considered, alongside training on how to communicate; that is, language barriers can stifle
communication, so it is on management to establish polices and language training. To
make the communication work, communication channels are needed, including channels for instant or informal communication, as they spur team communication.

Culture
Culture from the global perspective adds quite a few nuances to the previous discussion on innovation enablers. As before, the following is overlapping other enablers. On the organizational level, handling diversity related to language, time
zones, and cultural aspects requires attention. For managers not spending unnecessary time on people, communication is preferably short, structured, and task-
progress oriented. However, social-emotional communication is also necessary. To
show interest in the team, managers must follow up not only on goals, deadlines,
and related progress, but also act predicably and responsively to messages from the
team. Moreover, show respect by attending meetings on time and being present at
meetings with active participation. In a global team, it may be more difficult for a
member to raise their voice if another member is not acting professionally. Therefore, to avoiding bullying, potential team members are strongly advised to be evaluated on negative workplace acts before being invited to become a team member.

Management/leadership management
To set up a global innovation team may be even more challenging than an ordinary
innovation team. For global teams, an emergent, coaching, and transparent leadership style yields positive effects on performance. Further, managers who work on
task-oriented projects and who strive regularly to establish trust, guidelines, and
communication increase the chances of team success. Regarding communication,
as just mentioned; it is necessary to establish well functionally communication
channels, which represent the only way to communicate to the team and vice versa.
It is also needed for the team's work, as without functional communication channels, team members will become isolated, stalling progress.

Technology
Alongside communication channels, the technical equipment enables the global innovation team to work together. It is the glue that binds the team in knowledge sharing, collaborative workshops, relationship building, and so on. To enable a global team to get tighter, there is existing technical equipment, such as "transparent walls" where people can meet live and interact from a distance or in three-dimensional virtual reality environments. In the simplest application, by just adding video to an online meeting, trust and collaboration are likely to increase. From a manager's perspective, investment in proper technology to enable global innovation teams work should not be compromised. With technology comes education on how to use it. Too often, heavy investments are made in technology where its full potential is never reached due to a lack of instruction on how it works. To ease the work of the global innovation team, educate them in the use of the chosen technology. However, unethical application of technology for surveillance or monitoring leads to mistrust: Do not forget.

Trust
To build trust in a global innovation team, management must feel confident in the team and its members. To reach that level, management must develop and apply shared leadership in the team. To a certain extent, an ability to build trust depends on leadership and communication style, as well as the diverse cultures and the technology used. These variables are intertwined, meaning that trust develops alongside the progress of the other factors.

Innovation enablers from the global innovation team's perspective
This section considers the perspective of the global innovation team. Taking a team perspective means that the team acts as one unit, the team members together. Here, six aspects are discussed, as follows. To some extent, they overlap with the perspectives of both the organization and the team members, as all actions are conducted by an individual within a broader context (i.e., the organization).
– Collaboration
– Communication
– Culture
– Management
– Technology
– Trust

Collaboration
Collaboration from a global innovation team perspective relates to collaboration with parties external to the team, such as colleagues in different departments, suppliers, end-users, and so on. The benefit is that global teams can attract even more

diverse resources than is possible with co-located teams, as the geographical area is much greater. The challenge, however, is that the dispersed team members must work independently without the support of other team members (if not meeting virtually, of course). Hence, joint field studies may be impossible to arrange. In such cases, the use of technical equipment for information gathering, such as video recorders, templates for notes, and so forth, eases the work of sharing experiences.

Communication
From the perspective of a global innovation team, communication revolves around ways to communicate effectively given the dispersion of the members. As suggested above, informal communication is essential, easing the particular difficulty of not being able to meet in person. For that purpose, take the effort to identify communication tools that encourage communication in knowledge sharing and insights and are at the same time easy to use. Time zones may erect problems for how and when to communicate. Here, however, it is vital to discuss and find solutions sustainable for all team members.

Culture
At the level of the global innovation team, culture is similar to how it is at the organizational level; however, it is more condensed, as the team members represent the culture in person when attending a team meeting. The immediate challenges to solve include potential language barriers, communication behaviors, working hours, and so on. The team must establish a structure for meetings comprising both the content and the social aspects, such as norms for attendance and behavior at meetings. For progress, information about work tasks must be shared in the team, including actions and upcoming deadlines. To build an understanding of different cultures, one easy thing to do is to openly give examples of how certain things are done and why. Another is to create an awareness of national holidays, not necessarily celebrate them "all in" together but at least highlight them with a gentle "happy . . .," followed by a short version of something representing that specific holiday.

Management/leadership
Consideration of a global innovation team's perspective on management relies on the team to work as one, leading itself based on the set conditions and taking responsibility for communicating progress with management and for earning the trust that management hopefully strives to establish, by delivering on agreed goals. For co-leadership, when working remotely, team members must rely on each other, doing what they say they intend to. They will not accidentally meet at the coffee machine unless they have implemented technological tools enabling that sort of encounter. That is, team members need to be self-propelled and motivated to get things done.

Technology
Technology is what brings the global innovation team together. Therefore, the team must discuss what type of technology best suits their purpose in the project and the work environment at the different sites. As seen in the previous section about technology, the problem is not that there are no solutions out there, but that the team may be unaware of them. Even though management shouldn't be stingy regarding this kind of equipment, the team should not ask for something unneeded. To find the best solution within a reasonable budget, the team should carefully discuss ways to communicate formally and informally, build relationships, store common project material, and so forth. Technology providing the requested functionality can thereby be sought and evaluated.

Trust
For effectiveness in a global innovation team, it is essential to establish trust, collaboration, and job satisfaction. Trust can be achieved through various of ways, but one way is to as soon as possible learn about each other's behaviors, personal interests, and drivers, to mention a few. In the previous chapter on team-building activities (see chapter one), certain highlights were raised, and the same applies for global teams. For example, to meet for a team-building activity, however, the choice of technology must be considered (as traveling may be impossible).

Innovation enablers from the perspective of members of the global innovation team
The global innovation team members face unique challenges, to some extent as a result of working remotely. The individual team member's responsibilities are more but also more challenging than for co-located innovation teams. Here, eight key considerations are discussed, as follows:
- Collaboration
- Communication
- Culture
- Diverse knowledge
- Interaction
- Sense-making
- Technology
- Trust

Collaboration
Global teams built on diverse functions have a good setting for collaboration and have good chances for speedy processes. The basis of high-performing collaboration work globally is formed by putting enough effort into building relationships and trust

and spending enough time communicating and interacting. However, collaboration over a distance is challenging, as the feeling of being alone can be overwhelming. Since meetings online can make unavailable what is common in physical meetings, the choice of technology becomes important for collaboration. Therefore, try to choose tools that allow non-verbal communication, such as smiles, head shakes, eye contact, and gestures, which are easy to learn and use.

Communication
Each individual team member is central to the success of the communication. As all team members work globally, each must actively communicate, or they might risk being left out. The reason for this imperative is that there is no easy way to visit the team member to ask, "Hey, what up? We haven't heard from you for a while." Therefore, it is on each member to learn to communicate and use the chosen tools.

Culture
For the individual team member, he or she is part of a global setting, which means communicating with respect with team members of different cultural backgrounds, languages, and mannerisms. For the individual team member, two things are important. First, they must be open-minded to the other team members' cultures by reflecting on how they communicate and behave without being offended or irritated, just taking it in and reflecting. Second, they must contemplate their own ways of communicating and behaviors. These two areas of consideration offer a good chance to build a strong understanding of how all cultures may affect the common work in positive or negative ways. Time zone differences are common for global innovation teams, meaning that there will be compromises related to working hours regarding meetings in early mornings, during lunchtimes, or late evenings. Therefore, the team must continuously develop and follow norms, such as how to share knowledge and reach agreements, to ease the team's work, but also allows socializing through non-task conversation. Participate actively, invite team members to contribute, listen to others, do not multitask in meetings, and behave respectfully.

Interaction
Working remotely is not a hinderance to innovation. On the contrary, the greater the distance from the problem area, the more significant the results that may be developed. However, the level of interaction between team members makes a difference in trust building, building social capital, and collaboration. In this work, for team members to discover who to trust, they need to explore through interaction the who-knows-who and the who-knows-what. For global innovation teams, this activity becomes significant, as the team must rely on advice from people in other areas of expertise, impossible to meet in person.

Knowledge/diverse knowledge, function
Diverse knowledge supports innovation in global innovation teams. What is interesting for global teams, though, is that well-balanced teams, gender-wise, perform best Additionally, to get the most out of the knowledge of the people in a global innovation team, they should also be doers, as they contribute to high performance. For global innovations team, activity is significantly vital, as the team members must, to a large extent, solve emergent challenges alone.

Sense-making
Sense-making in ordinary innovation work is complex. For a global innovation team, sense-making is even more complex. The ambiguity that follows dispersity (e.g., relating to language barriers, interpretation of uncertainty, or different stakeholders and interests) needs to be addressed and discussed carefully. In co-located innovation work, sketches and digitized models can easily be shared on a screen to be discussed and to make decisions. For global teams, meetings to discuss physical models or other artifacts in the same location are impossible if not making multiple models to provide each team member. However, that can be expensive. Therefore, the importance of global innovation teams accessing virtual environments equally, for all participating, will increase, addressing their need to meet to discuss digital objects appearing as physical.

Technology
The individual team member in the global innovation team is in charge of the use of technology. Overall, the management and the team can establish boundaries, norms, expectations, and so on. With respect to the factors supporting collaboration, to enable collaboration the technology must allow team members to meet. However, as related to the use of technology, team members must set aside time to educate themselves on how to use it. Not seldom are there different tools depending on purpose. Make sure to learn them all. If management forgets to provide education, team members should ask for it. The cost of education is likely less than that of being unproductive.

Trust
Trust is earned, not to be taken for granted, as true for members of global innovation teams as in any relationship or collaboration. Teams should share a goal, and the team members should respect each other, with all contributing to the goal. Taking some time to get to know each other and sharing personal information without being too personal helps build cohesion and personal trust. Of course, at work, the easiest way to build trust is to deliver what is assigned. However, if obstacles arise, share them with other team members to find possible ways forward. Support each

other. In some cultures, asking for help is taboo, and instead problems are communicated as if everything is in order – while in reality, it is not. Delays are excused for "any reason available." This logic is a trap. In the team, discuss this potential trap and find ways to avoid it.

Creating global innovation teams – Consider this

Zoom out to take a systematic approach to the global innovation enablers, as previously demonstrated in chapter two, and a new figure emerges (see Fig. 5.1), slightly different from Fig. 2.2. Specifically, it incorporates the global level, which encompasses the organizational perspective. It contains several of the innovation enablers discussed earlier, but adds further nuance. At the core of the figure, the innovation team's members are separated to illustrate their different locations. For the team members to meet, they depend on technology to connect them, which to some extent becomes the most critical enabler of the global innovation team's work. Yes,

THE GLOBAL INNOVATION TEAM MODEL

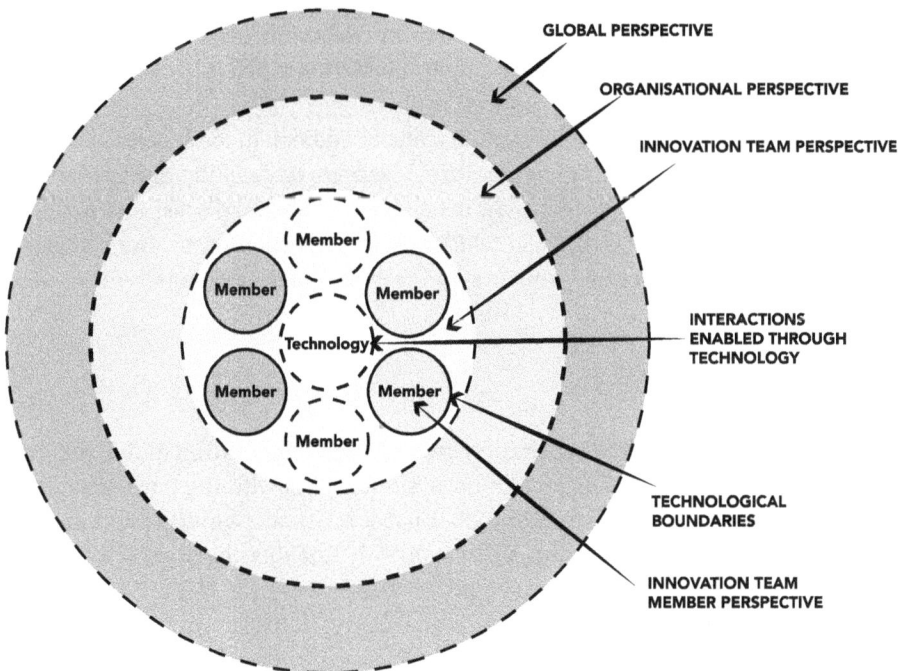

Fig. 5.1: The global innovation team, its context, and related viewpoints. The figure is inspired by Johnsson, M. (2021), Factors enabling global innovation teams. In *The XXXII ISPIM Innovation Conference – Innovating Our Common Future*, Berlin, Germany, 20–23 June, 2021.

they can work independently, but not together. Without the technology being fully functional, they cannot interact, making collaboration difficult.

Global innovation enablers are intertwined and closely related, as for the previous innovation enablers. Where it is even possible, they are difficult to separate. For example, culture is often defined as the behavior of people, meaning the culture is not the same across an organization, but can vary between locations or departments. Furthermore, the individual makes the culture through their actions (e.g., their communications and interactions), which in turn may be reflected by technology, management, and so forth. Culture also incorporates changes in behavior that may have been learned and practiced over generations. For a global innovation team, it means management may practice leadership differently even if they are part of the same organization, potentially leading to misunderstanding and conflict. Culture also refers to potential sense-making issues, as decision are made differently depending on where on earth the decision is made. In some countries, decisions are made by management, in other places, by consensus. For team members not used to it, making decisions can be very difficult. It will not be easier if members also differ in how they communicate verbally and through gestures, as loud people may seem more convincing than are quieter people. Therefore, the technological aspect cannot be underestimated. It is the only tool available to overcome all sorts of issues, enabling communication, interaction, trust building, and relationships, and thereby potentially skipping the storming phase, otherwise far too common, and reaching the high-performing phase.

At the kick-off of the global innovation team, in addition to the suggested content in Fig. 3.6 (i.e., the kick-off in chapter three), aspects to carefully discuss include what is mentioned above. In particular, team members should discuss and agree on ways to communicate, interact, build relationships, and establish trust for collaboration that makes the project fly – and discuss things that make the project fun.

Summary

Chapter five builds mainly on chapter two by means of adding global aspects affecting and influencing the global innovation team. As with the previously demonstrated innovation enablers, the global aspects are also intertwined and entangled, affecting each other directly or indirectly, making them very difficult to separate or isolate. Therefore, they should be seen as a system. Not to be forgotten, the global innovation team also needs preparation related to the group development process and the innovation process. It will benefit the support of a facilitator if the team is inexperienced in global innovation work.

A global innovation team is a team whose members cannot meet without traveling great distances. Other types of remote teams, such as dispersed, distributed, virtual teams, and so forth, may meet as they might be located in the same building, site, or region. In such cases, they are just a staircase or short trip away for a joint meeting or a nice coffee break meeting in person.

There are great advantages to working globally, as work can continue around the clock, reducing environmental impacts, saving working time, and avoiding people suffering from jetlag.

A global innovation team needs self-propelled team members who can act alone to solve tasks independently of support from other team members or managers. Furthermore, management must trust in the team, not trying to control it other than being interested in the team's progress and following up on planned tasks. As the global team members probably work in different countries, the culture will differ more significantly than other teams. Therefore, culture in all its meanings must be considered as part of the overall preparation by management and at the project kick-off, when norms and ways of working are established.

What stands out among the global innovation team enablers is technology. It is the main tool to enable the global innovation teams to do their work as teams. Through the technology, the team should be able to communicate formally and informally, socialize, interact, build relationships and trust, store work material, and so on. Therefore, the technology is necessary for the team should be investigated carefully. As a manager responsible for the investment and review of different options, consider also the cost of inefficient work.

Questions for reflections and discussions

In this chapter, the focus has been on global innovation teams, that is, innovation teams whose members are spread out globally, meeting through technical devices. The global perspective adds nuances to what has been said already, in addition to the innovation enablers discussed in chapter two, making the work even more complex. In the global setting, the individual team members work independently at each location. Of course, they should collaborate with colleagues in the same way as co-located innovation teams do. However, there is a risk they may feel lonely and isolated. Although the identified global innovation enablers tend to focus more on the team members than on the other perspectives, management is responsible for setting the conditions. Therefore, the suggestion is that management should discuss all perspectives, and the team and team members should focus on their perspectives.

As before, try to meet all together to discuss your perspectives, align your thoughts, and arrive at ways to progress.

Global innovation enablers – Factors that enable global innovation team's work

Collaboration – Functional innovation teams and collaborations internally between departments, and externally with suppliers, customers, and expert networks

Organization/management

- How do we, in our organization, engage other departments to collaborate with the global innovation team?
- How do we, in our organization, support the global innovation team's collaboration with, for example, other departments, clients, end-users, end-customers, suppliers, and so on, in the case they do not have access to them?
- How do we, in our organization, support the individual global innovation team members to establish collaboration with, for example, other departments, clients, end-users, end-customers, suppliers, and so on, if they struggle to work independently?

Innovation team

- How do we, in the global innovation team, establish collaboration with other departments, clients, end-users, end-customers, suppliers, and so on, in the case they are not at the same location as the team's expert of the specific topic is?
- How do we, in the global innovation team, support each other if anyone struggles to establish collaboration with other departments, clients, end-users, end-customers, suppliers, and so on.

Team member

- How do I, as a global innovation team member, engage in creating collaboration with other departments, clients, end-users, end-customers, suppliers, and so on, even though I must work independently?
- How do I, as a global innovation team member, seek help if I struggle to establish collaboration with other departments, clients, end-users, end-customers, suppliers, and so on.

Communication – Formal and informal communication channels dependent on intention and purpose

Organization/management

- How do we, in our organization, establish communication channels that encourage other departments to communicate with the global innovation team formally and informally?

- How do we, in our organization, support the global innovation team to establish communication channels that encourage internal formal and informal communication?
- How do we, in our organization, support the individual global innovation team members to communicate frequently with the other members and with colleagues in the same and other departments?

Innovation team
- How do we, in the global innovation team, establish communication channels and ways to communicate that encourage formal and informal communication to share, for example, information, insights, and progress on project tasks?

Team member
- How do I, as a global innovation team member, engage and build routines to frequently communicate internally and externally in formal and informal ways to share, for example, information, insights, and progress on project tasks?

Culture – Norms and rules for "how to do here"; tolerance for initiatives that go wrong; respect for other's culture

Organization/management
- How do we, in our organization, ensure that cultural differences in different locations do not negatively affect the global innovation team?
- How do we, in our organization, support the global innovation team to make the most of cultural differences in case there are any?
- How do we, in our organization, support the individual global innovation team members to educate themselves in other cultures and to develop respectfulness and understanding for potential differences.

Innovation team
- How do we, in the global innovation team, learn about cultural differences to develop, for example, understanding, respectfulness, trust, and ways to collaborate?

Team member
- How do I, as a global innovation team member, learn about the other team members' culture to develop my understanding of certain behaviors, and how do I ease for the other team members to learn about my culture and behavior?

Interaction – How to build relationships, trust, and social capital
Organization/management
– How do we, in our organization, encourage other departments to interact with the global innovation team?
– How do we, in our organization, encourage the global innovation team to interact internally and externally to develop, for example, relationships and trust?
– How do we, in our organization, support the individual global innovation team members to interact with the other team members and other colleagues to develop, for example, relationships and trust?

Innovation team
– How do we, in the global innovation team, interact to ensure everyone is included to develop, for example, relationships and trust?

Team member
– How do I, as a global innovation team member, interact in a way that increases the possibilities for developing, for example, relationships and trust?

Knowledge – Special knowledge concerning innovation and innovation work; diverse knowledge areas
Organization/management
– How do we, in our organization, ensure access to relevant expertise, supporting the global innovation team when needed?
– How do we, in our organization, support the global innovation team to diversify its knowledge base and encourage a well-balanced setting regarding gender?
– How do we, in our organization, support the individual global innovation team members to benefit from other team members' knowledge and reflect on the team constellation when seeking additional team members?

Innovation team
– How do we, in the global innovation team, keep alert of the present and coming potential need of knowledge contributing to the innovation work, and how do we communicate our needs to the management?

Team member
– How do I, as a global innovation team member, share my knowledge with the other team members so they can benefit from it, and how do I keep attention to

knowledgeable people of all genders for potential future members to contribute to a well-balanced team?

Management – Encouragement of exploration of new ideas
Organization/management
– How do we, in our organization, commit the management on all involved sites to support self-governance in the global innovation team?
– How do we, in our organization, support the global innovation team to establish self-governance, taking the lead and responsibility for the innovation project's progress together?
– How do we, in our organization, support the individual global innovation team members to manage and lead the innovation project as one unit in collaboration with the other team members?

Innovation team
– How do we, in the global innovation team, communicate about the innovation project's progress to management to ensure self-governance is working alright?

Team member
– How do I, as a global innovation team member, communicate about my work to the team and management to ensure self-governance is working alright?

Sense-making – Ways to make agreements and decisions for progress
Organization/management
– How do we, in our organization, engage stakeholders to add relevant information and perspectives to the global innovation team's sense- and decision-making work?
– How do we, in our organization, support the global innovation team to ease sense-making by, for example, accessing relevant information, providing language courses if needed, and supporting the establishment of decision-making tools, and so forth?
– How do we, in our organization, support the individual global innovation team members to collect relevant information, lower language barriers, and take part in choosing/developing decision-making tools, and so on?

Innovation team
–   How do we, in the global innovation team, ease the sense-making process, not wasting time because of lacking information, language barriers, or decision-making tools?

Team member
–   How do I, as a global innovation team member, contribute to ease sense-making by collecting and sharing relevant information, lowering potential language barriers, and engaging in the evaluation/development of decision-making tools?

Technology – Choice of technology to enable, e.g., communication and interaction
Organization/management
–   How do we, in our organization, provide technology enabling communication and interaction with the global innovation team and other colleagues and support its use, for example, in building relationships and cohesion but not for unethical monitoring or surveillance?
–   How do we, in our organization, support the global innovation team with technical equipment enabling, for example, formal and informal communication, interaction to build relationships and trust, storage of work material, and so forth, but not for unethical monitoring or surveillance?
–   How do we, in our organization, support the individual global innovation team members to learn about what technology is best for the team's purpose and take responsibility for understanding all relevant functions to make the most of the technology's functionality?

Innovation team
–   How do we, in the global innovation team, investigate what technology best fits the team's purpose and goals and support communication and interaction, building relationships and trust?

Team member
–   How do I, as a global innovation team member, engage in the investigation and conclusion of what technology fits our team best, and how do I take responsibility for learning how to use the technology we have or get.

Trust – Believe in each other (e.g., to solve tasks)

Organization/management
–   How do we, in our organization, commit the management to trust the global innovation team is doing its best despite working "out of control"?
–   How do we, in our organization, support the global innovation team to develop internal trust and trust for other departments and the management?
–   How do we, in our organization, support the individual global innovation team members to contribute to building trust by, for example, frequently communicating, interacting, and sharing knowledge and experience?

Innovation team
–   How do we, in the global innovation team, develop trust internally in the team and externally for other departments and management?

Team member
–   How do I, as a global innovation team member, contribute to building trust in the team and the management through, for example, my way of communication, interaction, and fulfilling work tasks.

6 A final word

It's a wrap

To wrap this book up, I'd like to start by thanking you for making it through. I hope you liked reading it as much as I enjoyed writing it. However, creating high-performing innovation teams is complex. Innovation efforts cover work even before an idea is hatched, through all its phases of development, including successful introduction and establishment on the market, subsequent lessons from the market, and the start of another innovation cycle. Adding team aspect to the innovation work makes it even more complex for all involved, including the organization as a whole and its managers, the innovation team, and that team's members.

Throughout the book, I have tried my best to be specific and to take things in order, accounting for different perspectives. I hope your work benefits from the time you've spent reflecting upon and discussing the questions related to the innovation enablers, innovation process, HIT process, and so on, from the different perspectives. Through all these years working with and developing my understanding of how to create high-performing innovation teams, I have learned that the faster one comes into action, the steeper is the learning curve. Even though unintentional, failure to consider the basics can create irreparable problems. Therefore, the best advice is to start small, reflect, learn, and advance. And, not to forget; first, set the direction of the innovation effort, then create the innovation team best fit for the mission.

I also learned through years of practice that the methodology described in this book applies in all types of organizations and businesses, which I, of course, find very satisfying. What determines the nature of the innovation team created is the desired scope and novelty of the innovation, as we learned that people tend to be more or less specialists in their area of expertise. Keep people's interests in mind, and fantastic solutions can be created.

https://doi.org/10.1515/9783110731934-006

Reach out or connect?

One more thing. If you want to reach out to me, feel free to send a message. Pointing your camera at the QR code by Fig. 6.1 will bring you to my LinkedIn page.

And, again, have fun!

Fig. 6.1: Link to Mikael Johnsson's LinkedIn profile.

Best wishes
Mikael Johnsson, PhD

Bibliography

Aagaard, A. & Gertsen, F. (2011), Supporting Radical Front End Innovation: Perceived Key Factors of Pharmaceutical Innovation. *Creativity and Innovation Management*, 20(4), 330–346.

Abouzeedan, A., Klofsten, M. & Hedner, T. (2013), Internetization Management as a Facilitator for Managing Innovation in High-Technology Smaller Firms. *Global Business Review*, 14(1), 121–136.

Adair, J. (2004), *Adair on Creativity and Innovation*. London: Thorogood Publishing Ltd.

Adamides, E.A. & Karacapilidis, N. (2006), Information technology support for the knowledge and social processes of innovation management. *Technovation*, 26(1), 50–59.

Adams, R., Bessant, J. & Phelps, R. (2006), Innovation management measurement: A review. *International Journal of Management Reviews*, 8(21), 21–47.

Adkins, L. (2010), *Coaching Agile Teams: A Companion for Scrum Masters, Agile Coaches, and Project Managers in Transition*. Massachusetts: Courier.

Ahmed, P.K. (1998b), Culture and climate for innovation. *European Journal of Innovation Management*, 1(1), 30–43.

Ahuja, G., Lampert, C.M. & Tandon, V. (2008), Moving Beyond Schumpeter: Management Research on the Determinants of Technological Innovation. *The Academy of Management Annals*, 2(1), 1–98.

Aiman-Smith, L., Goodrich, N., Roberts, D. & Scinta, J. (2005), Assessing your organization's potential for value innovation. *Research Technology Management*, 48(2), 35–42.

Akbar, H. & Tzokas, N. (2013), Charting the organisational knowledge creation process: An innovation-process perspective. *Journal of Marketing Management*, 29(13–14), 1592–1608.

Akgün, A.E., Byrne, J.C., Lynn, G.S. & Keskin, H. (2007), Team stressors, management support, and project and process outcomes in new product development projects. *Technovation*, 27, 628–639.

Alge, B.J., Ballinger, G.A. & Green, S.G. (2004), Remote Control: Predictors of Electronic Monitoring Intensity and Secrecy. *Personnel Psychology*, 57(2).

Alsharo, M., Gregg, D. & Ramirez, R. (2017), Virtual team effectiveness: The role of knowledge sharing and trust. *Information and Management*, 54(4), 479–490.

Amabile, T.M. (1988), A model of creativity and innovation in organizations. *Research in organizational behavior*, 10, 123–167.

Amabile, T.M. (1998), How to kill creativity. *Harvard Business Review*, 76(5), 76–87.

Amabile, T.M. & Gryskiewicz, N. (1989), The Creative Environment Scales: The Work Environment Inventory. *Creativity Research Journal*, 2, 231–254.

Amabile, T.M. & Kramer, S. (2012), How leaders kill meaning at work. *The McKinsey Quarterly*, 1, 124–131.

Amabile, T.M., Conti, R., Coon, H., Lazenby, J. & Herron, M. (1996), Assessing the work environment for creativity. *Academy of Management Journal*, 39(5), 1154–1184.

Amalia, M. & Nugroho, Y. (2011), An innovation perspective of knowledge management in a multinational subsidiary. *Journal of Knowledge Management*, 15(1), 71–87.

Anderson, N.R. & West, M.A. (1998), Measuring climate for work group innovation: development and validation of the team climate inventory. *Journal of Organizational Behavior*, 19, 235–258.

Anderson, T.D. (2011), Beyond eureka moments: supporting the invisible work of creativity and innovation. *Information Research*, 16(1), 1–24.

Anderson, T.D. (2013), The 4Ps of innovation culture: conceptions of creatively engaging with information. *Information Research*, 18(3), 1–16.

Andersson, R. (1996), *Uppfinnarboken – Om uppfinnandets innersta väsen*. Malmö: Liber-Hermods.

https://doi.org/10.1515/9783110731934-007

Andriopoulos, C. & Lewis, M.W. (2010), Managing Innovation Paradoxes: Ambidexterity Lessons from Leading Product Design Companies. *Long Range Planning*, 43(1), 104–122.

Anghern, A. & Nabeth, T. (1997), Leveraging Emerging Technologies in Management Education: Research and Experiences. *European Management Journal*, 15(3), 275–285.

Ardichvili, A., Cardozo, R. & Ray, S. (2000), A theory of entrepreneurial opportunity identification and development. *Journal of Business Venturing*, 18(1), 105–123.

Aronson, E. (1999), *The Social Animal*. New York: Worth Publishers.

Arranz, N. & de Arroyabe J.C.F. (2012), Can innovation network projects result in efficient performance? *Technological Forecasting & Social Change*, 79(3), 485–497.

Backström, T. & Olson, B.K. (2010), Kaikaku – a complement to emergence based development. In: *The first ICDC Conference*, Kobe, Japan.

Backström, T., Wilhelmson, L., Åteg, M., Olson, B.K. & Moström Åberg, M. (2011), The Role of Manager in the Post-Industrial Work System. In: *Studies in industrial renewal*, Segelod, E., Berglund. K., Bjurström, E., Dahlquist, E., Hallén, L., Johansson, L. (eds.), Eskilstuna: Mälardalens Högskola, 215–227.

Balsamo, T.J., Goodrich, N.E., Lee, J.M, Morse, T.F. & Roberts, D.A. (2008), Identify your innovation enablers and inhibitors. *Industrial Research Institute*, 51(6), 23–33.

Barczak, G., Griffin, A. & Kahn, K.B. (2009), Perspective: trends and drivers of success in NPD practices: results of the 2003 PDMA best practices study. *Journal of product innovation management*, 26(1), 3–23.

Barrick, M. & Mount, M. (1991), The big five personality dimensions and job performance: A meta-analysis. *Personnel Psychology*, 44(1), 1–26.

Batarseh, F.S., Daspit, J.J. and Usher, J.M. (2018), The collaboration capability of global virtual teams: relationships with functional diversity, absorptive capacity, and innovation. *International Journal of Management Science and Engineering Management*, 13(1), 1–10.

Batarseh, F.S., Usher, J.M. and Daspit, J.J. (2017a), Absorptive capacity in virtual teams: Examining the influence on diversity and innovation. *Journal of Knowledge Management*, 21(6). https://doi.org/10.1108/JKM-06-2016-0221.

Batarseh, F.S., Usher, J.M. and Daspit, J.J. (2017b), Collaboration capability in virtual teams: Examining the influence on diversity and innovation. *International Journal of Innovation Management*, 21(4). https://doi.org/10.1142/S1363919617500347.

Baucus, M.S., Norton Jr, W.I., Baucus, D.A. & Human, S.E. (2008), Fostering Creativity and Innovation without Encouraging Unethical Behavior. *Journal of Business Ethics*, 81, 97–115.

Baumann, O. & Martignoni, D. (2011), Evaluating the New: The Contingent Value of a Pro-Innovation Bias. *Schmalenbach Business Review*, 63(4), 393–415.

Baxter, M. (2002), *Product Design*. Cheltenham: Nelson Thornes Ltd.

Belbin, M. (1993), *Team Roles at Work*. Oxford: Butterworth Heineman.

Berghman, L., Matthyssens, P., Streukens, S. & Vandenbempt, K. (2013), Deliberate Learning Mechanisms for Stimulating Strategic Innovation Capacity. *Long Range Planning*, 46(1–2), 39–71.

Bergman, J., Jantunen, A. & Saksa, J-M. (2009), Enabling Open Innovation Process Through Interactive Methods: Scenarios and Group Decision Support Systems. *International Journal of Innovation Management*, 13(1), 139–156.

Berkout, A.J., Hartmann, D., Van der Duin, P. & Ortt, R. (2006), Innovating the innovating process. *International Journal if Technology Management*, 34(3/4), 390–404.

Bertola, P. & Teixeira, J.C. (2003), Design as a knowledge agent How design as a knowledge process is embedded into organizations to foster innovation. *Design Studies*, 24(2), 181–194.

Bessant, J. (2003), *High involvement innovation: building and sustaining competitive advantage through continuous change*. West Sussex: John Wiley & Sons Ltd.

Bessant, J. (2005), Enabling Continuous and Discontinuous Innovation: Learning From the Private Sector. *Public Money & Management*, 25(1), 35–42.

Bessant, J., von Stamm, B.M., Moeslein, K.M. & Neywer, A.-K. (2010), Backing outsiders: selection strategies for discontinuous innovation. *R&D Management*, 40(4), 345–356.

Bharadwaj, S.A. & Menon, A. (2000), Making Innovation Happen in Organizations: Individual Creativity Mechanisms, Organizational Creativity Mechanisms or Both? *Journal of Product Innovation Management*, 17(6), 424–434.

Billett, S. (2001), Learning through work: workplace affordances and individual engagement. *Journal of Workplace Learning*, 13(5), 209–214.

Birkinshaw, J. & Mol, M. (2006), How Management Innovation Happens. *MIT Sloan Management Review*, 47(4), 80–89.

Birkinshaw, J., Bessant., J. & Delbridge, R. (2007), Finding, Forming, and Performing: Creating Networks for Discontinuous Innovation. *California Management Review*, 49(3), 67–84.

Bosch-Sijtsema, P.M. and Haapamäki, J. (2014), Perceived enablers of 3D virtual environments for virtual team learning and innovation. *Computers in Human Behavior*, 37, 395–401.

Bossink, B. (2004), Managing Drivers of Innovation in Construction Networks. *Journal of Construction Engineering and Management*, 130(3), 337–345.

Bowonder, B., Dambal, A., Kumar, S. & Shirodkar, A. (2010), Innovation Strategies for Creating Competitive Advantage. *Research Technology Management*, 53(2), 19–32.

Bozeman, B. (2000), Technology transfer and public policy: a review of research and theory. *Research Policy*, 29, 627–655.

Bozic, N.Y. (2016), Integrated model of innovation competence. In: *The 27th ISPIM Innovation Conference*, Porto, Portugal.

Brennan, A. & Dooley, L. (2005), Networked creativity: a structured management framework for simulating innovation. *Technovation*, 25(12), 1388–1399.

Bright, D.S. & Godwin, L.N. (2010), Encouraging Social Innovation in Global Organizations: Integrating Planned and Emergent Approaches. *Journal of Asia-Pacific Business*, 11(3), 179–196.

Brooks, L.J. & Bowker, G. (2011), Playing at Work: Understanding the Future of Work Practices at the Institute for the Future. *Information, Communication & Society*, 5(1), 109–136.

Brown, C. (2005), Empowering innovation: extending services regionally. *World Patent Information*, 27(1), 37–41.

Bucic, t. & Ngo, l.v. (2012), Examining drivers of collaborative inbound open innovation: empirical evidence from Australian firms. *International Journal of Innovation Management*, 16(4), 1–24.

Buijs, J. (2007), Innovation Leaders Should be Controlled Schizophrenics. *Journal Compilation*, 16(2), 203–210.

Büschgens, T., Bausch, A. & Balkin, D. (2013), Organizing for radical innovation – A multi-level behavioral approach. *Journal of High Technology Management Research*, 24(2), 138–152.

Bush, J.B.Jr. & Frohman, A.L. (1991), Communication in a "Network" Organisation. *Business Credit*, 96(9), 21–26.

Byrne, C.L., Mumford, M.D., Barret, J.D. & Vessey, W.B. (2009), Examining the Leaders of Creativity Efforts: What Do They Do, and What Do They Think About. *Creativity and Innovation*, 18(14), 256–268.

Cabrales, À.L., Medina, C.C., Lavado, A.C. & Cabrera, R.V. (2008), Managing functional diversity, risk taking and incentives for teams to achieve radical innovations. *R&D Management*, 38(1), 35–50.

Camisón, C. & Villar-López, A. (2012), Organizational innovation as an enabler of technological innovation capabilities and firm performance. *Journal of Business Research*, 67(1), 2891–2902.

Castellano, S., Davidson, P. & Khelladi, I. (2017), Creativity techniques to enhance knowledge transfer within global virtual teams in the context of knowledge-intensive enterprises. *Journal of Technology Transfer*, 42(2), 253–266.

Cepeda, G. & Vera, D. (2007), Dynamic capabilities and operational capabilities: A knowledge management perspective. *Journal of Business Research*, 60(8), 426–437.

Cerne, M., Jaklic, M. & Škerlavaj, M. (2013), Decoupling management and technological innovations: Resolving the individualism–collectivism controversy. *Journal of International Management*, 19(2), 103–117.

Cetindamar, D., Phaal, R. & Probert, D. (2009), Understanding technology management as a dynamic capability: A framework for technology management activities. *Technovation*, 29(4), 237–246.

Chadwick, C. & Dabu, A. (2009), Human Resources, Human Resource Management, and the Competitive Advantage of Firms: Toward a More Comprehensive Model of Causal Linkages. *Organization Science*, 20(1), 253–272.

Chari, V.V., Golosov, M. & Tsyvinski, A. (2011), Prizes and patents: Using market signals to provide incentives for innovations. *Journal of Economic Theory*, 147(2), 781–801.

Charlier, S.D., Stewart, G.L., Greco, L.M. & Reeves, C.J. (2016), Emergent leadership in virtual teams: A multilevel investigation of individual communication and team dispersion antecedents. *Leadership Quarterly*, 27(5), 745–764.

Chen, J., Damanpour F. & Reilly R.R. (2009), Understanding antecedents of new product development speed: A meta-analysis. *Journal of Operational Management*, 28, 17–33.

Chen, M-H. (2007), Entrepreneurial Leadership and New Ventures: Creativity in Entrepreneurial Teams. *Entrepreneurial Leadership and New Ventures*, 16(3), 239–249.

Chen, M., Liou, Y., Wang, C.W., Fan, Y.W. & Chi, Y.P.J. (2007), TeamSpirit: Design, implementation, and evaluation of a Web-based group decision support system. *Decision Support Systems*, 43(4), 1186–1202.

Chen, M.Y-C., Lin, C.Y-Y., Lin, H-E. & Mc.Donough, E.F. (2012), Does transformational leadership facilitate technological innovation? The moderating roles of innovative culture and incentive compensation. *Asia Pac Journal Management*, 29(2), 239–264.

Cheng, C.C., Chen, J-S. & Tsou, H.T. (2012), Market-creating service innovation: verification and its associations with new service development and customer involvement. *Journal of Services Marketing*, 26(6), 444–457.

Chiesa, V., Coughlan, P. & Voss, C. (1996), Development of a technical innovation audit. *The Journal of product innovation management*, 13(2), 105–136.

Choo, C.W. (2001), The knowing organization as learning organization. *Education + Training*, 43(4/5), 197–205.

Chou, A.Y. & Chou, D.C. (2011), Course Management Systems and Blended Learning: An Innovative Learning Approach. *Decision Sciences Journal of Innovative Education*, 9(3), 463–484.

Chourides, P., Longbottom, D. & Murphy, W. (2003), Excellence in knowledge management: an empirical study to identify critical factors and performance measures. *Measuring Business Excellence*, 7(2), 29–45.

Christensen, C. (1997), *The Innovator's Dilemma*. Boston: Harvard Business School Press.

Chu, D. & Andreassi, T. (2011), Management of technological innovation. Case studies in biotechnology companies in Brazil. *Management Research: The Journal of the Iberoamerican Academy of Management*, 9(1), 7–31.

Clark, D. (2012), Innovation Management in SMEs: Active Innovators in New Zeeland. Journal of Small *Business and Entrepreneurship*, 23(4), 601–619.

Clark, R. (2003), Fostering the Work Motivation of Individuals and Teams. *Performance Improvement*, 42(3), 21–29.

Claver, E., Llopis, J., Garcia, D. & Molina, H. (1998), Organizational Culture for Innovation and New Technological Behavior. *The Journal of High Technology Management Research*, 9(1), 55–68.

Cobo, C. (2013), Mechanisms to identify and study the demand for innovation skills in world-renowned organizations. *On The Horizon*, 21(2), 96–106.

Cohen, W.M. & Levinthal, D.A. (1990), Absorptive Capacity: A New Perspective On Learning and Innovation. *Administrative Science Quarterly*, 35(1), 128–152.

Cooper, P. (2005), A study of innovators' experience of new product innovation in organisations. *R&D Management*, 35(5), 525–533.

Cooper, R.G. (2013), Where Are All the Breakthrough New Products? Using Portfolio Management to Boost Innovation. *Research-Technology Management*, 56(5), 25–33.

Cordero, R., Farris, G. & DiTomaso, N. (1998), Technical Professionals in Cross-functional Teams: Their Quality of Work Life. *Journal of Product Innovation Management*, 15(6), 550–563.

Cormican, K. & O'Sullivan, D. (2000), A Collaborative Knowledge Management Tool for Product Innovation. In: *The managing innovative manufacturing 2000 Conference*, Birmingham, UK, July 17th–19th.

Coviello, N.E. & Joseph, R.M. (2012), Creating Major Innovations with Customers: insights from Smali and Young Technology Firms. *Journal of Marketing*, 76(6), 87–104.

Creasy, T. & Carnes, A. (2017), The effects of workplace bullying on team learning, innovation and project success as mediated through virtual and traditional team dynamics. *International Journal of Project Management*, 35(6), 964–977.

Crespell, P. & Hansen, E. (2008), Managing for Innovation: Insights into a successful company. *Forest Products Journal*, 58(9), 6–17.

Dadriyansyah, G., Ibrahim, A. and Hassan, M.G. (2010), Virtual Integration as an Approach to Engender Product Innovation and Accelerate Product Development Time: A Literature Analysis. In: *The 17th International Conference on Industrial Engineering and Engineering Management*, Xiamen, China, October 29–31.

Dalohoun, D.N, Hall, A. & van Mele, P. (2009), Entrepreneurship as driver of a 'self-organizing system of innovation': the case of NERICA in Benin. *International Journal of Technology Management and Sustainable Development*, 8(2), 87–101.

Davison, G. & Blackman D. (2005), The role of mental models in innovative teams. *European Journal of Innovation Management*, 8(4), 409–423.

De Jong, J.P.J. & Vermeulen, P.A.M. (2003), Organizing successful new service development: a literature review. *Management Decision*, 41(9), 844–858.

Dekker, D.M., Rutte, C.G. and van den Berg, P.T. (2008), Cultural differences in the perception of critical interaction behaviors in global virtual teams. *International Journal of Intercultural Relations*, 32(5), 441–452.

Denning, S. (2011), Reinventing management: the practices that enable continuous innovation. *Strategy & Leadership*, 39(3), 16–24.

Denti, L. & Hemlin, S. (2012), Leadership and Innovation in Organizations: A Systematic Review of Factors That Mediate or Moderate the Relationship. *International Journal of Innovation Management*, 16(3).

Derven, M. (2016), Four drivers to enhance global virtual teams. *Industrial and Commercial Training*, 48(1), 1–8.

Dew, R. & Hearn, G. (2009), A new model of the learning process for innovation teams: Networked nominal pairs. *International Journal of Innovation Management*, 13(4), 521–535.

Dobni, C.B. (2006), The innovation blueprint. *Business Horizons*, 49(4), 329–339.

Donate, M.J. & Guadamillas, F. (2011), Organizational factors to support knowledge management and innovation. *Journal of Knowledge Management*, 15(6), 890–914.

Dooley, L., Cormican, K., Wreath, S. & O'Sullivan, D. (2000), Supporting Systems Innovation. International *Journal of Innovation Management*, 4(3), 277–297.

Dooley, L., Kirk D. & Philpott K. (2013), Nurturing life–science knowledge discovery: managing multi–organisation networks. *Production Planning & Control*, 24(2–3), 195–207.

Drake, A., Haka, S.F. & Ravenscroft, S.P. (2001), An ABC Simulation Focusing on Incentives and Innovation. *Accounting Education*, 16(3), 443–471.

Du Chantenier, E., Verstegen, J.A.A.M., Biemans, H.J.A. & Omta, O. (2009), The Challenges of Collaborative Knowledge Creation in Open Innovation Team. *Human Resource Development Review*, 8(3), 350–381.

Du Chatenier, E., Jos A.A.M., Verstegen, J.A.A.M., Harm, J.A., Biemans, H.J.A., Mulder, M. & Omta, O.S.W.F. (2010), Identification of competencies for professionals in open innovation teams. *R&D Management*, 40(3), 271–280.

Du Plessis, M. (2007), The role of knowledge management in innovation. *Journal of Knowledge Management*, 11(4), 20–29.

Dulaimi, M.F., Nepal, M.P. & Park, M. (2004), A hierarchical structural model of assessing innovation and project performance. *Construction Management and Economics*, 23(6), 565–577.

Duus, R. & Cooray, M. (2014), Together We Innovate: Cross-Cultural Teamwork Through Virtual Platforms. *Journal of Marketing Education*, 36, 244–257.

Eales-White, R. (1997), *Teambuilding: Att utveckla arbetslag*. Lund: Studentlitteratur.

Ebrahim, N.A., Ahmed, S. & Taha, Z. (2009), Virtual Teams: a Literature Review. *Australian Journal of Basic and Applied Sciences*, 3(3), 2653–2669.

Edmondson, A. (2012), Teamwork On the Fly. *Harvards Business Review*, 90(4), 72–80.

Edmondson, A. & Nembhard, I.M. (2009), Product Development and Learning in Project Teams: The Challenges Are the Benefits. *Journal of Product Innovation Management*, 26(2), 123–138.

Eikeland, O. (2006), The Validity of Action Research – Validity in Action Research. In: K. Aagaard Nielsen/L. Svensson (eds.), *Action Research and Interactive Research*. Maastricht: Shaker publishing, 193–240.

Eisenhardt, K.M. (1989), Building Theories from Case Study Research. *Academy of Management Review*, 14(4), 532–550.

Ekvall, C. (2008), *Richard Branson – Den globale entreprenören*. Malmö: Roos & Tegnér.

Ekvall, G. (1996), Organizational climate for creativity and innovation. *European Journal of Work and Organizational Psychology*, 5(1), 105–124.

Ellström, E., Ekholm, B. & Ellström, P.E. (2007), Two types of learning environment Enabling and constraining a study of care work. *Journal of Workplace Learning*, 20(2), 84–97.

Ellström, P.-E. & Nilsen P. (2014), Promoting Practice-Based Innovation Through Learning at Work. In: Billett, Harties C. & Gruber, H. (eds.), *International Handbook of Research in Professional and Practice-based Learning*. Dordrecht: Springer International Handbooks of Education. Springer, Dordrecht. https://doi.org/10.1007/978-94-017-8902-8_42

Eschenbächer, J., Seifert, M. & Thoben, K-D. (2011), Improving distributed innovation processes in virtual organisations through the evaluation of collaboration intensities. *Production, Planning & Control*, 22(5–6), 473–487.

Eschenbaecher, J. & Graser, F. (2011), Managing and Optimizing Innovation Processes in Collaborative and Value Creating Networks. *International Journal of Innovation and Technology Management*, 8(3), 373–391.

Esterhuizen, D., Schutte, C.S.L. & Toit, A.S.A. (2012), Knowledge creation processes as critical enablers for innovation. *International Journal of Information Management*, 32, 354–364.

Estrada, I., Martin-Cruz, N. & Pérez-Santana, P. (2013), Multi-partner alliance teams for product innovation: The role of human resource management fit. *Management, policy & practice*, 15(2), 161–169.

Eubanks, D.L., Palanski, M., Olabisi, J., Joinson, A. & Dove, J. (2016), Team dynamics in virtual, partially distributed teams: Optimal role fulfillment. *Computers in Human Behavior*, 61, 556–568.

Evans, K. & Waite, E. (2010), Stimulating the innovation potential of 'routine' workers through workplace learning. *Transfer: European Review of Labour and Research*, 16(2), 243–258.

Fairbank, J.F. & Williams, S.D. (2001), Leadership and Innovation in Organizations: A Systematic Review of Factors That Mediate Or Moderate The Relationship. *Creativity and Innovation Management*, 10(2), 68–74.

Farris, G.F. (1972), The effect of individual roles on performance in innovative groups. *R&D Management*, 3(1), 23–28.

Fellows, R. & Liu, A. (2002), *Research methods for construction*. Malden, Mass: Blackwell Science, 2nd ed., 133–141.

Feng, B., Jiang, Z-Z., Fan, Z-P. & Fu, N. (2009), A method for member selection of cross-functional teams using the individual and collaborative performances. *European Journal of Operational Research*, 203(3), 652–661.

Fields, G. (2006), Innovation, Time, and Territory: Space and the Business Organization of Dell Computer. *Economic Geography*, 82(2), 119–146.

Ford, D. & Paladino, A. (2013), Enabling Innovation through Strategic Synergies. *Journal of Product Innovation Management*, 30(6), 1058–1072.

Francois, J.P., Favre, F. & Negassi, S. (2002), Competence and Organization: Two Drivers of Innovation. *Economics of Innovation and New Technology*, 11(3), 249–270.

Franz, T.M. (2012), *Dynamics and Team Interventions: Understanding and Improving Team Performance*. Wiley-Blackwell.

Frostenson, S. (1997), *Fem kompententa team: Det lilla företaget i det stora företaget*. Lund: Studentlitteratur.

Fruchter, R. & Bosch-Sijtsema, P. (2011), The WALL: Participatory design workspace in support of creativity, collaboration, and socialization. *AI and Society*, 26(3), 221–232.

Fu, X. (2012), How does openness affect the importance of incentives for innovation? *Research Policy*, 41(3), 512–523.

Gaimon, C. & Bailey, J. (2013), Knowledge Management for the Entrepreneurial Venture. *Production and Operations Management*, 22(6), 1429–1438.

Gamatese, J.A. & Hallowell M. (2011), Enabling and measuring innovation in the construction industry. *Construction Management and Economics*, 29(6), 553–567.

Gebauer, H., Worch, H. & Truffer, B. (2012), Absorptive capacity, learning processes and combinative capabilities as determinants of strategic innovation. *European Management Journal*, 30, 57–73.

Gibbert, M., Leibold, M. & Probst, G. (2002), Five Styles of Customer Knowledge Management, and How Smart Companies Use Them To Create Value. *European Management Journal*, 20(5), 459–469.

Gibson, C.B. and Gibbs, J.L. (2006), Unpacking the Concept of Virtuality: The Effects of Geographic Dispersion, Electronic Dependence, Dynamic Structure, and National Diversity on Team Innovation. *Administrative Science Quarterly*, 51, 451–495.

Gieskes, J. & Van der Heijden, B. (2004), Measuring and Enabling Learning Behaviour in Product Innovation Processes. *Learning Behaviour in Product Innovation*, 13(2), 109–125.

Gil, F., Rico, R., Alcover, C.M. & Barrasa, Á. (2005), Change-oriented leadership, satisfaction and performance in work groups: Effects of team climate and group potency. *Journal of Managerial Psychology*, 20(3/4), 312–328.

Gomes, J.F., de Weerd Nederhof, P.C., Pearson, A.W. & Cunha, M.P. (2003), Is more always better? An exploration of the differential effects of functional integration on performance in new product development. *Technovation*, 23(3), 185–191.

Gressgård, L.J. (2011), Virtual team collaboration and innovation in organizations. *Team Performance Management*, 17(1), 102–119.

Gumusluoglu, L. & Ilsev, A. (2009), Transformational leadership, creativity, and organizational innovation. *Journal of Business Research*, 62(1), 461–473.

Guzzo, R.A. & Dickson, M.W. (1996), Team in Organizations: Recent Research on Performance and Effectiveness. *Annual Review of Psychology*, 47(1), 307–338.

Hackman, J.R. (1990), *Groups that work (and those that don't)*, San Francisco: Jossey-Bass.

Hackman, J.R. (2002), *Leading Teams: Setting the Stage for Great Performances*. Boston: Harvard Business School Press.

Hallgren, E.W. (2009), How to Use an Innovation Audit as a Learning Tool: A Case Study of Enhancing High-Involvement Innovation. *Creativity and Innovation Management*, 18(1), 48–58.

Hammond, J.M., Harvey, C.M., Koubek, R.J., Gilbreth, L.M. & Darisipudi, A. (2005), Distributed Collaborative Design Teams: Media Effects on Design Processes. *International Journal of Human-Computer Interaction*, 18, 145–165.

Han, J-Y. & Hovav, A. (2012), To bridge or to bond? Diverse social connections in an IS project team. *International Journal of Project Management*, 31(3), 378–390.

Han, S.J., Chae, C., Macko, P., Park, W. and Beyerlein, M. (2017), How virtual team leaders cope with creativity challenges. *European Journal of Training and Development*, 41(3), 261–276.

Haner, U-E. (2005), Spaces for Creativity and Innovation in Two Established Organizations. *Creativity and Innovation Management*, 14(3), 288–298.

Harborne, P. & Johne, A. (2003), Creating a Project Climate for Successful Product Innovation. *European Journal of Innovation Management*, 6(2), 118–132.

Hardakker, G., Ahmed, P.K. & Graham, G. (1998), An integrated response towards the pursuit of fast time to market of NPD in European manufacturing organisations. *European Business Review*, 98(3), 172–177.

Hassainen, A. & Dale, C. (2012), Drivers and barriers of new product development and innovation in event venues: A multiple case study. *Journal of Facilities Management*, 10(1), 75–92.

Haucap, J. & Wey, C. (2004), Unionisation Structures and Innovation Incentives. *The Economic Journal*, 114(494), 149–165.

Hauschildt, J. & Kirchmann, E. (2001), Teamwork for Innovation – The "Troika" of Promotors. *R&D Management*, 31(1), 41–49.

Hauser, H. (1998), Organizational culture and innovativeness of firms – an integrative view. *International Journal of Technology Management*, 16 (1/2/3), 239–256.

Hayton, J.C. (2003), Strategic human capital management in SMEs: An empirical study of entrepreneurial performance. *Human Resource Management*, 42(4), 375–391.

Hayton, J.S.C. & Kelly, D.J. (2006), A competency-based framework for promoting corporate entrepreneurship. *Human Resource Management*, 45(3), 407–427.

Haywood, M. (1998), *Managing Virtual Teams: Practical Techniques for High-Technology Project Managers*. Boston: Artech House.

Hazy, J.K. & Backström. T. (2013), Human interaction dynamics (HID): An emerging paradigm for management research. *Emergence: Complexity & Organization*, 15(4), i–ix.

Hecker, A. & Ganter, A. (2013), The Influence of Product Market Competition on Technological and Management Innovation: Firm-Level Evidence from a Large-Scale Survey. *European Management Review*, 10(1), 17–33.

Heffner, M. & Sharif, N. (2008), Knowledge fusion for technological innovation in organizations. *Journal of Knowledge Management*, 12(2), 79–93.

Hemlin, S. & Olsson, L. (2011), Creativity-stimulating leadership: A critical incident study of leaders' influence on creativity in research groups. *Creativity and Innovation Management*, 20(1), 49–58.

Hemphälä, J. & Magnusson, M. (2012), Networks for Innovation – But What Networks and What Innovation? *Creativity and Innovation Management*, 21(1), 3–16.

Henttonen, K. & Blomqvist, K. (2005), Managing distance in a global virtual team- the evolution of trust through technology mediated relational communication. *Strategic Change*, 14(2), 107–119.

Hidalgo, A. & Albors, J. (2008), Innovation management techniques and tools: a review from theory and practice. *R&D Management*, 38(2), 113–127.

Highsmith, J. (2009), *Agile Project Management: Creating Innovative Products*. Crawfordsville: Addison-Wesley.

Hine, D. & Ryan, N. (1999), Small service firms – creating value through innovation. *Managing Service Quality*, 9(6), 411–422.

Hoegl, M. (2005), Smaller teams-better teamwork: How to keep project teams small. *Business Horizons*, 48(3), 209–214.

Hoegl, M., Parboteeah, K.P. & Gemuenden, H.G. (2003), When teamwork really matters: task innovativeness as a moderator of the teamwork–performance relationship in software development projects. *Journal of Engineering and Technology Management*, 20(4), 281–302.

Hollen, R.M.A., van Den Bosch, F.A. J. & Volberda, H.W. (2013), The Role of Management Innovation in Enabling Technological Process Innovation: An Inter-Organizational Perspective. *European Management Review*, 10(1), 35–50.

Holthausen, R.W., Larcker, D.F. & Sloan, R.G. (1994), Annual bonus schemes and the manipulation of earnings. *Journal of Accounting and Economics*, 19(1), 29–74.

Holton, J.A. (2001), Building trust and collaboration in a virtual team. *Team Performance Management*, 7(3/4), 36–47.

Honarpour, A., Jusoh, A. & Nor, K.Md. (2012), Knowledge Management, Total Quality Management and Innovation: A New Look. *Journal of Technology Management & Innovation*, 7(3), 22–31.

Horth, D. & Vehar, J. (2012), Becoming a Leader Who Fosters Innovation. *Center of Creative Leadership*, 1–25.

Hosseini, M.R., Bosch-Sijtsema, P., Arashpour, M., Chileshe, N. & Merschbrock, C. (2017), A qualitative investigation of perceived impacts of virtuality on effectiveness of hybrid construction project teams. *Construction Innovation*, 18(1), 109–131.

Hülsheger, U.R., Anderson, N., & Salgado, J.F. (2009), Team level predictors of innovation at work: a comprehensive meta analysis spanning three decades of research. *Journal of Applied psychology*, 94(5), 1128.

Hung, R.Y-Y, Lien, B.Y-H., Fang, S-C. & McLean, G.N. (2010), Knowledge as a facilitator for enhancing innovation performance through total quality management. *Total Quality Management*, 21(4), 425–438.

Hunter, S.T. & Cushenbery, L. (2011), Leading for Innovation: Direct and Indirect Influences. Advances in *Developing Human Resources*, 13(3), 248–265.

Hurmelinna-Luukkanen, P. (2011), Enabling collaborative innovation – knowledge protection for knowledge sharing. *European Journal of Innovation Management*, 14(3), 303–321.

Ileris, K. (2013), *Kompetens*. Lund: Studentlitteratur.

Im, S., Montoya, M.M. & Workman, J.P. (2013), Antecedents and consequences of creativity in product innovation teams. *Journal of Product Innovation Management*, 30(1), 170–185.

Inderst, R. (2009), Innovation management in organizations. *European Economic Review*, 53(8), 871–887.

Inderst, R. & Klein, M. (2007), Innovation, endogenous overinvestment, and incentive pay. *The Rand Journal of Economics*, 38(4), 881–904.

Isaksen, S.G. & Ekvall, G. (2010), Managing for Innovation: The Two Faces of Tension in Creative Climates. *Creativity and innovation management*, 19(2), 73–88.

Ismail, M. (2005), Creative climate and learning organization factors: their contribution towards innovation. *Leadership & Organization Development Journal*, 26(8), 639–654.

Jablokow, K.W. & Booth, D.E. (2006), The impact and management of cognitive gap in high performance product development organizations. *Journal of Engineering and Technology Management*, 23, 313–336.

Jagersma, P.K. (2003), Innovate or die. *Journal of Business Strategy*, 24(1).

Jasper, S. (2019), *The Effect of Time Zone Disparity on the Performance of Dispersed Innovation Teams in the Australian Biotechnology Industry*. Doctoral thesis, School of Graduate School of Business and Law. Melbourne: RMIT University.

Jenssen, J.I. & Nybakk, E. (2009), Inter-Organizational Innovation Promoters in Small, Knowledge-Intensive Firms. *International Journal of Innovation Management*, 13(3), 441–466.

Johannessen, J.-A. & Olsen, B. (2011), Projects as communicating systems: Creating a culture of innovation and Performance. *International Journal of Information Management*, 31(1), 30–37.

Johansson, F. (2005), *Medicieffekten*. Stockholm: BookHouse Publishing AB.

Johnsson, M. (2009), *Sälj skinnet innan björnen är skjuten*. Kolbäck: Raft Förlag.

Johnsson, M. (2016), *Innovation Enablers and Their Importance for Innovation Teams*. Doctorial thesis. Karlskrona: Blekinge Institute of Technology.

Johnsson, M. (2017), How understanding of agile innovation work affects innovation teams. In: *ISPIM Innovation Summit – Building the Innovation Century*. Melbourne, Australia on 10–13 December 2017.

Johnsson, M. (2017), The emergence process of innovation teams. In: *The XXVIII ISPIM Conference – Composing the Innovation Symphony*, Vienna, Austria on 18–21 June 2017.

Johnsson, M. (2017a), Innovation Enablers for Innovation Teams – A Review. *Journal of Innovation Management*, 5(3), 75–121.

Johnsson, M. (2017b), Creating High-performing Innovation Teams. *Journal of Innovation Management*, 5(4), 23–47.

Johnsson, M. (2018), The innovation facilitator: characteristics and importance for innovation teams. *Journal of Innovation Management*, 6(2), 12–44.

Johnsson, M. (2021), Factors enabling global innovation teams. In: *The XXXII ISPIM Innovation Conference – Innovating Our Common Future*. Berlin, Germany on 20–23 June 2021.

Johnsson, M. Svensson, E. & Swenningsson, K. (2020), Success factors when implementing innovation teams. In: *The XXXI ISPIM Conference – Innovation in the times of crisis*. Virtual event, June on 7–10, 2020.

Johnsson, M. Swenningsson, K. & Svensson, E. (2019), Problems when implementing innovation teams. In: *The XXX ISPIM Conference – Celebrating Innovation: 500 Years Since Da Vinci. Florence*, Italy on 16–19 June, 2019.

Johnsson, M., Ekman, S., Wiktorsson, M. & Karlsson, T. (2010), A model-based process for developing environmental innovations: Four cases where the RAFT-model has been used in environmental innovations. In: *The XXVII IASP Conference*, Daedak, South Korea on 24–28 September, 2013.

Johnstone, C., Pairaudeau, G. & Pettersson, J.A. (2011), Creativity, innovation and lean sigma: a controversial combination? *Drug Discovery Today*, 16(1/2), 50–57.

Judge, W.Q., Fryxell, G.E. & Dooley, R.S. (1997), The New Task of R&D Management: Creating Goal-directed Communities for Innovation. *California Management Review*, 39(3), 72–85.

Kadefors. A. (2003), Trust in project relationships – inside the black box. *International Journal of Project Management*, 22(3), 175–182.

Kairisto-Mertanen, L., Penttilä, T. & Nuotio, J. (2011), On the definition of innovation competencies. In: Torniainen, I., Mahlamäki-Kultanen, S., Nokelainen P. & Paul, I. (eds.), *Innovations for competence management*. Conference proceedings. Series C, reports and other current publications, part 83, Lahti University of Applied Sciences, Esa print Oy. 25–33.

Kamhawi, E.M. (2012), Knowledge management fishbone: a standard framework of organizational enablers. *Journal of Knowledge Management*, 16(5), 808–828.

Karlsson, H., Johnsson, M. & Backström, T. (2010), Interview Supported Innovation Audit: how does a complementary interview affect the understanding of an innovation audits results when the interview is based on the audit statements. In: *The 3rd ISPIM Innovation Symposium*, Quebec, Canada on 12–15 December, 2010.

Karlsson, L., Löfstrand, M., Larsson, A., Törlind, P., Larsson, T., Elfström, B.-O. & Isaksson, O. (2005), Information Driven Collaborative Engineering: Enabling Functional Product Innovation. In: *CCE '05; the Knowledge Perspective in Collaborative Engineering*. Sopron, Hungary, 14t-15th April, 2005.

Kask, T. (2011), Strategic decisions as drivers of innovation: the case of MicroLink. *Baltic Journal of Management*, 6(3), 300–319.

Kathleen, K.M. (2012), Sustainability and Innovation. Creating Change that Engages the Workforce. *Journal of Corporate Citizenship*, 46, 175–187.

Katzenbach, J. & Smith, D. (1993), *The wisdom of teams: creating the high performing organization*. Cambridge: Harvard business school press.

Katzenback, J.R. and Smith, D.K. (1993), *The Wisdom of Teams: Creating the High-Performance Organization*. Boston: Harvard Business School Press.

Kay, L. (2011), The effect of inducement prizes on innovation: evidence from the Ansari X Prize and the Northrop Grumman Lunar Lander Challenge. *R&D Management*, 41, 360–377.

Kayabasi, A., Duran, C. & Çentindere (2013), An Analysis of the Relationship Between the Elements Encouraging Innovation and Innovation Performance for SMEs. *European Journal of Business and Economics*, 4, 1–8.

Kelly, T. (2005), *Ten faces of Innovation*. New York: The Crown Publishing Group.

Kelly, T. (2016), *The Art of Innovation*. London: Profile Books Publishing.

Kesting, P. & Ulhöj J.P. (2010), Employee-driven innovation: extending the license to foster innovation. *Management Decision*, 48(1), 65–84.

Kianto, A. (2011), Enabling Innovation in Knowledge Worker Teams. *International Journal of Intellectual Capital*, 8(1), 30–49.

Kihlbom, G. (2005), *Släpp medarbetarna loss*. Uppsala: Konsultförlaget.

Kindström, D., Kowalkowski, C. & Sandberg, E. (2012), Enabling service innovation: A dynamic capabilities approach. *Journal of Business Research*, 66(8), 1063–1073.

King, N. & Anderson, N. (2002), *Managing Innovation and Change: A Critical Guide for Organizations*. London: Thomson.

Kirkegaard, O.L. (1976), *Gummi-Tarzan*. Stockholm: Tidens förlag.

Kleinknecht, A. (1987), Measuring R and D in Small Firms: How Much Are We Missing? *The Journal of Industrial Economics*, 36(2), 253–256.

Klitmøller, A. & Lauring, J. (2013), When global virtual teams share knowledge: Media richness, cultural difference and language commonality. *Journal of World Business*, 48(3), 398–406.

Koberg, C.S., Uhlenbruck, N. & Sarason, Y. (1996), Facilitators of Organizational Innovation: The Role of Life-Cycle Stage. *Journal of Business Venturing*, 11(2), 133–149.

Kodama, M. (2000), Creating New Services Based on the Formation of a Strategic Community with Customers: A Case Study of Innovation Involving IT and Multimedia Technology in the Field of Veterinary Medicine. *Networking Veterinary Medicine Services*, 9(3), 171–184.

Kollmann, T. & Stöckmann, C. (2010), Antecedents of strategic ambidexterity: effects of entrepreneurial orientation on exploratory and exploitative innovations in adolescent organisations. *International Journal of Technology Management*, 52(1/2), 153–174.

Kramer, J-P., Marinelli, E., Iammarino, S. & Diez, J.R. (2011), Intangible assets as drivers of innovation: Empirical evidence on multinational enterprises in German and UK regional systems of innovation. *Technovation*, 31(9), 447–458.

Kristiansen, M. & Bloch-Poulsen J. (2010), Employee Driven Innovation in Team (EDIT) – Innovative Potential, Dialogue. *International Journal of Action Research* 6(2–3), 155–195.

Kuckertz, A., Kohtamäki, M. & Droge gen.Körber, C. (2010), The fast eat the slow – the impact of strategy and innovation timing on the success of technology-oriented ventures. *International Journal of Technology Management*, 52(1/2), 175–188.

Lahiri, N. (2010), Geographic Distribution of R&D Activity: How Does It Affect Innovation Quality? *The Academy of Management Journal*, 53(5), 1194–1209.

Laine, T., Korhonen, T. & Martinsuo, M. (2016), Managing program impacts in new product development: An exploratory case study on overcoming uncertainties. *International Journal of Project Management*, 34(4), 717–733.

Laloux, F. (2014), *Reinventing Organizations. A Guide to Creating Organizations Inspired by the Next Stage of Human Consciousness*. Bryssel: Nelson Parker.

Langley, A. (1999), Strategies for theorizing from process data. *Academy of Management Review*, 24(4), 691–710.

Lans, H. (1997), *Uppfinn framtiden*. Stockholm: Svenska Ingenjörssamfundet.

Larsson, A. (2003), Making sense of collaboration: the challenge of thinking together in global design teams. In: The 2003 international ACM SIGGROUP conference on Supporting group work, 153–160.

Larsson, A. (2007), Banking on social capital: towards social connectedness in distributed engineering design teams. *Design Studies*, 28(6), 605–622.

Larsson, A., Törlind, P., Mabogunje, A. & Milne, A. (2002), Distributed design teams: embedded one-on-one conversations in one-to-many. In: *Common Ground: Design Research Society International Conference*. Held 5–7 September 2002, London, UK, Staffordshire University Press, p. 234.

Laursen, K. (2011), User–producer interaction as a driver of innovation: costs and advantages in an open innovation model. *Science and Public Policy*, 38(9), 713–723.

Leavy, B. (2005), A leader's guide to creating an innovation culture. *Strategy & Leadership*, 33(4), 38–45.

Lee, L. T-S. & Sukoco B.M. (2011), Reflexivity, stress, and unlearning in the new product development team: the moderating effect of procedural justice. *R&D Management*, 41(4), 410–423.

Lei, D. (2003), Competition, cooperation and learning: the new dynamics of strategy and organisation design for the innovation net. *International Journal of Technology Management*, 26(7), 694–716.

Lencioni, P. (2002), *The Five Dysfunctions of a Team: A Leadership Fable*. San Francisco: Jossey-Bass.

LePine J.A., Buckman, B.R., Crawford, E.R. & Methot, J.R. (2011), A review of research on personality in teams: Accounting for pathways spanning levels of theory and analysis. *Human Resource Management Review*, 21(4), 311–330.

Lerner, J. & Wulf, J. (2007), Innovation and Incentives: Evidence From Corporate R&D. *The Review of Economics and Statistics*, 89(4), 634–644.

Lettice, F. & Thomond, P. (2008), Allocating resources to disruptive innovation projects: challenging mental models and overcoming management resistance. *International Journal of Technology Management*, 44(1/2), 140–159.

Li, V., Mitchell, R. & Boyle, B. (2016), The Divergent Effects of Transformational Leadership on Individual and Team Innovation. *Group and Organization Management*, 41(1), 66–97.

Liao, S-H. & Wu, C-C. (2010), System perspective of knowledge management, organizational learning, and organizational innovation. *Expert Systems with Applications*, 37(2), 1096–1103.

Linder, F. & Wald, A. (2011), Success factors of knowledge management in temporary organizations. *International Journal of Project Management*, 29(7), 877–888.

Liu, M-S. (2013), Impact of knowledge incentive mechanisms on individual knowledge creation behavior – An empirical study for Taiwanese R&D professionals. *International Journal of Information Management*, 32(5), 442–450.

Loan, P. (2006), Review of The New Knowledge Management: Complexity, Learning and Sustainable Innovation. *On the Horizon*, 14(3), 130–138.

Logman, M. (2007), Logical brand management in a dynamic context of growth and innovation. *Journal of Product & Brand Management*, 16(4), 257–268.

Lombardo, M.M. & Eichinger, R.W. (1995), *The Team Architect User's Manual*. Minneapolis: Lominger Limited.

Longo, F. (2007), Implementing managerial innovations in primary care: Can we rank change drivers in complex adaptive organizations? *Health Care Management Review*, 32(3), 213–225.

López-Fernández, M.C., Serrano-Bedina, A.M. & Gómez-López, R. (2011), Factors Encouraging Innovation in Spanish Hospitality Firms. *Cornell Hospitality Quarterly*, 52(2), 144–152.

Love, J. & Roper, S. (2009), Organizing innovation: Complementarities between cross-functional teams. *Technovation*, 29(3), 192–203.

Lubaktin, M., Florin, J. & Lane. P. (2001), Learning together and apart: A model of reciprocal interfirm learning. *Human Relations*, 54(10), 1353–1382.

Lukeš, M. (2012), Supporting Entrepreneurial Behaviour and Innovation in Organizations. *Central European Business Review Research Papers*, 1(2), 29–36.

Lumpkin, G.T. & Dess, G. (2001), Linking Two Dimensions of Entrepreneurial Orientation to Firm Performance: The Moderating Role of Environment and Industry Life Cycle. *Journal of Business Venturing*, 16(5), 429–451.

Lundin, R.A. & Söderholm, A. (1995), A Theory of The Temporary Organization. *Scandinavian Journal of Management*, 11(4), 437–455.

Majumdar, S.K. (1999), Sluggish Giants, Sticky Cultures, and Dynamic Capability Transformation. *Journal of Business Venturing*, 15(1), 59–78.

Manley, K. & McFallan, S. (2006), Exploring the drivers of firm-level innovation in the construction industry. *Construction Management and Economics*, 24(9), 911–920.

Manning, S., Larsen, M.M. & Bharati, P. (2015), Global delivery models: The role of talent, speed and time zones in the global outsourcing industry. *Journal of International Business Studies*, 46(7), 850–877.

Manole, I. (2014), Virtual Teams and E-Leadership in the Context of Competitive Environment-Literature Review. *Journal of Economic Development, Environment and People*, 3(3), 72–76.

Manral, L. (2011), Managerial cognition as bases of innovation in organization. *Management Research Review*, 34(5), 576–594.

Mansfeld, M.N., Hölzle, K. & Gemünden, H.G. (2010), Personal Characteristics of Innovators – An Empirical Study of Roles in Innovation Management. *International Journal of Innovation Management*, 14(6), 1129–1147.

Mansikkamäki, P., Mäntysalo, M. & Rönkkä, R. (2007), Integrative Technologies Complicate Communication during Development Work Context: Industry-Academy Collaboration. *Systemics, Cybernetics and Informatics*, 5(3), 9–15.

Manso, G. (2011), Motivating Innovation. *The Journal of Finance*, 66(5), 1823–1860.

Maqsood, T. & Finegan, A. (2009), A knowledge management approach to innovation and learning in the construction industry. *International Journal of Managing Projects in Business*, 2(2), 297–307.

Marion, R. & Uhl-bien, M. (2002), Leadership in complex organizations. *The Leadership Quarterly*, 12(4), 389–418.

Marion, T.J., Friar, J.H. & Cullinane, T. (2012), A Multi Disciplinary New Product Development Course for Technological Entrepreneurs. *Journal of the Academy of Business Education*, 13, 71–84.

Markides, C. (1998), Strategic innovation in established companies. *Sloan Management Review*, 39(3), 31–42.

Martinsuo, M., Hensman, N., Artto, K., Kujala, J. & Jaafari, A. (2006), Project-Based Management as an Organizational Innovation: Drivers, Changes, and Benefits of Adopting Project based Management. *Project Management Journal*, 37(3), 87–97.

Masoulas, V. (1998), Organizational requirements definition for intellectual capital management. *International Journal of Technology Management*, 16(1/2), 126–144.

Matjaž, M., Kajzer, S., Potocan, V., Rosi, B. & Knez-Riedl, J. (2006), Interdependence of systems theories – potential innovation supporting innovation. *Kybernetes*, 35(7/8), 942–954.

Maturana, H. & Varela, F. (1987), *The three of knowledge*. Boston: Shambhala.

Maurer, I. (2010), How to build trust in inter-organizational projects: The impact of project staffing and project rewards on the formation of trust, knowledge acquisition and product innovation. *International Journal of Project Management*, 28(7), 629–637.

McAdam, R. (2000), Knowledge Management as a Catalyst for Innovation within Organizations: A Qualitative Study. *Knowledge and Process Management*, 7(4), 233–241.

McDonough III, E.F. (2000), Investigation of Factors Contributing to the Success of Cross-Functional Teams. *Journal of Product Innovation Management*, 17(3), 221–235.

McGreevy, M. (2006a), Team working: part 1 – an evaluation of current thinking. *Industrial and commercial training*, 38(5), 259–264.

McGreevy, M. (2006b), Team working: part 2 – how are teams chosen and developed. *Industrial and commercial training*, 38(7), 365–370.

McGurk, J. & Baron, A. (2012), Knowledge management – time to focus on purpose and motivation. *Strategic HR Review*, 11(6), 316–321.

Mele, C., Spena, T.R. & Colurcio, M. (2012), Co-creating value innovation through resource integration. *International Journal of Quality and Service Sciences*, 2(1), 60–78.

Menon, A., Chowdhury, J. & Lukas B.A. (2002), Antecedents and outcomes of new product development speed: An interdisciplinary conceptual framework. *Industrial Marketing Management*, 31(4), 317–328.

Mentzas, G. (2004), A Strategic Management Framework for Leveraging Knowledge Assets. *International Journal of Innovation and Learning*, 1(2), 1–30.

Meslec, N. and Curşeu, P.L. (2015), Are balanced groups better? Belbin roles in collaborative learning groups. *Learning and Individual Differences*, 39, 81–88.

Michanek, J. & Breiler, A. (2004), *Idéagenten – en handbok i idea management*. Jönköping: Brain Books AB.

Milton, A. & Rodgers, P. (2013), *Research methods for product design*. London: Laurence King Publishing Ltd.

Mitchell, R.J. & Boyle B. (2008), A theoretical model of transformational leadership's role in diverse teams. *Leadership & Organization Development Journal*, 30(5), 455–474.

Mol, M.J. & Birkinshaw, J. (2009), The sources of management innovation: When firms introduce new management practices. *Journal of Business Research*, 62(12), 1269–1280.

Mooi, E.A. & Frambach, R.T. (2012), Encouraging innovation in business relationships – A research note. *Journal of Business Research*, 65(7), 1025–1030.

Morgan, C.W., Blake, A. & Poyago-Theotoky, J.A. (2004), The management of technological innovation: lessons from case studies in the UK food and drink industry. *International Journal of Biotechnology*, 5(3/4), 334–353.

Morris, M.H., Allen, J., Schindehutte, M. & Avila, R. (2006), Balanced Management Control Systems as a Mechanism for Achieving Corporate Entrepreneurship. *Journal of Managerial Issues*, 18(4), 468–493.

Morris, S. (2008), Virtual team working: Making it happen. *Industrial and Commercial Training*, 40(3), 29–133.

Muethel, M., Siebdrat, F. & Hoegl, M. (2011), When Do We Really Need Interpersonal Trust in Globally Dispersed New Product Development Teams? *R&D Management*, 46(1), 31–46.

Mumford, M.B. & Licuanan, B. (2004), Leading for innovation: Conclutions, issues, and directions. *The Leadership Quarterly*, 15(1), 163–171.

Mumford, M.D., Connely, M.S., Baughman, W.A. & Marks, M.A. (1994), Creativity and problem solving: Cognition, adaptability, and wisdom. *Roeper Review*, 16(4), 241–247.

Mumford, M.D., Hunter, S.T. & Byrne, C.L. (2009), What is fundamental? The Role of Cognition in Creativity and Innovation. *Industrial and organizational psychology*, 2(3), 353–356.

Nagji, B. & Tuff, G. (2012), Managing Your Innovation Portfolio. *Harvard Business Review 3*, May 2012, 66–74.

Nakata, C. & Im, S. (2010), Spurring Cross Functional Integration for Higher New Product Performance: A Group Effectiveness Perspective. *Journal of Product Innovation Management*, 27(4), 554–571.

Nanda, T. & Singh, T.P. (2008), Determinants of creativity and innovation in the workplace: a comprehensive review. *International Journal of Technology, Policy and Management*, 9(1), 84–106.

Narasimhalu, A.D. (2005), Innovation Cube: Triggers, Drivers and Enablers for Successful Innovations. In: *The XVI ISPIM Conference*. Porto, Portugal on 19–22 June, 2005.

Nerkar, A.A., McGrath, R.G. & MacMillan, I.C. (1996), Three Facets of Satisfaction and Their Influence on the Performance of Innovation Teams. *Journal of Business Venturing*, 11, 167–188.

Neuman, G.A., Wagner, S.H. & Christiansen, N.D. (1999), The relationship between work team personality composition and the job performance of teams. *Group & Organization Management*, 24(1), 28–45.

Newton, K. (1998), The high performance workplace: HR–based management innovations in Canada. *International Journal of Technology Management*, 16 (1/2/3), 177–192.

Nicolaou, N., Shane, S., Cherkas, L. & Spector, T.D. (2009), Organizational Behavior and Human Decision Processes. *Organizational Behavior and Human Decision Processes*, 110(2), 108–117.

Noke, H. & Radnor, Z.J. (2004), Navigating innovation: a diagnostic tool supporting the process. *Journal of Manufacturing Technology Management*, 15(2), 172.

Noke, H., Perrons, R.K. & Hughes, M. (2008), Strategic dalliances as an enabler for discontinuous innovation in slow clockspeed industries: evidence from the oil and gas industry. *R&D Management*, 38(2), 129–139.

Nonaka, I. & Takeuchi, H. (1995), *The knowledge-creating company: How Japanese companies create the dynamics of innovation*. New York: Oxford University Press.

Norman, D.A. (1999), Affordance, conventions, and design. *Interactions*, 6(3), 38–41.

Nybakk, E., Crespell, P. & Hansen, E. (2011), Climate for Innovation and Innovation Strategy as Drivers for Success in the Wood Industry: Moderation Effects of Firm Size, Industry Sector, and Country of Operation. *Silva Fennica*, 45(3), 415–430.

O'Brian, C. & Smith, S.J.E. (1995), Strategies for encouraging and managing technological innovation. *International Journal of Production Economics*, 41(1), 303–310.

O'Connor, G.C. & McDermott C.M. (2004), The human side of radical innovation. *Journal of Engineering and Technology Management*, 21(1), 11–30.

O'Reilly, C.A. & Tushman, M.L. (2004), The Ambidextrous Organization. *Harvard Business Review*, 82(4), 74–81.

O'Reily, C. & Pfeffer, J. (2000), *Hidden Value: How Great Companies Achieve Extraordinary Results with Ordinary People*. Boston: Harvard Business School Press.

O´Connor, G.C. & DeMartino, R. (1997), Organizing for Radical Innovation: An Exploratory Study of the Structural Aspects of RI Management Systems in Large Established Firms. *Journal of Product Innovation Management*, 23(6), 475–497.

Ocker, R.J. and Hiltz, S.R. (2012), Learning to work in partially distributed teams: The impact of team interaction on learning outcomes. In: *Hawaii International Conference on System Sciences*, IEEE Computer Society, 88–97.

OECD (2005), *Oslo Manual – Guidelines for Collecting and Interpreting Innovation Data*. Eurostat. available at: https://webgate.acceptance.ec.europa.eu/eurostat/web/products-manuals-and-guidelines/-/oslo, retrieved 2022-04-08.

Olaisen, J. & Revang, O. (2017), Working smarter and greener: Collaborative knowledge sharing in virtual global project teams. *International Journal of Information Management*, 37(1), 1441–1448.

Olsen, J.E. & Haslett, T. (2002), Strategic Management in Action. *Systemic Practice and Action Research*, 15(6), 449–464.

Olson, J. & Olson, L. (2012), Virtual team trust: Task, communication and sequence. *Team Performance Management*, 18(5), 256–276.

Olson, J.D., Appunn, F.D., Mc Allister, C.A., Walters, K.K. & Grinnell, L. (2014), Webcams and virtual teams: An impact model. *Team Performance Management*, 20(3–4), 148–177.

Olsson, A., Wadell, C., Odenrick, P. & Norell Morgendahl, M. (2010), An action learning method for increased innovation capability in organisations. *Action Learning: Research and Practice*, 7(2), 167–179.

Orcutt, L.H. & AlKadri, M.Y. (2009), Overcoming Roadblocks to Innovation: Three Case Studies at the California Department of Transportation. *Transportation Research Record*, 2109(1), 65–73.

Ottosson, S. (2012), *Dynamisk Produktutveckling*, 2nd ed. Floda: Tervix AB.

Overvest, M. & Veldman, J. (2008), Managerial Incentives for Process Innovation. *Managerial and Decision Economics*, 29(7), 539–545.

Paasi, J., Valkokari, K., Rantala, T., Hytönen, H., Nystén-Haarala, S. & Huhtilainen, L. (2010), Innovation Management Challenges of a System Integrator in Innovation Networks. *International Journal of Innovation Management*, 14(6), 1047–1064.

Painter, G., Posey, P., Austrom, D., Tenkasi, R., Barrett, B. and Merck, B. (2016), Sociotechnical systems design: coordination of virtual teamwork in innovation. *Team Performance Management*, 22(7–8), 354–369.

Palacios, P., Gil, I. & Garragos, F. (2009), The impact of knowledge management on innovation and entrepreneurship in the biotechnology and telecommunications industries. *Small Business Economy*, 32(3), 291–301.

Paladino, A. (2007), Investigating the Drivers of Innovation and New Product Success: A Comparison of Strategic Orientations. *Journal of Product Innovation Management*, 24(6), 534–553.

Panayides, P. (2006), Enhancing innovation capability through relationship management and implications for performance. *European Journal of Innovation Management*, 9(4), 466–483.

Panesar, S.S. & Markeset, T. (2008), Development of a framework for industrial service innovation management and coordination. *Journal of Quality in Maintenance Engineering*, 14(2), 177–193.

Park, J.S. (2005), Opportunity recognition and product innovation in entrepreneurial hi-tech start-ups: a new perspective and supporting case study. *Technovation*, 25(7), 739–752.

Parolin, S.R.H., Vasconcellos, E., Volpato, M. & Laurindo, A.M. (2013), Barriers and Facilitators of Collaborative Management in Technological Innovation Projects. *Journal of Technology Management & Innovation*, 8(3), 151–164.

Pattersson, M.L. (2009), Innovation as a system. *Research-technology Management*, 52(5), 42–51.

Pearce, C.L. & Ensley, M.D. (2004), A reciprocal and longitudinal investigation of the innovation process: The central role of shared vision in product and process innovation teams (PPITs). *Journal of Organizational Behavior*, 25(2), 259–278.

Pearson, A.E. (2002), Though-Minded Ways to Get Innovative. *Harvard Business Review*, 80(8), 117–124.

Peñarroja, V., Orengo, V., Zornoza, A., Sánchez, J. & Ripoll, P. (2015), How team feedback and team trust influence information processing and learning in virtual teams: A moderated mediation model. *Computers in Human Behavior*, 48, 9–16.

Peschl, M.F. & Fundneider, T. (2012), Spaces Enabling Game-Changing and Sustaining Innovations: Why Space Matters For Knowledge Creation and Innovation. *Journal of Organisational Transformation and Social Change*, 9(1), 41–61.

Petty, E.R. (1983), Engineering Curricula for Encouraging Creativity and Innovation. *European Journal of Engineering Education*, 8(1), 29–43.

Pinar, T., Zehir, C., Kitapçi, H. & Tanriverdi, H. (2014), The Relationships between Leadership Behaviors Team Learning and Performance among the Virtual Teams. *International Business Research*, 7(5).

Radnor, Z. & Robinson J. (2000), Benchmarking Innovation: A Short Report. *Creativity and Innovation Management*, 9(1), 3–13.

Räsänen, M., Putkonen, A. & Kairisto-Mertanen, L. (2015), Innovation process-competences needed to make it succeed. In: *CINet conference*. Stockholm, Sweden on 13–15 September, 2015.

Ribeiro-Soriano, D. & Urbano, D. (2010), Employee-organization relationship entrepreneurship: an overview. *Journal of Organizational Change Management*, 23(4), 349–359.

Richtnér, A. & Åhlström, P. (2010), Top Management Control and Knowledge Creation in New Product Development International. *Journal of Operations & Production Management*, 30(10), 1006–1031.

Richtner, A. & Frishammar, J. (2012), *Innovationsledning och kreativitet i svenska* företag. Stockholm: VINNOVA.

Rigtering, J.P.C. & Weitzel, U. (2013), Work Context and Employee Behaviour as Antecedents for Intrapreneurship. *International Entrepreneurship and Management Journal*, 9(3), 337–360.

Ringelmann, M. (1913b), Recherches sur les moteurs animes: Travail de rhomme [Research on animate sources of power: The work of man]. *Annales de l'Institut National Agronomique*, 2e serie – tome XII, 1–40.

Ritala, P. & Hurmelinna-Laukkanen, P. (2009), What's In It For Me? Creating and Appropriating Value in Innovation-Related Coopetition. *Technovation*, 29(12), 819–828.

Robert, L., Denis, A. & Hung, Y.T. (2009), Individual swift trust and knowledge-based trust in face-to-face and virtual team members. *Journal of Management Information Systems*, 26(2), 241–279.

Robinson, A.G. & Schroeder, D.M. (2006), *Ideas are free: how the idea revolution is liberating people and transforming organizations*. San Francisco: Berrett-Koehler Publishers.

Rogers, E.W. (1998), Enabling Innovative Thinking: Fostering the Art of Knowledge Crafting. *International Journal of Technology Management*, 16 (1/2/3), 11–23.

Romero, D. & Molina, A. (2011), Collaborative Networked Organisations and Customer Communities: Value Co-Creation and Co-Innovation in the Networking Era. *Production Planning & Control*, 22(5–6), 447–472.

Rosing, K., Frese, M. & Bausch, A. (2011), Explaining the Heterogeneity of The Leadership-Innovation Relationship: Ambidextrous Leadership. *The Leadership Quarterly*, 22(5), 956–974.

Ross, T., Mitchell, V.A. & May, A.J. (2012), Bottom-Up Grassroots Innovation in Transport: Motivations, Barriers and Enablers. *Transportation Planning and Technology*, 35(4), 469–489.

Rousseau, V., Aubé, C. & Tremblay, S. (2013), Team coaching and innovation in work teams: An examination of the motivational and behavioral intervening mechanisms. *Leadership and Organization Development Journal*, 34(4), 344–364.

Rubin, I.M., Plovnick, M.S. and Fry, R.E. (1977), Task Oriented Team Development. McGraw-Hill, New York.

Sack, R.L. (2009), The pathophysiology of jet lag. Travel Medicine and Infectious Disease, 7(2), 102–110.

Salge, T.O., Bohné, T.M., Farchi, T. & Piening, E.P. (2012), Harnessing the Value of Open Innovation: The Moderating Role of Innovation Management. *International Journal of Innovation Management*, 16(3).

Sampson, R.C. (2007), R&D Alliances and Firm Performance: The Impact of Technological Diversity and Alliance Organization on Innovation. *Academy of Management Journal*, 50(29), 364–386.

Schraub, E.M., Michel A., Shemla M. & Sonntag K. (2014), The roles of leader emotion management and team conflict for team members' personal initiative: A multilevel perspective. *European Journal of Work and Organizational Psychology*, 23(2), 263–276.

Schweder, R.A. & Sullivan, M.A. (1993), Cultural Psychology: Who Needs It? *Annual Review of Psychology*, 44(1), 497–523.

Scott, C.P.R. & Wildman, J.L. (2015), Culture, Communication, and Conflict: A Review of the Global Virtual Team Literature. In J. L. Wildman & R. L. Griffith (Eds.), *Leading Global Teams*. New York: Springer, 13–32.

Scozzi, B., Garavelli, C. & Crowson, K. (2005), Methods for modeling and supporting innovation processes in SMEs. *European Journal of Innovation Management*, 8(1), 120–137.

Searle, R.H. & Ball, K.S. (2003), Supporting Innovation through HR Policy: Evidence from the UK. *Creativity and Innovation Management*, 12(1), 50–62.

Seshadri, V. & Elangovan, N. (2019), Role of Manager in Geographically Distributed Team; A Review. *Journal of Management*, 6(1), 122–129.

Shang, S.S.C., Lin, S-F. & Wu, Y-L. (2009), Service innovation through dynamic knowledge management. *Industrial Management & Data Systems*, 109(3), 322–337.

Sheikh, S. (2012), Do CEO compensation incentives affect firm innovation? *Review of Accounting and Finance*, 11(1), 4–39.

Smart, P., Bessant, J. & Gupta, A. (2007), Towards technological rules for designing innovation networks: a dynamic capabilities view. *International Journal of Operations & Production Management*, 27(10), 1069–1092.

Smith, M., Busi, M., Ball, P. & Van Der Meer, R. (2008), Factors Influencing an Organisation's Ability to Manage Innovation: A Structured Literature Review and Conceptual Model. *International Journal of Innovation Management*, 12(4), 655–676.

Smith, S., Smith, G. & Shen, Y-T. (2012), Redesign for Product Innovation. *Design Studies*, 33(2), 160–184.

Smyth, H., Gustafsson, M. & Ganskau, E. (2010), The value of trust in project business. *International Journal of Project Management*, 28(2), 117–129.

Solé, R. & Goodwin, B. (2000), *Signs of life – How complexity pervades biology*. New York: Basic Books.

Spena, T.R. & Colurcio, M. (2010), A cognitive-relational view of innovation in the agri-food industry: The fresh-cut business. *International Journal of Innovation Management*, 14(2), 307–329.

Steele, J. & Murray, M. (2004), Creating, supporting and sustaining a culture of innovation. *Engineering, Construction and Architectural Management*, 11(5), 316–322.

Stempfle, J. (2011), Overcoming Organizational Fixation: Creating and Sustaining an Innovation Culture. *Journal of Creative Behavior*, 45(2), 116–129.

Strannegård, L. (2003), *Flipp eller flopp: om misslyckandets dynamik*. Stockholm: Raster förlag.

Tahirsylaj, A.S. (2012), Stimulating creativity and innovation through Intelligent Fast Failure. *Thinking Skills and Creativity*, 7(3), 265–270.

Tan, R. (2013), Seven Stimuli to Identify Opportunities of Innovation: A Practice of Training Innovative Engineers and Some Findings in China. *American Journal of Industrial and Business Management*, 3, 725–739.

Taylor, A. & Helfat, C.E. (2009), Organizational Linkages for Surviving Technological Change: Complementary Assets, Middle Management, and Ambidexterity. *Organization Science*, 20(4), 718–739.

Tidd, J & Bessant, J. (2013), *Managing innovation: integrating technological, market and organizational change*, 5th ed. West Sussex: John Wiley & Sons Ltd.

Tidd, J & Bessant, J. (2020), *Managing innovation: integrating technological, market and organizational change*, 7th ed. West Sussex: John Wiley & Sons Ltd.

Tidd, J. & Bessant, J. (2009), *Managing Innovation: integrating technological, market and organizational change*, 4th ed. West Sussex: John Wiley & Sons Ltd.

Timmermans, O., Van Linge, R., Van Petegem, P., Van Rompaey, B. & Denekens, J. (2011), Team learning and innovation in nursing, a review of the literature. *Nurse Education Today*, 32(1), 65–70.

Tranfield, D., Young, M., Parington, D., Bessant, J. & Sapsed, J. (2003), Knowledge Management Routines for Innovation Projects: Developing A Hierarchical Process Model. *International Journal of Innovation Management*, 7(1), 27–49.

Trott. P. (2012), *Innovation Management and New Product* Development, 5th ed. Essex: Pearson Education Ltd.

Tuckman, B.W. (1965), Developmental sequence in small groups. *Psychological Bulletin*, 63(6), 384–399.

Tuckmann, B.W. & Jensen, M.A.C. (1977), Stages of Small-Group Development Revisited. *Group and Organization Management*, 2(4), 419–427.

Tzabbar, D. and Vestal, A. (2015), Bridging the social chasm in geographically distributed R&D teams: The moderating effects of relational strength and status asymmetry on the novelty of team innovation. *Organization Science*, 26(3), 811–829.

Un, A.C. & Montoro-Sanchez, A. (2010), Innovative capability development for entrepreneurship. A theoretical framework. *Journal of Organizational Change Management*, 23(4), 413–434.

Utterback, J., Vedin, B.-A., Alavarez, E., Ekman, S., Sanderson, S.W., Tether, B. & Verganti, R. (2006), *Design-Inspired Innovation*. London: World Scientific Publishing.

Vaghely, I.P. & Julien, P.-A. (2008), Are opportunities recognized or constructed? An information perspective on entrepreneurial opportunity identification. *Journal of Business Venturing*, 25, 73–86.

Vale, P.A. & Addison, M. (2002), Promoting Entrepreneurship and Innovation in a Large Company: Creating a Virtual Portfolio. *Journal of Change Management*, 2(4), 334–343.

Van der Panne, G., Van Beers, C. & Kleinknecht, A. (2003), Success and Failure of Innovation: A Literature Review. *International Journal of Innovation Management*, 7(3), 309–338.

Van Manen, M. (1990), *Researching Lived Experience. Human Science for an Action Sensitive Pedagogy*. London: State University of New York Press.

Vandenberg, R.J., Richardson, H.A. & Eastman, L.J. (1999), The impact of high involvement work processes on organizational effectiveness: A second-order latent variable approach. *Group & Organizational Management*, 24(3), 300–339.

Vashishtha, V.K., Makade, R. & Mehla, N. (2011), Advancement of Rapid Prototyping in Aerospace Industry – A Review. *International Journal of Engineering Science and Technology*, 3(3), 2486–2493.

Vincenzo, F. Di & Mascia D. (2011), Social capital in project-based organizations: Its role, structure, and impact on project performance. *International Journal of Project Management*, 30, 5–14.

Von Hippel, E. & Tyre, M. (1995), How "Learning by Doing" is Done: Problem Identification in Novel Process Equipment. *Research Policy*, 24(1), 1–12.

Warwick, Rl. Wehlan, E., Parise, S., de Valk, J. & Aalbers, R. (2011), Creating Employee Networks That Deliver Open Innovation. *MIT Sloan Management Review*, 53(1), 37–44.

Weisenfeld, U. (2003), Engagement in Innovation Management: Perceptions and Interests in the GM Debate. *Engagement in Innovation Management*, 12(4), 211–220.

Weiss, M., Hoegl, M. & Gibbert, M. (2011), Making Virtue of Necessity: The Role of Team Climate for Innovation in Resource-Constrained Innovation Projects. *Journal of Product Innovation Management*, 28(S1), 196–207.

West, M. & Sacramento, C.A. (2012), *Creativity and Innovation: The Role of Team and Organizational Climate. I: Handbook of Organizational Creativity*. London: Academic press.

West, M., Hirst, G., Richter A. & Shipton H. (2004), Twelve steps to heaven: Successfully managing change through developing innovative teams. *European Journal of Work and Organizational Psychology*, 13(2), 269–299.

Wheelan, S.A. (2009), Group Size, Group Development, and Group Productivity. *Small Group Research*, 40(2), 247–262.

Wheelan, S.A. (2013), *Creating Effective Teams – A Guide for Members and Leaders*. London: SAGE Publications, Inc.

Wheelan, S.A., Åkerlund, M. & Jacobsson, C. (2021), *Creating Effective Teams*, 6th edition. London: SAGE Publications.

Whyte, W.F., Greenwood, D.J. & Lazes, P. (1989), Participatory action research: Through practice to science in social research. *American Behavioral Scientist*, 32(5), 513–551.

Xu, Q., Chen, J., Xie, Z., Liu, J., Zheng, G. & Wang, Y. (2006), Total Innovation Management: a novel paradigm of innovation management in the 21st century. *Journal of Technology Transfer*, 32(1), 9–25.

Yang, Y. & Konrad, A.M. (2011), Diversity and organizational innovation: The role of employee involvement Journal of Organizational Behavior. *Journal of Organizational Behaviour*, 32, 1062–1083.

Yesil, S., Büyükbese, T. & Koska, A. (2013), Exploring the Link Between Knowledge Sharing Enablers, Innovation Capability and Innovation Performance. *International Journal of Innovation Management*, 17(4).

Yu, D. & Hang, C.C. (2010), A Reflective Review of Disruptive Innovation Theory. *International Journal of Management Reviews*, 12(4), 435–452.

Zuidema, K.R. & Kleiner, B.H. (1994), Self-directed work groups gain popularity. *Business Credit*, 96(9), 21–26.

Åhlström, P. & Karlsson, C. (2009), Longitudinal field studies. In: C.E. Karlsson (eds.), *Researching Operations Management*. New York: Routledge, 198–232.

Index

https://doi.org/10.1515/9783110731934-008

www.ingramcontent.com/pod-product-compliance
Lightning Source LLC
Chambersburg PA
CBHW081105220326

41598CB00038B/7241